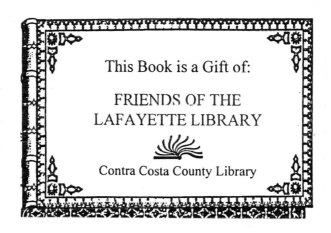

Korean War
Almanac and
Primary Sources

Korean War
Almanac and
Primary Sources

Sonia G. Benson
Gerda-Ann Raffaelle, Editor

GALE GROUP

THOMSON LEARNING

oit • New York • San Diego • San Francisco
on • New Haven, Conn. • Waterville, Main
London • Munich

Sonia G. Benson

Staff

Gerda-Ann Raffaelle, *U•X•L Editor*
Carol DeKane Nagel, *U•X•L Managing Editor*
Thomas L. Romig, *U•X•L Publisher*

Robyn V. Young, *Project Manager, Imaging and Multimedia Content*
Robert Duncan, *Senior Imaging Specialist*
Kim Davis, *Permissions Associate, Text*
Tracey Rowens, *Senior Art Director, Cover Design*
Pamela A. E. Galbreath, *Senior Art Director, Page Design*

LM Design, *Typesetter*

Rita Wimberley, *Senior Buyer*
Evi Seoud, *Assistant Manager, Composition Purchasing and Electronic Prepress*

Front cover photograph of Republic of Korea troops in camouflage reproduced by permission of AP/Wide World Photos, Inc. Back cover photograph of United Nations soldiers at the 38th parallel reproduced by permission of Archive Photos, Inc.

Library of Congress Cataloging-in-Publication Data

Benson, Sonia.

    Korean War : almanac and primary sources / Sonia G. Benson ; Gerda-Ann Raffaelle, editor.

        p. cm.

    Includes bibliographical references and index.

    Summary: A comprehensive overview of the Korean War, including biographies and full or excerpted memoirs, speeches, and other source documents.

    ISBN 0-7876-5691-7 (hc. : alk. paper)

    1. Korean War, 1950–1953—Juvenile literature. 2. Korea—History—20th century—Juvenile literature. 3. United States—Biography—Juvenile literature. [1. Korean War, 1950–1953. 2. Korean War, 1950–1953—Sources.] I. Raffaelle, Gerda-Ann. II. Title.

DS918 B386 2001
951.904'2–dc21

2001044242

Printed in the United States of America

10 9 8 7 6 5 4 3 2 1

Contents

Primary Sources:

Reader's Guide

A long with being the "forgotten war" that no one wants to think about and the "wrong war" that the world powers probably should have avoided, the Korean War was a war that lacked definition. It had no exact beginning or end. The traditional dates are 1950 to 1953, from the North Koreans' invasion of South Korea to the signing of the armistice. Many historians, however, place the beginning of the war in 1945, when the United States and the Soviet Union began their occupations of the country, splitting it in two in a way that the Koreans had never imagined. Though the fighting ended in 1953, the country is still divided: many Koreans have not seen nor heard from family and loved ones—mother, father, sister, husband, friend, cousin—nor have they been allowed to return to their homeland for fifty years. For them, the war is not over.

The Korean War was neither civil war nor foreign conquest. Although the initial armed conflict was between the communist government of North Korea and the Westernized dictatorship in South Korea, these two opposing factions were created and supported by outsiders. In effect, Korea became a playing field for the cold war powers, so much so that many histories of the war written in the United States barely mention the Korean people and their struggles at all. But an estimated two million Korean civilians died during the war, leaving the survivors to rebuild a thoroughly decimated country.

Korean War: Almanac and Primary Sources explores the Korean War through thirteen chapters and twelve documents. The Almanac chapters provide a solid overview of the war, from its underlying causes to its major battles through its drawn-out peace process. The twelve primary source documents include excerpted speeches, memoirs, oral histories, war correspondents' reports, and government documents pertaining to the war. Each of the primary source documents is divided into these sections:

- **Introductory material** places the document and its author in an historical context

- **Things to remember** offers readers important background information about the featured text

- **Excerpt** presents the document in its original format

- **What happened next** discusses the impact of the document on both the speaker and his or her audience

- **Did you know?** provides interesting facts about each document and its author

Additionally, each excerpt is accompanied by a glossary running alongside the document that defines terms, people, and ideas discussed within the document.

Throughout the volume are numerous sidebar boxes that highlight people and information of special interest, while eighty-five black-and-white photographs help illustrate the material covered in the text. Each chapter and primary source entry offers a list of additional sources students can refer to for more information, including sources used in writing the text. Finally, the volume begins with a timeline of important events in the Korean War and a "Words to Know" section that introduces students to difficult or unfamiliar terms. It concludes with a general bibliography and a subject index so students can easily find the people, places, and events discussed throughout *Korean War: Almanac and Primary Sources.*

Related Source

Korean War: Biographies presents the life stories of twenty-five people who played pivotal roles in the Korean War, from the leaders of the world powers who created the situation that led to war to the leaders of Korea who found themselves on either side of a demarcation line despite their wanting the same thing: a unified country. This volume contains fifty photographs, numerous sidebar boxes, sources for further study, a timeline of events, a glossary, and a subject index.

Comments and Suggestions

We welcome your comments on this work as well as your suggestions for topics to be featured in future editions of *Korean War: Almanac and Primary Sources*. Please write: Editors, *Korean War: Almanac and Primary Sources*, U•X•L, 27500 Drake Rd., Farmington Hills, MI 48331–3535; call toll-free: 1–800–877–4253; fax: 248–414–5043; or send e-mail via www.galegroup.com.

Acknowledgments

Following is a list of the copyright holders who have granted us permission to reproduce excerpts from primary source documents in *Korean War: Almanac and Primary Sources.* Every effort has been made to trace copyright; if omissions have been made, please contact us:

Apel, Otto F., Jr. From *MASH: An Army Surgeon in Korea.* University Press of Kentucky, 1998. Copyright © 1998 by The University Press of Kentucky. All rights reserved. Reproduced by permission of The University Press of Kentucky.

Beech, Keyes. From *Tokyo and Points East.* Doubleday & Company, Inc., 1954. Copyright, 1954, by Keyes Beech ©. All Rights Reserved.

Higgins, Marguerite. From *War in Korea: The Report of a Woman Combat Correspondent.* Doubleday & Company, Inc., 1951. Copyright, 1951, by Marguerite Higgins. All Rights Reserved. Reproduced by permission.

Kim Il Sung. "What Should We Do and How Should We Work This Year?," from *On Juche in Our Revolution.* Foreign Languages Publishing House, 1980.

Korean War Timeline

1905 Japan declares Korea its protectorate.

1907 Widespread rebellion against Japanese rule rages through Korea. The Japanese brutally repress the Korean rebels, killing thousands.

1910 Japan annexes Korea, beginning a thirty-five-year colonial rule.

March 1, 1919 Protestors against Japanese rule read a Proclamation of Independence in Seoul, the capital of Korea, initiating a massive nationwide protest, later known as the March First Movement. The Japanese respond with deadly force.

1919 The first Korean Communist Party is formed in Siberia, a region in the Soviet Union.

1919 The Korean Provisional Government is formed in Shanghai, China; Korean independence leader Syngman Rhee, residing in the United States, is named its president.

1931 Japan invades Manchuria, China, extending its industrial empire from Korea into Manchuria.

1937 The Japanese enter full-scale war with China.

1941 A half million Korean men are forced to serve in the Japanese military in World War II.

August 6, 1945 The United States drops an atomic bomb on Hiroshima, Japan. Three days later it drops another on Nagasaki, Japan.

August 8, 1945 The Soviet Union enters the Pacific theater of World War II, assembling its troops in Manchuria and preparing to march into Korea.

August 10, 1945 Two U.S. officials select the 38th parallel as the dividing line across Korea. The United States then issues an order stating that Americans will accept the Japanese surrender to the south of the 38th parallel and Soviets will receive the surrender to the north of it.

August 15, 1945 As Japan surrenders, Korean leaders headed by Yŏ Un-hyŏng and Pak Hŏn-yŏng begin to prepare for an interim government, forming the Committee for the Preparation of Korean Independence (CPKI). By the end of the month, 145 branches of the CPKI, called "People's Committees," set up as local governments throughout the country.

September 5, 1945 U.S. troops arrive in Korea south of the 38th parallel, establishing the U.S. military government.

September 6, 1945 The CPKI elects fifty-five leaders to head the new Korean People's Republic (KPR), hoping to create an independent Korean government. The U.S. military government refuses to recognize the KPR.

October 1945 Exiled Korean leader Syngman Rhee arrives in Seoul on the plane used by General Douglas MacArthur, commander of the U.S. forces in the Far East.

August 1946 Communist Chinese leader **Mao Zedong** is interviewed by American journalist Anna Louise Strong, out of which comes his "Nuclear Weapons Are Paper Tigers" statement.

1946–47 The Soviet Union and the United States try to create a joint trusteeship in Korea, but talks fail.

September 1947 The United States passes the matter of Korea to the United Nations (UN).

January 12, 1948 Korean guerilla leader **Kim Il Sung** delivers his "What Should We Do and How Should We Work This Year?" speech.

May 1948 Members of the United Nations Temporary Commission on Korea (UNTCOK) arrive in Seoul to supervise elections in Korea. The North Koreans refuse to allow them north of the 38th parallel.

May 10, 1948 The Republic of Korea's first National Assembly is elected without participation of the north.

August 15, 1948 Rhee is inaugurated as president of the Republic of Korea (ROK or South Korea).

September 9, 1948 The Democratic People's Republic of Korea (DPRK or North Korea) is created; Kim Il Sung is elected its premier.

December 1948 The Soviet Union withdraws its troops from North Korea.

1948–49 Guerrilla resistance to the rule of Rhee in the southern provinces of the Republic of Korea rages; a year of brutal police action follows.

1949 The Soviets successfully test their first atomic bomb.

January 1949 Dean Acheson is appointed U.S. Secretary of State; under him, the cold war policy of containment flourishes.

August 1949 General Omar N. Bradley is named the first permanent chairman of the Joint Chiefs of Staff, serving as a top military advisor to two presidents, Harry S. Truman and Dwight D. Eisenhower, through the course of the war.

October 1, 1949 Mao Zedong proclaims the establishment of the People's Republic of China, having driven Chinese Nationalist leader Chiang Kai-shek and his forces to the island of Taiwan (formerly Formosa).

December 1949 The United States withdraws its troops from Korea.

1949–50 Skirmishes periodically erupt across the 38th parallel, initiated by both the South and North Korean armies.

February 1950 At a conference in Wheeling, West Virginia, Senator Joseph McCarthy announces that there are communists working in the U.S. State Department.

June 25, 1950 Ninety thousand North Korean People's Army troops cross the 38th parallel, attacking the ROK Army at five key locations.

June 25, 1950 The UN Security Council passes a U.S.-proposed resolution condemning North Korea's "armed attack on the Republic of Korea" and calling for "the immediate cessation of hostilities" and withdrawal of NKPA troops to the 38th parallel.

June 26, 1950 U.S. ambassador to the Republic of Korea John J. Muccio organizes the evacuation of the families of Americans stationed in Korea as well as all American embassy workers.

June 27, 1950 Seoul falls to the North Koreans. War correspondent **Bill Shinn** describes that event and its aftermath in *The Forgotten War Remembered,* published in 1996.

June 27, 1950 The United Nations passes a resolution that its members are to "furnish such assistance to the Republic of Korea as may be necessary to repel the armed attack and to restore international peace and security to the area."

June 30, 1950 Truman authorizes MacArthur to use ground forces in Korea. He also approves a naval blockade of North Korea. The president does not consult with Congress and calls this a "police action under the United Nations," rather than declaring war.

July 5, 1950 Task Force Smith, a small U.S. unit of 406 men—the first to fight in Korea—is shattered by the North Koreans at Osan.

July 10, 1950 The UN Security Council agrees to create a unified Korean command with MacArthur serving as commander in chief of the UN forces. Rhee places the Republic of Korea Army in the service of MacArthur.

July 14–16, 1950 North Koreans shatter two regiments of General William F. Dean's Twenty-fourth Division at the Kum River.

July 19, 1950 The city of Taejon falls to the North Koreans.

July 26–29, 1950 U.S. soldiers kill an estimated three hundred unarmed South Korean civilians at the No Gun Ri Bridge.

August 1950 The People's Republic of China, alarmed with U.S. intervention in Korea, begins to move troops into Manchuria.

August 1950 The North Korean Army continuously attacks UN defenses of the city of Taegu, which is the temporary capital of the Republic of Korea.

August 1, 1950 Soviet delegate to the UN Security Council Jacob A. Malik introduces a resolution to invite representatives of the People's Republic of China and both Koreas to the Security Council to discuss the war. The resolution is defeated after debate.

August 1–3, 1950 UN forces in Korea are forced to retreat to the Pusan Perimeter in the south of the peninsula.

August 5, 1950 North Koreans successfully attack at the Naktong Bulge, penetrating the Pusan Perimeter defense.

August 17, 1950 The U.S. Marines strike the enemy at the Naktong Bulge and shatter them.

September 15, 1950 MacArthur leads the newly created X Corps in a massive and highly successful amphibious assault on the port city of Inchon.

September 23, 1950 General Walton H. "Johnnie" Walker leads the Eighth Army's breakout from the Pusan Perimeter and drives north to meet the X Corps.

September 24, 1950 China cables the United Nations to protest the strafing of sites in Manchuria by U.S. aircraft.

September 27, 1950 UN forces recapture Seoul.

September 30, 1950 ROK troops cross the 38th parallel, followed by other UN units.

October 14–18, 1950 Communist Chinese Forces (CCF) Commander Peng Dehuai moves 180,000 troops from Manchuria into North Korea.

October 15, 1950 Truman and MacArthur meet at Wake Island.

October 19–20, 1950 UN forces capture the already abandoned capital of North Korea, Pyongyang, and continue north toward the Korea-China border.

October 26–31, 1950 Chinese troops attack UN forces in several places near China's border with North Korea.

November 1, 1950 China launches the first Chinese offensive against the UN forces. Walker orders a retreat for the Eighth Army.

November 6–7, 1950 The Chinese troops mysteriously withdraw into the mountains, even though they are winning the battles.

Mid-November 1950 The X Corps advances to the Chosin (Changjin) Reservoir, separated from the Eighth Army.

November 24, 1950 The Eighth Army advances toward the Yalu River at the North Korea-China border.

November 25, 1950 CCF forcefully attack the Eighth Army, beginning the second Chinese offensive.

November 27, 1950 The Chinese strike at seven different fronts in Chosin, particularly targeting the well-trained marines under the command of General Oliver P. Smith.

November 28, 1950 The Eighth Army begins its withdrawal.

November 28–December 5, 1950 The X Corps retreats from the Chosin Reservoir to Hagaru in some of the worst fighting in the Korean War.

December 3, 1950 MacArthur orders a withdrawal of all UN forces to the 38th parallel. ROK General **Paik Sun Yup** recalled in his memoirs, *From Pusan to Panmunjon,* published in 1992, that on that day the South Korean army's "dream of national reunification by force was dashed forever."

December 4, 1950 War correspondent **Keyes Beach** arrives in Hagaru and follows the retreating marines. He records their stories over the next couple weeks and publishes them four years later in *Tokyo and Points East.*

December 11, 1950 105,000 UN troops and nearly 100,000 Korean civilians begin a two-week evacuation from Hungnam, North Korea.

December 23, 1950 Eighth Army commander Walker dies in a jeep accident.

December 26, 1950 Lieutenant General Matthew B. Ridgway, appointed to replace Walker as the commander of the Eighth Army, arrives in Korea.

1951 Journalist **Marguerite Higgins** publishes *War in Korea: The Report of a Woman Combat Correspondent* and wins a Pulitzer Prize for the reports she filed on the war.

January 1, 1951 The Chinese launch their third offensive, pushing UN forces fifty miles south of the 38th parallel.

January 4, 1951 Seoul is recaptured by the enemy.

January 15–February 11, 1951 Ridgway sends out patrols to find the enemy. They cover significant distance without resistance.

February 1951 Preparations for a prison camp begin on an island called Koje-do in South Korea.

February 11, 1951 The Chinese counterattack Ridgway's patrols in the battle at Chipyong-ni, but the UN forces stand, killing many Chinese.

March 14–15, 1951 Seoul is back in UN control; the Eighth Army is again approaching the 38th parallel.

April 11, 1951 MacArthur is relieved of command; Ridgway replaces him as commander of the UN forces; General James A. Van Fleet succeeds Ridgway as commander of the Eighth Army.

April 11, 1951 **Harry S. Truman** addresses Congress, explaining the reasons for MacArthur's dismissal. Eight days later, **Douglas MacArthur** addresses Congress, outlining his views on the Korean War.

April 21, 1951 UN forces enter a three-day battle with the Chinese and North Koreans; UN forces are victorious. **Ted White** recounts fighting in this offensive as a member of the last all-African American unit in the U.S. Army, the Twenty-fourth Regiment of the Twenty-fifth Infantry Division, in *No Bugles, No Drums,* published in 1993.

May 1951 CCF continues to strike at UN forces, but without much success.

Summer 1951 Otto F. Apel Jr. arrives in Korea for a one-year term as a doctor in a Mobile Army Surgical Hospital. He will publish his memoirs, *MASH: An Army Surgeon in Korea,* in 1998.

June 1951 Chinese and UN forces dig in across from each other at the crater known as the Punchbowl, beginning two years of stationary trench warfare.

June 23, 1951 After meeting with American diplomat George F. Kennan, Soviet ambassador Malik broadcasts a message on UN radio, stating that the Soviet people believe a cease-fire and an armistice can be arranged.

July 10, 1951 The first armistice meeting convenes.

July 16, 1951 Rhee and other Korean officials declare their unwillingness to accept a cease-fire while Korea remains divided.

August 1951 The Communists call off the armistice talks because, they claim, UN aircraft were bombing neutral zones.

August 1951 Assistant Secretary of Defense Anna Rosenberg establishes the Defense Advisory Committee on Women in the Service to recruit women into military service and improve the working conditions of those already enlisted.

September 13–26, 1951 A violent battle is fought at Heartbreak Ridge, in which many die on both sides and little ground is exchanged. This is typical of the fighting during the armistice talks.

October 1951 Armistice meetings resume at Punmanjom, a small village near the 38th parallel.

October 31, 1951 Civilian internees and American prisoners of war set off on a forced nine-day march to prison camps in North Korea. Forty years later captured missionary **Larry Zellers** writes of the brutal ordeal in *In Enemy Hands: A Prisoner in North Korea.*

November 23, 1951 In the armistice negotiations, a new demarcation line is established at the front, with a demilitarized zone that stretches out two kilometers on each side of the line.

January 1952 The two sides at the armistice talks enter a long and difficult stalemate over the issue of repatriating prisoners of war who do not wish to return to their country.

February–March 1952 The Communists accuse the United States of engaging in biological warfare.

May 1952 Mark W. Clark replaces Ridgway as commander of the Far East Forces and the UN command.

May 7, 1952 Inmates at the United Nations' Koje-do prisoner of war camp kidnap the camp commander and begin making demands. The acting commander yields to the prisoners' requests.

March 5, 1953 Soviet Premier Joseph Stalin dies and is replaced by Georgy M. Malenkov, who soon broadcasts a speech expressing the Soviet Union's desire for peace in Asia.

April 20–May 3, 1953 The first exchanges of Korean War POWs begins with "Little Switch," a transfer of sick and wounded prisoners.

June 18, 1953 As truce negotiations near completion, Rhee secretly orders the release of about twenty-five thousand North Korean POWs who did not wish to be repatriated, effectively sabotaging the armistice agreements.

July 11, 1953 With promises of enormous economic aid and the continued presence of U.S. troops to provide security in South Korea, Rhee agrees not to obstruct the armistice.

July 27, 1953 The armistice agreement is signed by both sides. At ten o'clock P.M. the fighting stops.

August 5–September 6, 1953 "Operation Big Switch," the exchange of all POWs between the opposing sides, takes place.

1954 The Geneva Conference raises the issue of the unification of Korea; discussions continue for two months without progress.

1960 Civil disorder in the Republic of Korea arises from dissatisfaction with the corruption and violence within Rhee's government. At the age of eighty-five, Rhee is forced to resign and flee to Hawaii.

1994 Kim Il Sung dies, after being the absolute leader of Korea for forty-six years.

1997 **Survivors of the No Gun Ri incident** of July 26–29, 1950 present to the South Korean and United States governments a petition for compensation and an apology for the massacre of their family members. Initially their petition was rejected, but in January 2001 President Bill Clinton acknowledged the loss of life at No Gun Ri.

Words to Know

A

agenda: a list or outline of things to be discussed, planned, or undertaken.

airborne operation: a military action involving movement of troops into a combat area by aircraft, often referring to a mission using parachutes.

aircraft carrier: a warship with a huge deck on which planes take off and land.

amphibious attack: an invasion that uses the coordinated efforts of land, sea, and air forces.

annex: to take over a nation that was independent, making it a dependent part of another nation.

annihilate: to destroy or kill.

armistice: talks between opposing forces in which they agree to a truce or suspension of hostilities.

army: two or more military corps under the command of a general; an army usually consists of between 120,000 and 200,000 troops. Chinese armies were generally composed of three 10,000-men divisions and resembled the U.S. Army's corps.

artillery: large weapons, such as howitzers, rockets, and 155-millimeter guns, that shoot missiles and generally take a crew to operate.

assimilation: the effort to eliminate the cultural practices and identity of a minority group or conquered people, and to replace them with the dominating group's culture and identity.

atomic bomb: a powerful bomb created by splitting the nuclei of a heavy chemical, such as plutonium or uranium, in a rapid chain reaction, resulting in a violent and destructive shock wave as well as radiation.

autocrat: a person who rules with unlimited authority.

automatic weapon: a weapon that fires repeatedly without needing reloading or other extra actions by the person shooting it.

B

battalion: a military unit usually made up of about three to five companies. Generally one of the companies is the headquarters unit, another the service unit, and the rest are line units. Although the numbers differ greatly, a battalion might consist of about 35 officers and about 750 soldiers.

battleships: huge combat ships used in Korea primarily for their big guns as support to the ground forces.

bazooka: a light and portable rocket launcher or antitank weapon fired from the shoulder that consists of a large tube that launches antitank ammunition.

beriberi: a disease caused by inadequate nutrition that attacks the digestive system as well as the heart and nervous system.

biological warfare: the act of spreading disease germs or other living organisms through enemy territory, using the germs as a weapon with which to kill or disable the enemy.

boycott: a refusal to participate in something (purchasing from a store, working, attending an organization) until stated conditions are met.

brainwashing: the use of carefully planned psychological techniques to try to change the way someone thinks and believes, often against the will of, or even without the knowledge of, the person.

buffer zone: a neutral area between the territories of opposing forces.

bug-out: to panic and run away from a battle in confusion; a disorderly retreat without permission.

bunker: a reinforced underground room dug into a battle area for protection against enemy gunfire and bombs.

C

camouflage: disguise to look like the surrounding plants and environment.

capitalism: an economic system in which individuals, rather than the state, own the property and businesses, and the cost of goods are determined by the free market.

casualties: those who are killed, wounded, missing, or taken prisoner in combat.

China Lobby: a group of Americans during the late 1940s and early 1950s who fervently supported Chinese Nationalist leader Chiang Kai-shek in his struggles against the Communist Chinese, and who held a romanticized and sometime patronizing view of the Chinese people and their relations with Americans.

civilian: someone who is not in the military or any other security forces.

classified: kept away from public view; being placed in a category (as a document) in which only select people have access to it.

cold war: the struggle for power, authority, and prestige between the communist Soviet Union and the capitalist Western powers of Europe and the United States from 1945 until 1991.

collaborator: someone who cooperates with, or helps out, enemies to his or her own nation.

colonial rule: rule imposed upon one nation by another, more powerful, nation.

commandant: commanding officer.

communism: an economic theory that does not include the concept of private property. Instead, the public (usually represented by the government) owns the goods and the means to produce them in common.

company: the basic army unit, composed of a headquarters and two or three platoons. A company is generally made up of about 100 soldiers commanded by a major or captain. There are four or five companies to a battalion. Army and Marine Corps regiments during the Korean War followed the same system of designating their companies by a letter. In First Battalion, A, B, C were rifle companies, D was a weapons company. In Second Battalion, E, F, G were rifle companies, H was a weapons company, and so on. To avoid confusion, the letter designations became words: H Company was How Company, etc.

compound: a walled-in area within which there are buildings, usually places of residence.

concessions: things that are given up and granted to the other side in an argument or conflict.

conservative: in politics, a person who seeks to maintain traditions, preserve established institutions, and promote a strong, authoritative government; conservatives are anticommunist and may tend to favor big business and power in the hands of an aristocracy or elite.

corps: a military unit consisting of two or more divisions under the command of a lieutenant general; there are usually between 30,000 and 60,000 personnel in a corps.

Corsair: a single-pilot fighter plane used by navy and marine forces.

coup d'etat: the overthrow of an existing government through force or violence.

cruiser: a fast, lightly armored warship, smaller and with less armor but faster than a battleship.

D

delegate: a person who represents another person, a group, or a nation.

demilitarized zone (DMZ): an area in which military presence and activity are forbidden.

destroyers: small, fast battleships with guns, depth charges, and torpedoes, used to support the main battleship.

diplomat: a professional representative of a nation who helps handle affairs and conduct negotiations between nations.

disarmament: taking away a group's weapons and other military equipment in order to render it unable or less able to make war.

division (or infantry division): a self-sufficient military unit, usually about 15,000 to 16,000 strong, under the command of a major general. Communist Chinese army divisions were closer to 10,000 soldiers strong.

dysentary: a disease caused by infection resulting in severe diarrhea.

E

egalitarian: promoting equality; allowing each person in a group more or less equal powers.

evacuate: to remove people from a dangerous area or a military zone.

exile: forced or voluntary absence from one's home country.

G

gauntlet: a terrible ordeal; a ritual in which an individual is forced to run through a formation of two facing rows of people armed with clubs or other weapons who are striking him or her from both sides.

Geneva Convention: a series of agreements about the treatment of prisoners of war and the sick, wounded, and dead in battle, signed by many nations.

grenade: a small explosive weapon that can be thrown, usually with a pin that is pulled to activate it and a spring-loaded safety lever that is held down until the user wants to throw the grenade; once the safety lever is released, the grenade will explode in seconds.

gross national product (GNP): a measurement of the output of goods and services of a nation.

guerrilla warfare: an irregular form of combat; in Korea it usually involved small groups of warriors who hid in mountains, enlisted the help of the local population, and used ambushes and surprise attacks to harass or even destroy much larger armies.

H

hawkish: advocating for all-out war or military action.

heat exhaustion: also called heat prostration; the symptoms that arise when one physically exerts oneself in hot weather, including dizziness, nausea, weakness, and sweating.

hierarchy: organization by rank; in most hierarchies, the higher the rank, the greater the individual's power and authority.

howitzers: short cannons.

humanitarian: promoting the good of humanity.

I

impasse: the position of being faced with a problem for which there seems no solution; a stalemate.

imperialism: one nation imposing its rule over another country outside of its borders.

impressed: forced to enlist as a soldier.

indoctrination: to thoroughly teach or train someone with a particular, and one-sided, set of beliefs, practices, or principles.

industry: manufacturing and production activities; the plants and businesses in which systematic labor is employed to create the goods and necessities for a nation's use.

infantry: the branch of an army that is composed of soldiers trained to fight on foot.

infantry division: a self-sufficient military unit, usually about 15,000 to 16,000 soldiers strong, under the command of a major general. Communist Chinese army divisions were closer to 10,000 soldiers strong.

infiltrate: to enter into enemy lines by passing through gaps in its defense.

integration: the act of bringing all the groups of individuals within an organization into the whole as equals; the elimination of separate facilities and structures for different racial groups.

intelligence (military): information about the enemy.

interim government: a government formed after the ruling government in a nation is eliminated; when necessary, an interim government fills in until a permanent one can be established.

international trusteeship: the government of a country by the joint rule of several countries that have committed to act in what they deem to be the country's best interest.

intervention: the act of a third party who steps into an on-going fight in the attempt to interfere in its outcome or stop it altogether.

isolationism: the view that a country should take care of its problems at home and not interfere in conflicts in other countries.

J

Joint Chiefs of Staff: an agency within the Department of Defense serving to advise the president and the secretary of defense on matters of war. The Joint Chiefs of Staff consists of a chairman, a vice chairman, the chief of staff of the army, the chief of naval operations, the chief of staff of the air force, and the commandant of the marine corps.

K

Kuomintang: originally a democratic and moderately socialist party founded by Chinese revolutionary leader Sun

Yat-sen in 1912, the Kuomintang came into the hands of Chinese Nationalist leader Chiang Kai-shek in the late 1920s and became heavily committed to eliminating the Chinese Communists. In 1949, the Communists, under Mao Zedong, defeated Chiang Kai-shek and the Kuomintang and forced them to withdraw to the Chinese island of Taiwan.

L

leftists: people who advocate change and reform, usually in the interest of gaining greater freedoms and equality for average citizens and the poor; some leftist groups aspire to overthrow the government; others seek to change from within.

limited warfare: warfare with an objective other than the enemy's complete destruction, as in holding a defensive line during negotiations.

logistics: the military science of tending to the acquisition, upkeep, and transportation of military equipment, goods, and personnel.

M

machine-gun emplacement: a prepared position for a powerful automatic weapon.

malnourished: having a poor diet lacking in proper nutrients, resulting in ill health.

mine: a buried explosive set to go off if it is disturbed.

minesweeper: a warship that drags the bottom of the sea to remove or deactivate mines.

missionary: a person who takes on organized religious work with the purpose of converting people to his or her faith.

mop up: the clearing of an area of all enemy troops or resistance.

morale: the way that a person or a group of people feels about the job they are doing or the mission they are working on.

mortar: a muzzle-loading cannon that shoots high in the air.

N

napalm: a jellylike material that turns to flame as it is shot from bombs and flame throwers; napalm is known for sticking to its targets as it burns them.

nationalize: to place ownership, usually of a factory or a business, in the hands of the government.

Nationalists (Chinese): the ruling party led by Chiang Kai-shek in China from the 1920s until 1949, when the Nationalists were defeated by the Communists in the Chinese Civil War and forced to withdraw to the island of Taiwan. The Kuomintang party eventually became known as "Nationalists."

P

parasite: an insect or animal that lives off another animal, usually hurting the host animal; a person who lives off someone else.

paratroopers: soldiers who are trained to jump from airplanes with parachutes.

Pentagon: the headquarters of the Department of Defense and therefore of all U.S. military activity.

perimeter: the outside limits of a geographical area.

perimeter defense: fighting the enemy around the outer limits of an area.

platoon: a military unit composed of three squads.

POW: prisoner of war.

protectorate: a dependent nation subject to the control of a more powerful nation, but not officially a part of the more powerful nation.

provisional government: a temporary government, often formed in another country in opposition to a colonial or repressive government in the home country.

Provisional Korean Government: a government in exile, formed in Shanghai, China, during Japanese rule of Korea (1910–45), that elected leaders and fought for the cause of an independent Korea, but had no actual power within occupied Korea.

W

war correspondent: someone who provides news stories to a newspaper or television or radio news program from the battlefront or on location in a war.

warlord: a leader with his own military whose powers are usually limited to a small area that, in most cases, he took by force.

warmongering: pushing for war.

Western nations: the noncommunist nations of Europe and America.

Y

youth gang: a group of young people acting together toward some end; usually used in its negative sense of an adolescent group that works outside the law, often terrorizing others and committing illegal acts.

Z

zealot: fanatic; someone who pursues his or her objectives with extreme passion and eagerness.

Korean War
Almanac and
Primary Sources

Almanac

Background to the War: The Japanese Occupation

1

Korea is a peninsula lying between the island of Japan and the mainland countries of China and Russia in eastern Asia. It is a beautiful land, with statuesque mountains running most of its six-hundred-mile length. In total area, it is about the size of Great Britain. Korea's geographical position alone explains a great deal about its history. As a small country surrounded by big and powerful nations, Korea has often suffered the effects of its neighbors' troubles. There is a Korean proverb historians often quote: "The shrimp is broken when the whales fight." Korea has indeed been crushed in hostilities between China and Japan; Russia and Japan; and the Western powers (the United States and Western Europe) and the communist powers (the Soviet Union and the People's Republic of China) in the Korean War (1950–53). (The Soviet Union was the first communist country and was made up of fifteen republics, including Russia. It existed as a unified country from 1922 to 1991. Communism is a set of political beliefs that advocates the elimination of private property. It is a system in which goods are owned by the community as a whole rather than by specific individuals and are available to all as needed.)

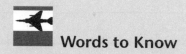

Words to Know

annex: to take over a nation that was independent, making it a dependent part of another nation.

assimilation: the effort to eliminate the cultural practices and identity of a minority group or conquered people, and to replace them with the dominating group's culture and identity.

capitalism: an economic system in which individuals, rather than the state, own the property and businesses, and the cost of goods are determined by the free market.

collaborator: someone who cooperates with, or helps out, enemies to his or her own nation.

colonial rule: rule imposed upon one nation by another, more powerful, nation.

communism: an economic system that does not include the concept of private property. Instead, the public (usually the government) owns the goods and the means to produce them in common.

diplomat: a professional representative of a nation who helps handle affairs and conduct negotiations between nations.

exile: forced or voluntary absence from one's home country.

guerrilla warfare: an irregular form of combat; in Korea it usually involved small groups of warriors who hid in mountains, enlisted the help of the local population, and used ambushes and surprise attacks to harass or even destroy much larger armies.

industry: manufacturing and production activities; the plants and businesses in which systematic labor is employed to create the goods and necessities for a nation's use.

Kuomintang: originally a democratic and moderately socialist party founded by Chinese revolutionary leader Sun Yat-sen in 1912, the Kuomintang came into the hands of Chinese Nationalist leader Chiang Kai-shek in the late 1920s and became heavily committed to eliminating the

Over the years, Korea has had periods of great progress and other eras of decline. For example, in the seventh century the Korean peninsula was unified and ruled by a native government. Scholarship, creativity, and culture flourished, and it is said that at this time Korean civilization was more advanced than almost any in Europe. In other periods, Korea agreed to recognize China as its "elder brother," thus becoming a tributary state, one that ruled itself independently but paid taxes to the controlling country and acted according to the wishes of

Chinese Communists. In 1949, the Communists, under Mao Zedong, defeated Chiang Kai-shek and the Kuomintang and forced them to withdraw to the Chinese island of Taiwan (formerly Formosa).

missionary: a person who takes on organized religious work with the purpose of converting people to his or her faith.

Nationalists (Chinese): the ruling party led by Chiang Kai-shek in China from the 1920s until 1949, when the Nationalists were defeated by the Communists in the Chinese Civil War and forced to withdraw to the island of Taiwan (formerly Formosa). The Kuomintang party eventually became known as "Nationalists."

protectorate: a dependent nation subject to the control of a more powerful nation, but not officially a part of the more powerful nation.

provisional government: a temporary government, often formed in another country in opposition to a colonial or repressive government in the home country.

puppet state: a government that seems independent, but in fact obeys the command of an outside ruler.

reprisal: violence or other use of force by one side in a conflict in retaliation for something bad that was done by the other side; a system of getting even for harm done.

tenant farmers: a worker who farms land owned by someone else and usually pays part of the crop to the owner in return.

tributary state: a nation that rules itself independently but pays taxes to—and deals with other nations under the instructions of—a larger country.

warlord: a leader with his own military whose powers are usually limited to a small area that, in most cases, he took by force.

Western nations: the noncommunist nations of Europe and America.

the controlling country in its dealings with other nations. This relationship often served both countries well. From China, Korea received a steady stream of culture and education, and from Korea, China received monetary benefits and military protection.

From the sixteenth century on, both Japan and China invaded Korea periodically as Korea experienced periods of instability in its government. By the nineteenth century, Western nations began seeking trade with Korea, but Korea wanted

EAST CENTRAL ASIA, 1945

nothing to do with outside forces. For a time, Korea existed in true isolation, becoming known as the Hermit Kingdom. No foreigners were allowed to enter the nation and there was great suspicion of anything foreign or new.

In 1876, Korea broke its isolation by signing a treaty of friendship with Japan, which was becoming modernized through its relationships with the West. Six years later, Korea signed a trade agreement with the United States, followed quickly by trade agreements with other European nations. Diplomats (people who help handle affairs and conduct negotiations between nations) from Europe and the United States arrived, and with them came Protestant missionaries (people who conduct religious or charitable work in a territory or foreign country). As Korea opened itself to the world, Japan saw an opportunity to build a great Japanese empire in Korea based on industry (manufacturing and production activities) and capitalism (an economic system in which individuals, rather than the state, own the property and businesses, and the cost and distribution of goods are determined by the free market). The Japanese wanted to rule Korea so it could serve as one of their industrial centers and as a bridge into Manchuria, an area in northern China just north of the Korean border. In Manchuria, the Japanese hoped to build a large industrial empire.

Japan takes over

Japan fought and won wars with China and Russia over Korea during the later part of the nineteenth century. By 1905, Japan declared Korea a protectorate, a dependent nation subject to Japanese control. To the great dismay of the Koreans, the United States recognized Japan's interests in Korea.

The Koreans, unwilling to submit to Japanese rule, organized large-scale rebellions. In 1907, there were revolts throughout the country involving tens of thousands of Koreans. The Japanese troops reacted brutally, killing thousands of dissenters. Pictures of peasants being executed by Japanese firing squads were put on public display, discouraging others who might rebel.

In 1910, Japan annexed Korea; that is, they incorporated it as a part of Japan with the help of a very weak Korean monarch whom they had helped to the throne. Because Korean popular resistance was strong, the Japanese did not announce the annexation for one week after the agreement was signed. They took this time to arrest people who opposed their rule, and they shut down Korean newspapers and broke up Korean national organizations.

Life under the Japanese: 1910–1945

After annexation, Japan installed a colonial governor in Korea who held tremendous power over the people. The Japanese also sent in a large and powerful colonial police force and quickly began enlisting Koreans to serve in it: in essence, forcing them to restrict the rights of their own countrypeople.

In the first years of its rule in Korea, Japan was mainly interested in obtaining a source of food to supply its own people. Consequently, Japan built up Korea's agricultural base, but much at the expense of the Koreans. Many small farmers lost their land to the Japanese, becoming tenant

Korean protesters of the March First Movement are executed by a Japanese firing squad as other Japanese soldiers keep back a large crowd of sympathizers and spectators, May 14, 1919. *Reproduced by permission of the Corbis Corporation.*

farmers who had to give so much of their crops to landlords that they could barely get by themselves. Many upper-class Korean farmers held on to their land and became prosperous under the Japanese; they were often hated by the impoverished tenant farmers.

Modernization of Korea did occur under the Japanese. By the 1920s, Japan began to build up Korea's industry. By the 1930s, there was a massive electrical/chemical industry in the north. During the Japanese rule, new and modern roads, railways, and communication systems spread throughout the peninsula.

Korean resistance

Although there were Koreans who viewed the Japanese influence as progress (particularly the new class of landlords and businesspeople who profited from the improvements), the majority of Koreans detested Japanese rule. In the first eight years after annexation, two hundred thousand Koreans were imprisoned as rebels. In 1919, a group of students led a revolt that would come to be known as the March First Movement. Trying to get the attention of the Western powers, the protestors read a Proclamation of Independence in the capital city of Seoul. From this small beginning, a massive, nationwide protest arose, including approximately five hundred thousand people. The Japanese, taken by surprise, responded with the full force of their troops. According to Korean records, the Japanese killed seventy-five hundred Koreans, wounded fifteen thousand, and arrested forty-five to put down the uprising. Although not successful in gaining independence for Korea, the movement helped to build empowerment and national unity, which paved the way for nationalist groups that would later emerge.

During the 1920s, the Koreans continued to organize against the Japanese. Their resistance methods included organized guerrilla warfare, usually involving small groups of warriors who hid in mountains, enlisted the help of the population, and used ambushes and surprise attacks to harass or even destroy much larger armies.

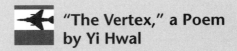

"The Vertex," a Poem by Yi Hwal

During the Japanese occupation, hundreds of thousands of Koreans made their way to Manchuria and Siberia, a huge but sparsely populated region of Russia comprised of the northern third of Asia. For many who had joined in the rebellions or were suspected of doing so by the Japanese, exile was the only way to survive and escape prison. Moving north to the frozen mountains of Manchuria was a frightening and lonely prospect, as Yi Hwal expressed in this poem written in 1940:

> In the night rain
> I hear the whistle of a distant train
> A sharp shrill sound trailing off to the north
> North, north across the fields.
> Where are they going, these travelers
> Packed in coaches through the night?
> How many have said good-bye to their country,
> Wandering souls filled with blighted hopes?

Source: Yi Hwal, "The Vertex." Translated by Yi In-su and reprinted in The Land and People of Korea, by S. E. Solberg. New York: HarperCollins, 1991.

Reprisals for the 1919 March First Movement caused thousands to flee Korea, many settling in Manchuria and Siberia, a huge but sparsely populated region of Russia comprised of the northern third of Asia. In the new Korean communities here, Korean newspapers and schools arose. In Siberia, the first Korean Communist Party was founded. Russian communist leader Vladimir Lenin (1870–1924) joined forces with Koreans in fighting the anticommunist Japanese, who allied with remaining czarists—noncommunist Russian

Korean Names

Korean names almost always consist of three Chinese characters that are pronounced with three Korean syllables. The family name comes first and the remaining two characters form the given name. One of these two given names often identifies the generation, and the two given name syllables are often hyphenated.

There are about three hundred family names in Korea, but most people have one of the common last names. These are Kim, Lee or Yi, Park or Pak, An, Chang, Cho, Ch'oe, Cho'ng, Han or Hahn, Kang, Yu, and Yun. People in Korea do not refer to each other by their given names unless they are very close.

Because the family name comes first in Korean, there is no need to invert names as we do in the English language. After the first mention of Paik Sun Yup, for example, we would refer to him as Paik, his family name, as we would refer to Douglas MacArthur after first mention as MacArthur. The exception to this is Korean independence leader Syngman Rhee, who changed his name to conform to Western traditions. His family name is Rhee and he would normally be called Rhee Syngman in Korea.

groups who believed in the monarchy—in the area. The North Korean People's Army to this day considers its origins to be in this resistance movement against the Japanese.

Leaders arise from anti-Japanese movement

By the 1930s, a strong and popular anti-Japanese guerrilla leader emerged named Kim Il Sung (1912–1994). Born into a peasant family, Kim had moved with his family to Manchuria in the 1920s. At the age of seventeen, he was arrested for organizing the Communist Youth League. On his release after a year in jail, he organized the Korean Revolutionary Army in Manchuria, and led it in guerrilla tactics. He was so effective against the Japanese that they established special squads to chase him and his guerrilla army. Around 1940, Kim sought refuge in the Soviet Union, where some historians believe he received military and leadership training during World War II (1939–45).

The Provisional Government of the Republic of Korea was formed in Shanghai, China, in 1919, and proclaimed independence for Korea. (A provisional government is a temporary one, often formed in exile in another country.) Syngman Rhee (1875–1965), a Korean independence leader then living in the United States, was declared its leader. Rhee had been raised in an elite Korean family and received his early education in China, but during his youth he had turned his back on tradition, preferring to study Western society and politics. As the Japanese started moving into Korea at the end of the nineteenth century, he

protested strongly against their imperialism (ruling a country outside one's own nation's borders) and was arrested as a rebel. After being brutally tortured, Rhee spent six years in jail. While in prison he converted to Christianity and, upon his release in 1904, he went to the United States. He did his undergraduate and graduate work there, receiving his Ph.D. in political science from Princeton University. In 1920, Rhee went to Shanghai, to take his office as president of the Korean provisional government, but he was expelled from the position in 1924 after disagreements with other members.

War over China

In 1931, Japan invaded Manchuria, creating a new puppet state called Manchukuo in 1932. (A puppet state is a government that seems independent, but in fact obeys the command of an outside ruler.) Japan then expanded its empire of electrical/chemical plants, extending it through Korea and into Manchuria.

A group of Asian women who survived Japanese enslavement during World War II protest in front of the Japanese Embassy in Washington, D.C, in September 2000. They filed suit against the Japanese government in an American court, seeking an apology. *Reproduced by permission of the Corbis Corporation.*

China: The Other Neighbor

At the turn of the twentieth century, the monarchy in China was severely weakened by the exploitation of European nations and their trade demands. In 1911, Chinese leader Sun Yat-sen (1866–1925) led a successful revolution against the monarchy (a government having a hereditary chief of state with life tenure) and became president of the new republic. A year later he resigned his position so that Yüan Shih-k'ai (pronounced you-ahn shir-kie; 1859–1916), the commander of the northern forces, could become president. Yüan attempted to become a dictator (someone who rules absolutely and often oppressively), and Sun and his revolutionary forces were soon fighting his repressive government. This was the beginning of decades of fragmented government in China, with warlords (often military leaders who control parts of a country, particularly when the central government is not in control) and other rulers seizing power in local districts, and larger powers warring with each other for central control.

Yüan died in 1916, and China fell to the rule of rival warlord states. Sun's revolutionary party, called the Kuomintang (pronounced KWOE-min-TANG), set up a government in the south. An opposing Nationalist government formed in the north, ruled mainly by warlords. In 1921, the Chinese Communist Party was founded. Sun tried to get help for his party from the West but was unsuccessful, so he allied with the communists and got aid from the Soviet Union.

In 1926, a year after Sun's death, General Chiang Kai-shek (1887–1975) led

In 1937, the Japanese entered full-scale war with China for control of the Chinese mainland. Japan then launched an all-out assimilation policy in Korea: an effort to eliminate the Korean culture and identity entirely and replace it with Japanese. Korean schools could only teach in Japanese, and students were not allowed to speak the Korean language at all. In 1939, Koreans were compelled to change their names to Japanese names, and Korean newspapers and magazines were once again shut down. Koreans were encouraged to maintain Japanese shrines and adopt the belief that the Japanese emperor was divine. The Japanese police were so strong that few dared to rebel.

Chiang Kai-shek. *Reproduced by permission of AP/Wide World Photos.*

Nationalist government. A new communist government then arose in opposition to Chiang's Kuomintang. With China in a state of civil disruption, Japan invaded Manchuria, setting up its puppet state of Manchukuo in 1932. In 1937, Japan invaded China proper, and by 1940 northern China, the coastal areas, and other regions of China were occupied by the Japanese.

When the Japanese surrendered at the end of World War II (1939–45) and began to evacuate China, the Chinese Nationalists under Chiang Kai-shek, and the Chinese Communists under Mao Zedong (Mao Tse-tung; 1893–1976), scrambled to occupy the territories that Japan was leaving behind, leading to full-scale civil war between the Nationalists and the Communists.

the Kuomintang army to victory in the north. He reversed Sun's alliance with the Communist Party and established a

World War II in Korea

When World War II (1939–45) erupted in the Pacific in 1941, a half million Korean men were forced to serve in the Japanese military. The Japanese also forced some 150,000 young Korean women into sexual servitude in Japanese military brothels on the battlefields. Many of these women, who came to be known as "comfort women," died from the terrible conditions and rough treatment, or never returned home because of the trauma and shame they felt. As Japanese men went off to war, Japan's industries required a new source of labor. Koreans by the thousands were forced to work in Japanese plants and mines, often in unsafe conditions, under terms little better than slavery.

At the end of World War II in 1945, when the Japanese surrendered, the Koreans were already divided among themselves. The Japanese system of rule had virtually wiped out the middle class. There were masses of landless and impoverished Koreans on the one hand, and a few wealthy landowners and capitalists, most of whom had collaborated with the Japanese, on the other. Along with their desire for independence and hatred for the Japanese, many Korean peasants were motivated to correct the injustices and inequalities that had long been their lot. As the war drew to a close, they envisioned an independent government that could address their needs.

Where to Learn More

Breen, Michael. *The Koreans: Who They Are, What They Want, Where Their Future Lies*. New York: St. Martin's Press, 1999.

Cumings, Bruce. *Korea's Place in the Sun: A Modern History*. New York: W. W. Norton, 1997.

Hart-Landsberg, Martin. *Korea: Division, Reunification, and U.S. Foreign Policy*. New York: Monthly Review Press, 1998.

McNair, Sylvia. *Enchantment of the World: Korea*. Chicago: Children's Press, 1986.

Solberg, S. E. *The Land and People of Korea*. New York: HarperCollins, 1991.

Web sites

Savada, Andrea Matles, and William Shaw, eds. "South Korea: A Country Study." The Federal Research Division, Library of Congress. [Online] http://lcweb2.loc.gov/frd/cs/krtoc.html (accessed on August 14, 2001).

The Cold War Comes to Korea: 1945–1948

2

In the five-year period from 1945 to 1950, after World War II (1939–45) and before the start of the Korean War in 1950, the fate of Korea became entwined with intense power struggles between the Western nations (Europe and the United States) and the Union of Soviet Socialist Republics (USSR or Soviet Union). As World War II drew to a close, the Allies (the United States, the British Commonwealth, the Soviet Union, and other European nations) began to divide up territories that had been controlled by the soon-to-be-defeated enemies, mainly Germany and Japan. Presiding at these early negotiations, which began in 1943, were U.S. President Franklin D. Roosevelt (1882–1945), Soviet Premier Joseph Stalin (1879–1953), and British Prime Minister Winston Churchill (1874–1965).

By World War II's end in 1945, Stalin had negotiated tremendous Soviet power in eastern Europe. Although the Soviets were an ally, the Western nations were worried by this Soviet communist expansion. (The Soviet Union was made up of fifteen republics, including Russia, and existed as a unified communist country from 1922 to 1991. Communism is a set

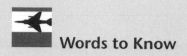

Words to Know

atomic bomb: a powerful bomb created by splitting the nuclei of a heavy chemical, such as plutonium or uranium, in a rapid chain reaction, resulting in a violent and destructive shock wave as well as radiation.

cold war: the struggle for power, authority, and prestige between the Communist Soviet Union and the capitalist Western powers of Europe and the United States from 1945 until 1991.

collaboration: cooperating with, or helping out, an enemy to one's nation.

colonial rule: rule imposed upon one nation by another, more powerful, nation.

communism: an economic system that does not include the concept of private property. Instead, the public (usually represented by the government) owns the goods and the means to produce them in common.

conservative: in politics, a person who seeks to maintain traditions, preserve established institutions, and promote a strong, authoritative government; conservatives are anticommunist and may tend to favor big business and power in the hands of an aristocracy or elite.

diplomat: a professional representative of a nation who helps handle affairs and conduct negotiations between nations.

exile: forced or voluntary absence from one's home country.

imperialism: one nation imposing its rule over another country outside of its borders.

interim government: a government formed after the ruling government in a nation is eliminated; when necessary, an interim government fills in until a permanent one can be established.

international trusteeship: the government of a country by the joint rule of several countries that have committed to act in what they deem to be the country's best interest.

nationalize: to place ownership, usually of a factory or a business, in the hands of the government.

Provisional Korean Government: a government in exile, formed in Shanghai, China, during Japanese rule of Korea (1910–45), that elected leaders and fought for the cause of an independent Korea, but had no actual power within occupied Korea.

refugee: someone who is fleeing to a different country to escape danger in his or her own nation.

38th parallel: the 38th degree of north latitude as it bisects the Korean Peninsula, chosen by Americans as the dividing line between what was to be Soviet-occupied North Korea and U.S.-occupied South Korea in 1945.

Western nations: the noncommunist nations of Europe and America.

of political beliefs that advocates the elimination of private property. It is a system in which goods are owned by the community as a whole rather than by specific individuals and are available to all as needed. The United States, on the other hand, has a capitalist economy, in which individuals, rather than the state, own the property and businesses, and the cost and distribution of goods are determined by the free market.) Distrust grew to such proportions that at times it appeared that World War III was at hand. These tensions were the beginning of the cold war, a period of political anxiety and military rivalry between the United States and the Soviet Union that stopped short of full-scale war. The cold war between these two giants had devastating consequences for the Korean nation that continue right into the twenty-first century.

The Soviet Union joins the war in the Pacific as Japan surrenders

The Soviet Union fought in Europe during World War II, but it was not involved in the war in the Pacific against the Japanese until the end of the war. When Russia entered the war in the Pacific, it did so at the request of the Allies, who were planning to invade the Japanese homeland. They wanted the Soviets to intervene with the Japanese troops stationed in Manchuria, an area in northern China where Japan had built up its army into a massive force, so those troops would be occupied outside of Japan at the time the Allies invaded. By asking the Russians to participate in the fight in the Pacific, the United States seemed willing to give them control of parts of Asia, including Korea.

The Allies asked the Soviets to intervene in Manchuria before it was clear that the atomic bomb was going to be available to the United States to use as a weapon on Japan. The Allied invasion of Japan never took place, but the Soviet entry into the war in the Pacific did. On August 6, 1945, the United States dropped an atomic bomb on Hiroshima, Japan. On August 8, the Soviets entered the war in the Pacific, assembling its troops in Manchuria. On August 9, the United States dropped another atomic bomb on Nagasaki, Japan. Japan surrendered on August 14, and World War II was over. The Soviets were still in Manchuria.

Two men stand guard on a dirt road at the border between northern and southern Korea, November 1946. *Reproduced by permission of the Corbis Corporation.*

The 38th parallel

As the war closed, the Russians, already stationed at the Korean borders, continued their march into Korea. U.S. troops in Asia were spread so thin that there was no way to get them to Korea before the Soviet troops arrived. Nonetheless, the United States acted quickly, fearing that once the Soviet Union was established as the liberator in Korea, a pro-Soviet

KOREA, 1945

CHINA

U.S.S.R.

- Musan
- Chongjin
- Hyesan
- Yalu
- Manpo
- Kimchaek
- Sinuiju
- Taedong
- Hamhung
- Wonsan
- Pyongyang

100 miles
100 kilometers

38th Parallel

- Chunchon
- Seoul
- Inchon
- Han

Sea of Japan

KOREA

- Kunsan

Yellow
Sea

- Nam
- Mokpo
- Pusan
- Yosu

JAPAN

communist nation would form there. On August 10, without consulting the Soviets or the Koreans, two U.S. officials selected the 38th parallel (the 38th degree of north latitude as it bisects the Korean peninsula) as the dividing line across Korea. On August 15, General Douglas MacArthur (1880–1964), the Allied supreme commander of U.S. forces in the southwest Pacific, issued a general order for the Japanese to surrender throughout Asia. This order included an arrangement for Korea in which the Americans were to accept the Japanese surrender south of the 38th parallel, and the Soviets would receive the surrender north of it. The Soviets accepted the arrangement without comment and stopped their march at the 38th parallel, even though there was nothing to stop them from occupying the whole country.

The Allied powers did not believe Korea would be ready to rule itself right away after so many years under colonial rule. (Korea had struggled under Japanese imperialism—ruling a country outside one's own nation's borders—since 1905.) Prior to the war's end, the Allies had agreed that Korea should be allowed to form an independent nation once liberated from the Japanese, but only "in due course" (meaning, not right away). Roosevelt and Stalin had agreed that the Allies would set up an international trusteeship (control by several countries) to govern Korea for no more than five years. But Roosevelt died in 1945, before an agreement about the trusteeship was reached.

Korea prepares for independence

After four decades of Japanese imperialism, most Koreans wanted to get rid of all reminders of colonial rule. When the Japanese defeat was assured, the Koreans immediately went to work to create an independent Korean government. First they formed the Committee for the Preparation of Korean Independence (CPKI). The committee quickly spread throughout Korea, with 145 branches by the end of August 1945. These branches were called People's Committees, and in many places they served effectively as the local government. On September 6, 1945, the CPKI elected fifty-five leaders to head the Korean People's Republic. This new Korean government favored reforms that would redistribute land and wealth, help workers, and uphold human rights for all Korean people.

The United States arrives in the south

Major General John Reed Hodge was appointed commanding general of the U.S. armed forces in Korea as soon as the war ended. The U.S. State Department was not able to make his mission in Korea very clear to him because the United States until that time had little understanding of Korea.

While MacArthur instructed Hodge to treat the Koreans as a liberated people, Hodge also received orders from the U.S. secretary of state to "create a government in harmony with U.S. policies." Hodge, a very competent leader in battle but a poor diplomat (foreign relations negotiator), instructed his officers to treat Korea as an "enemy of the state," as quoted in Bruce Cumings's history, *Korea's Place in the Sun: A Modern History*.

A strange collaboration between the American military in Korea and the Japanese developed. Although the Japanese had been the United States's enemy in the war just weeks before, for some reason many U.S. leaders found them easier to understand than the Koreans. Thus, instead of arriving to expel the former colonial rulers, Hodge actually had leaflets dropped in southern Korea telling the citizens to continue to obey the same Japanese authorities they had been forced to obey before the surrender. When the U.S. troops arrived in Korea on September 5, 1945, they were welcomed by the Japanese police force. The Koreans, who anxiously awaited the U.S. soldiers as their liberators, were stunned to see them treating the Japanese as their allies in Korea.

The Koreans' hopes for independence under their new government were soon dampened as well. The Americans never accepted the Korean People's Republic, viewing it as pro-communist. The new U.S. military government, the Korean Military Advisory Group (KMAG), had no interest in the reforms sought by the Koreans. Additionally, the United States was initially unwilling to recognize any group as a government until an agreement was reached by the Allies about a trusteeship to oversee Korea. To maintain law and order until such a trusteeship came into being, Hodge decided to leave the Japanese colonial rule intact. In September 1945, at the ceremony given for the surrender of the Japanese, Hodge announced that the colonial government would continue to rule as it had before the war, with the Japanese leaders, even the Japanese governor general, remaining in place.

The uproar from the Koreans in the south against Japanese rule was so strong that within days Hodge agreed to replace the Japanese leaders with Koreans. The Japanese leaders, however, were asked to recommend Koreans to take their places. Because of this, most leaders in postwar southern Korea were those Koreans who had collaborated with the Japanese

Syngman Rhee in 1919, at that time president of the Provisional Government of the Republic of Korea.
Reproduced by permission of AP/Wide World Photos.

during the colonial rule, and many of the Korean people viewed them as traitors. Although the Japanese civil servants and soldiers were shipped back to Japan within four months, the Koreans did not forget the alliance between the Americans and the Japanese. Uprisings against the U.S. military government were soon common in the south.

Occupation in the south

In order to fight the communist elements in southern Korea without starting an all-out revolution, the United States began seeking Korean leaders who had not been affiliated with the Japanese rulers. Several conservative nationalist leaders—who were both anticommunist and proindependence—were brought in from the Provisional Government of the Republic of Korea in Shanghai, China (see Chapter 1). In October 1945, Syngman Rhee (1875–1965), a Korean independence leader who had been living in the United States, arrived in the capital city of Seoul. The seventy-year-old Rhee and his Austrian wife arrived in MacArthur's plane. For decades Rhee had been doing everything he could to educate the U.S. government to the evils of Japanese rule in Korea, but up to this point he was generally paid little heed. Rhee was staunchly anticommunist.

New factions arose in southern Korea. One was made up of the tiny Korean minority of wealthy landowners and capitalists, who formed a party called the Korean Democratic Party (KDP). The United States gave its approval to this party and began to form an interim government (a government formed to fill in until a permanent one is established). In October 1945, the U.S. military government established an eleven-person "advisory council" to work with the American military governor. This council was supposed to represent the Korean population; in fact, it was archly conservative and mainly comprised of members of the KDP.

In November 1945, the Americans began to train Koreans in military maneuvers. The old Korean National Police (KNP), the nationwide police force with which the Japanese had tyrannized the Koreans, was also revamped and called the "constabulary" by the Americans. It was comprised of about 85 percent of the same Koreans who had been employed by the Japanese. Hodge then began his battle against the Korean People's Republic, using the KNP to dismantle the People's Committees that remained active in the countryside.

South Korean artillerymen cleaning the mechanism of a 105-millimeter field piece in preparation for an inspection by members of the U.S. Military Advisory Group, July 1949. *Reproduced by permission of Double Delta Industries, Inc.*

Korean Place Names

The Korean language is written in its native land in *Han'gul,* meaning "great letters," a script using characters that are very different from the Roman alphabet that is used to write English. When Korean names, places, and other words are spelled in English, the words are written more or less as they are pronounced. In the Korean language, however, there are sounds that the Roman alphabet cannot produce exactly. Because of this, when reading about Korea, place names can be spelled in slightly different ways, with different consonants (Pusan = Busan), or with a variety of diacritical marks (Pyongyang = P'yong'an). Generally speaking, however, when reading a Korean place name in the Roman alphabet, the word itself reflects the pronunciation.

Place names in Korean often have a special addition or two to make them more specific. For example, the village of No Gun is generally referred to as No Gun Ri; *ri* means "village." Similarly, the island of Koje is often called Koje-do; *do* means "island."

Northern Korea after the split

The Soviets entering northern Korea after World War II were welcomed enthusiastically by the many Koreans who sought reforms under the new People's Committees. The Soviets were not such a welcome sight to landlords, businesspeople, Japanese civilians, and anticommunists, many of whom fled to southern Korea on their arrival. Unlike the Americans in the south, the Soviets left the People's Committees intact and joined in their reform efforts, especially in eliminating the hated Japanese colonial government. Many Korean soldiers and anti-Japanese activists had taken refuge from the Japanese in the Soviet Union, particularly in Siberia, the vast part of Russia that comprises one-third of Asia. The Russians brought these soldiers back to Korea with Soviet training and installed them in key positions in the People's Committees. One of these refugees was the popular and successful guerrilla leader Kim Il Sung (1912–1994). (See Chapter 1.)

Unlike southern Korea, which was mainly agricultural, northern Korea had most of the nation's industry. Under Soviet supervision, the industries were quickly nationalized (became owned by the government), which was easy to accomplish because they had been owned by the Japanese. Land reforms were put into place that took farms away from landlords, redistributing the land among the people. Within one year of the Soviet arrival in northern Korea, those Koreans who had been part of the KNP in colonial times were expelled. There was little killing, but in that first year between one and two million people—landlords, capitalists, police, and others who had collaborated with the Japanese—became refugees in southern Korea.

The new northern Korean government did not allow opposition. There was no freedom of speech or press. The powerful new security forces that took the place of the KNP were well trained: they avoided corruption and unnecessary cruelty. Instead of using brutality as the Japanese had done, the northern Koreans adopted the technique of converting their opponents, persuading them to change their beliefs. The police system was set up to try to learn everyone's thoughts, at least as they pertained to politics. Northern Koreans were encouraged to report to the authorities if a neighbor or relative said anything that might be anticommunist. Detailed records of seemingly innocent remarks were kept at special offices in every village; suspects and their families, friends, and associates were carefully watched.

Where to Learn More

Blair, Clay. *The Forgotten War: America in Korea, 1950–1953.* New York: Times Books, 1987.

Breen, Michael. *The Koreans: Who They Are, What They Want, Where Their Future Lies.* New York: St. Martin's Press, 1998.

Clark, Mark W. *From the Danube to the Yalu.* New York: Harper and Brothers, 1954.

Cumings, Bruce. *Korea's Place in the Sun: A Modern History.* New York: Norton, 1997.

Goulden, Joseph C. *Korea: The Untold Story of the War.* New York: Times Books, 1982.

Hart-Landsberg, Martin. *Korea: Division, Reunification, and U.S. Foreign Policy.* New York: Monthly Review Press, 1998.

Hasting, Max. *The Korean War.* New York: Simon & Schuster, 1987.

Liem, Channing. *The Korean War: An Unanswered Question.* Albany, NY: The Committee for a New Korea Policy, 1992.

Varhola, Michael J. *Fire and Ice: The Korean War, 1950–1953.* Mason City, IA: Savas Publishing, 2000.

Whelan, Richard. *Drawing the Line: The Korean War, 1950–1953.* Boston: Little, Brown, 1990.

Web sites

Savada, Andrea Matles, and William Shaw, eds. "South Korea: A Country Study." The Federal Research Division, Library of Congress. [Online] http://lcweb2.loc.gov/frd/cs/krtoc.html (accessed on August 14, 2001).

A Divided Korea Heads for War: 1948–1950

3

By 1947, an overpopulated southern Korea, without industry or energy sources, was quickly going into an economic tailspin, with widespread famine and unemployment. A new and stronger right wing (a group composed of anticommunists who generally supported a government by the wealthy or elite) was forming, and youth gangs were terrorizing the leftists (those who sought reform and equality, some of whom were communist). Conflicts among the Koreans were becoming more violent and more frequent. Something needed to be done and quickly.

Talks were held between the United States and the Soviet Union in 1946 and again in 1947 to try to create a joint trusteeship over Korea, with the idea that a few nations jointly govern the country. In 1947, the Soviets proposed to the United States that both powers withdraw their troops from Korea at the same time, leaving the Koreans to create their own independent nation. The United States knew its position in Korea was too difficult to defend. In September, despite Russia's strong objections, the United States passed the matter of Korea on to the United Nations.

Left versus Right: Definitions

The terminology used to express the opposing sides in modern politics has at its base the opposites left and right. In politics, leftism is a vague term used to include people who hold radical political views seeking change and reform, usually including more freedom, more equality, and better conditions for common people. Leftism may include communism, which is a kind of economic practice that eliminates private property, under which production of goods and the distribution of goods are owned by the state or the population as a whole. But many leftists are not communists. They seek reform either within the existing government or through revolution.

The right wing in politics holds conservative views and generally seeks to maintain traditions, preserve established institutions, and establish a strong, authoritative government. The right wing is always anticommunist and may tend to favor big business and power in the hands of an aristocracy or elite.

The United Nations Temporary Commission on Korea (UNTCOK) was then formed; its members arrived in the capital city of Seoul in May 1948.

The Soviet Union and the northern Koreans did not believe that the UN had authority to decide the future of Korea. The northern Koreans blocked UNTCOK from entering its part of the country to set up the elections and refused to participate in any way. Korean independence leader Syngman Rhee (1875–1965) urged going forward with the elections without the northern vote, a plan that was clearly in his favor. (In order to fight the communist elements in southern Korea without starting an all-out revolution, the United States had sought out Rhee, who was staunchly anticommunist, to come help lead a new independent Korea after World War II. He was already in place in southern Korea. See Chapter 2.) Many in southern Korea strongly objected, believing that an election in which only the south participated would doom any possibility of reunification. Several prominent leaders from southern Korea went to the north to try to work out some kind of arrangement with the northern Koreans, but they did not succeed before the elections.

There was much controversy within the UN about holding such a one-sided vote, but the election went on without the Koreans north of the 38th parallel. The elections filled two hundred of the three hundred seats in the new Korean National Assembly, reserving one hundred seats for northerners. The new government was to rule over all of Korea.

On May 10, 1948, the Republic of Korea's first Korean National Assembly was elected. It adopted a constitution

A festive ceremony in Seoul to celebrate the birth of a new nation: the Republic of Korea, August 15, 1948. Soldiers of the constabulary are lined on the right of the crowd. *Reproduced by permission of the Corbis Corporation.*

establishing a presidential form of government and four-year terms for the president. Syngman Rhee was inaugurated president of the Republic of Korea (ROK) on August 15, 1948. With the new South Korean flag now flying over Seoul, Rhee cracked down on his opposition, using the national police as his own machine for repression. Political arrests abounded, and freedom of the press was restricted.

Members of a Democratic People's Republic of Korea government delegation arrive in Moscow, in the Soviet Union, March 1949. Kim Il Sung is at front left, observing the honor guard. *Reproduced by permission of AP/Wide World Photos.*

North Korea forms a new government

Northern Korea then announced upcoming elections for a new Korean government. On September 9, 1948, the Democratic People's Republic of Korea (DPRK) was created, and popular guerrilla leader Kim Il Sung (1912–1994) was elected as its premier. He claimed to be the legitimate leader of all the people of Korea, saying he had been elected not only in the north, but in underground elections in the south as well. The Soviet Union withdrew all of its troops from North Korea at the end of 1948.

The cold war heats up

In 1949, while the United States was getting its troops out of Korea, several world events made a wave of change in public attitude. First, by 1948 and 1949, the Soviet Union had become very aggressive in Europe. Then the Russians successfully tested their first atomic bomb in September 1949.

As tension was building, an unprepared American public was shocked when Communist Chinese leader Mao Zedong (Mao Tse-tung; 1893–1976) proclaimed the establishment of the People's Republic of China on October 1, 1949, having driven the American-backed Chinese Nationalist leader Chiang Kai-shek (1887–1975) and his forces to the island of Taiwan (formerly Formosa). The United States government cut off aid to Chiang, seeing no hope for the Nationalists, who had lost most of their popular support in China through corruption and incompetence. The American public was horrified, believing that Chiang Kai-shek was a strong and heroic ruler. Cold war propaganda began to abound, spurred on by sensational media stories and attention-seeking politicians. (The cold war refers to the political tension and military rivalry that begun after World War II between the United States and the Soviet Union, which stopped short of full-scale war and persisted until the breakup of the Soviet Union in 1991.) Fingers pointed everywhere, and U.S. leaders, especially in the White House and the State Department, were accused of selling out China and being communist sympathizers.

From scattered uprisings to guerrilla warfare

Meanwhile, hostilities between South Korean factions mounted. Small battles arose daily, often between peasants and the national police or youth gangs. In certain parts of South Korea there were large pockets of leftists, particularly in places where the People's Committees remained strong, such as the provinces of Chölla, Kyöngyang, and Kangwön, and the island of Cheju (pronounced SHE-shoo). (People's Committees were formed as local branches of the Committee for the Preparation of Korean Independence [CPKI], the first organized effort after World War II for Korean independence and unity. In many places they served effectively as the local government.)

Cheju-do

In 1948, guerrilla warfare broke out on Cheju-do (*do* means island), an island with a population of three hundred thousand. Cheju, blissfully isolated from the rest of Korea and its conflicts, had been existing peacefully, governed by its People's Committee. But in 1948, the national police started a brutal campaign there to eliminate the People's Committee. At the

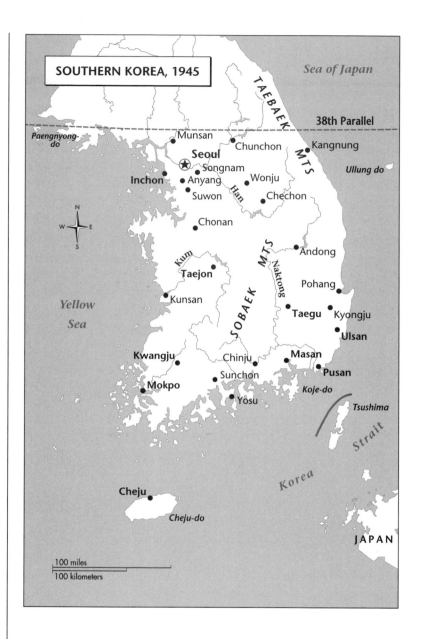

SOUTHERN KOREA, 1945

time of the national elections in May 1948, there were protest demonstrations in Cheju over the attempts to eliminate the People's Committee and institute police rule. Over two thousand young demonstrators were arrested; one was tortured to death.

The people of Cheju-do had had enough; a guerrilla army of about four thousand was quickly formed and it began to attack police stations, blow up bridges, and cut communica-

A village on Cheju-do, circa 1986. *Reproduced by permission of the Corbis Corporation.*

tions lines on the island. The guerrillas, working in small groups, had taken control of most of the villages on the interior of the island by June 1948, and they managed to maintain their control for some time. It was not until a year later, in April 1949, that the American embassy reported that the guerrillas had been stopped. The price, however, was costly. The national police and the youth gangs who came in to put down the uprisings were ruthless, taking an appalling toll on the population of Cheju-do. American sources cited fifteen thousand to twenty thousand islander deaths, but the governor of Cheju cited a much higher figure of sixty thousand deaths. Out of four hundred villages on Cheju-do, only one hundred seventy villages remained after this warfare. Terrified people fled across the water to Japan as their homes and villages were demolished. The people of Cheju have long kept silent about the atrocities that befell them, but in the 1980s the survivors began to record the tales of torture, murder, and rape to which they were subjected by the youth gangs and the national police.

Soldiers turn rebel

In October 1948, some South Korean soldiers who had been sent to fight the rebels in Cheju-do decided instead to turn against the government. They took control of the port city of Yosu and restored the People's Committee. While the town was in rebel hands, trials began for police and landlords, among others, and some executions took place. As the rebellion spread, red flags and DPRK (North Korean) flags flew over surrounding villages. After one week of this rebellion, the Korean army regained control of Yosu. Many of the townspeople fled; those who remained were beaten and tortured. More than five hundred townspeople in Yosu were shot on suspicion of having helped the guerrillas.

By early 1949, there were an estimated thirty-five hundred to six thousand guerrilla rebels in South Korea, especially strong in South Chölla, North Kyöngysang, and Kyöngju. Syngman Rhee's entire army, backed by its American advisors, killed an estimated six thousand guerrillas between November 1949 and March 1950, claiming to have eliminated them entirely.

Fighting begins between North and South

By 1949, Rhee was determined to go to war with the north, hoping to unify Korea under his own regime. Rhee had been intent on one thing throughout his whole career: to be the ruler of an independent Korea. However, Rhee was not popular with American leaders. Even the future commander of the UN forces in Korea, General Mark W. Clark, who was very sympathetic to Rhee, described him as a zealot (fanatic) and an autocrat (a person who rules with unlimited authority) in his book *From the Danube to the Yalu:* "By the time of the Korean War, Rhee had been working for independence and unity so long that he had come to identify himself as the living embodiment of Korean patriotism, the sole prophet who could show the way to unity and freedom for the Koreans. Opposition to Rhee's ideas seemed to him to be anti-Korean, not anti-Rhee." Rhee badly needed strong U.S. backing to begin his mission to take over North Korea by force, but the United States, with no wish to be involved in a war in Asia, repeatedly told him there would be no U.S. support in an unprovoked attack against the north.

Kim Il Sung, too, wanted to reunify Korea under his leadership. But when the first battles began in 1949, it was for the most part the south that was on the attack, and this was probably because Kim was still preparing his army for war. In 1947, Kim had sent thirty thousand troops to Mao Zedong to fight with the communists in the civil war in China. With Mao's victory in 1949, the troops were gradually coming back to Korea, trained and well seasoned in war. And Kim had been building his forces by buying military equipment from the Soviets and training his own troops.

A bloody border battle between north and south took place in May 1949, started by the south. Small but vicious battles continued at the border until the war began.

States of preparedness in 1950

In January 1950, U.S. Secretary of State Dean Acheson (1893–1971) delivered a speech to the press, outlining the areas of concern for military defense. Korea was not mentioned among the countries that the United States was prepared to defend. This may have been the news Kim Il Sung was hoping for. It greatly disturbed Syngman Rhee.

Without strong military support from the United States, the Republic of Korea Army (called the ROKs) was not very prepared for war. There were about ninety-five thousand troops in the ROKs in 1950, almost all of them members of the national police, or constabulary, that had been formed by the U.S. military government. They were undertrained and poorly equipped. Because Rhee was so eager to go to war, the United States had deliberately underequipped the ROKs, so they would not do something foolish. The United States had not provided the ROKs with tanks, either, thinking that they would be useless in Korea's mountainous countryside. Heavy weapons and vehicles were in short supply, and most of the ROK artillery units were only one-quarter armed. When the United States had withdrawn its troops in July 1949, it had left behind a five-hundred-man Korean Military Advisory Group (KMAG), which was still working on building up the ROK troops.

The American military itself was drastically reduced since the end of World War II. At the end of the war there had been twelve million men and women in military service, but by 1948 there were only 1.5 million. Weapons and equipment were in short supply.

The North Korean People's Army (NKPA), founded in February 1948, was significantly stronger than the ROKs. By mid-year in 1950, the NKPA had strength of about 135,000 troops. Most of the officers in the NKPA had fought in the Chinese Civil War or with the Soviets in World War II. The NKPA had 150 Soviet-made armored tanks and were equipped with heavy weaponry. When the Soviets withdrew their occupation troops at the end of 1948, they, like the Americans, left behind a military advisory group.

On June 24, 1950, unknown to South Korea or its American advisors, ninety thousand North Korean People's Army troops—two-thirds of the entire army—gathered on the 38th parallel, prepared for battle.

Where to Learn More

Blair, Clay. *The Forgotten War: America in Korea, 1950–1953*. New York: Times Books, 1987.

Breen, Michael. *The Koreans: Who They Are, What They Want, Where Their Future Lies*. New York: St. Martin's Press, 1999.

Clark, Mark W. *From the Danube to the Yalu*. New York: Harper and Brothers, 1954.

Cumings, Bruce. *Korea's Place in the Sun: A Modern History*. New York: Norton, 1997.

Goulden, Joseph C. *Korea: The Untold Story of the War*. New York: Times Books, 1982.

Hart-Landsberg, Martin. *Korea: Division, Reunification, and U.S. Foreign Policy*. New York: Monthly Review Press, 1998.

Hasting, Max. *The Korean War*. New York: Simon & Schuster, 1987.

Liem, Channing. *The Korean War: An Unanswered Question*. Albany, NY: The Committee for a New Korea Policy, 1992.

Varhola, Michael J. *Fire and Ice: The Korean War, 1950–1953*. Mason City, IA: Savas Publishing, 2000.

Whelan, Richard. *Drawing the Line: The Korean War, 1950–1953*. Boston: Little, Brown, 1990.

Web sites

Savada, Andrea Matles, and William Shaw, eds. "South Korea: A Country Study." The Federal Research Division, Library of Congress. [Online] http://lcweb2.loc.gov/frd/cs/krtoc.html (accessed on August 14, 2001).

The Invasion of South Korea: June 25–30, 1950

O n the evening of June 24, 1950, a Saturday night, the South Korean (ROK) Army's entire front line defense force consisted of four infantry divisions and a regiment. Normally there would have been about thirty-eight thousand troops at the 38th parallel (the dividing line between northern and southern Korea), but for the first time in months, the ROK Army felt confident enough to issue leaves to soldiers on the front. On that crucial night, only about one-third of the force was on duty.

Throughout the night, the North Korean People's Army (NKPA) prepared for an offensive. To its ten thousand troops already stationed at the 38th parallel, the NKPA had added eighty thousand more men, amassing seven divisions equipped with one hundred fifty Soviet-made T-34 tanks. Without being detected, the North Koreans took up positions along the front across Korea, even rebuilding train tracks in the night for the transport of soldiers in the morning.

The North Korean invasion of June 25

The North Koreans positioned themselves to strike at five key places. All of the strikes occurred between 4:00 and

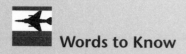

Words to Know

army: two or more military corps under the command of a general; an army usually consists of between 120,000 and 200,000 troops. Chinese armies were generally composed of three 10,000-men divisions and resembled the U.S. Army's corps.

battalion: a military unit usually made up of about three to five companies. Generally one of the companies is the headquarters unit, another the service unit, and the rest are line units. Although the numbers differ greatly, a battalion might consist of about 35 officers and about 750 soldiers.

boycott: a refusal to participate in something (purchasing from a store, working, attending an organization) until stated conditions are met.

casualties: those who are killed, wounded, missing, or taken prisoner in combat.

civilian: someone who is not in the military or any other security forces.

company: the basic army unit, composed of a headquarters and two or three platoons. A company is generally made up of about 100 soldiers commanded by a major or captain. There are three to five companies to a battalion. Army and Marine Corps regiments during the Korean War followed the same system of designating their companies by a letter. In First Battalion, A, B, C were rifle companies, D was a weapons company. In Second Battalion, E, F, G were rifle companies, H was a weapons company, and so on. To avoid confusion, the letter designations became words: H Company was How Company, etc.

corps: a military unit consisting of two or more divisions under the command of a lieutenant general; there are usually between 30,000 and 60,000 personnel in a corps.

division (or infantry division): a self-sufficient unit, usually about 15,000 to

5:00 A.M. on June 25, 1950. Two full divisions and a battalion of T-34 tanks struck on a route beginning with Kaesong (a South Korean city positioned on the 38th parallel) and leading to the capital city of Seoul. A fifteen-car train packed with North Korean soldiers moved across the 38th parallel and right into Kaesong. The Twelfth Regiment of the ROK First Division, stationed at Kaesong, was very nearly wiped out in this initial attack. The First Division's Thirteenth Regiment, about fifteen miles east of Kaesong, and the Eleventh Regiment in reserve near Seoul, fought bravely against the North Koreans in desperate conditions for two days.

16,000 strong, under the command of a major general. Communist Chinese army divisions were closer to 10,000 soldiers strong.

evacuate: to remove people from a dangerous area or a military zone.

grenade: a small explosive weapon that can be thrown, usually with a pin that is pulled to activate it and a spring-loaded safety lever that is held down until the user wants to throw the grenade; once the safety lever is released, the grenade will explode in seconds.

intervention: the act of a third party who steps into an ongoing fight in the attempt to interfere in its outcome or stop it altogether.

Joint Chiefs of Staff: an agency within the Department of Defense serving to advise the president and the secretary of defense on matters of war. The Joint Chiefs of Staff consists of a chairman, a vice chairman, the chief of staff of the army, the chief of naval operations, the chief of staff of the air force, and the commandant of the marine corps.

resolution: the formal statement of an organization's intentions or opinions on an issue, usually reached by vote or general agreement.

ROK: an acronym standing for Republic of Korea; "ROK" was frequently used to refer specifically to South Korean soldiers.

suicide mission: an activity taken on with the knowledge that carrying it out will mean one's own death.

38th parallel: the 38th degree of north latitude as it bisects the Korean Peninsula, chosen by Americans as the dividing line between what was to be Soviet-occupied North Korea and U.S.-occupied South Korea in 1945.

The largest NKPA attack occurred at the Uijongbu Corridor (pronounced wee-jong-boo), a broad valley leading southward through western Korea, with good roads that lead right from the 38th parallel into Seoul. There, two full NKPA divisions armed with eighty tanks met the highly trained ROK Seventh Division. The Seventh put up a good fight and inflicted many casualties on the NKPA, but was forced to withdraw. The retreat of the Seventh Division exposed the First Division, which then fell back to Seoul.

The ROK Sixth Division was stationed near Chunchon at the time of attack. Despite the fact that the NKPA had about

eleven thousand men to the ROK's twenty-four hundred, the ROK Army had its greatest success at Chunchon, stopping the NKPA in its tracks for three days.

There were two smaller attacks on the coasts. On the east coast, the ROK's Eighth Division was attacked in the Taebaek mountains and was quickly forced to withdraw. The Seventeenth ROK Regiment held the Ongjin peninsula on the west coast. When the NKPA attacked, one battalion was wiped out and two managed to evacuate.

As the NKPA infantry divisions attacked on the ground, two full forces of the North Korean Air Force began bombing sites in Seoul, especially Kimpo Airport.

Men of the U.S. First Marine Division move up the road from Inchon to Seoul, South Korea, past a knocked-out Soviet-made T-34 North Korean tank. *Reproduced by permission of Double Delta Industries, Inc.*

Fighting tanks

In the first weeks of the war, the North Korean People's Army was almost unstoppable. The North Koreans were better prepared, better armed, and better disciplined than the South Koreans and had more troops ready for action. Perhaps the biggest single asset of the North Koreans in their invasion of the south was their strategic use of the Soviet-made T-34 tanks they had amassed before attacking. This 35-ton armored vehicle had been the Soviet Union's main battle tank during World War II (1939–45). It had a high-velocity 85-millimeter gun and could be driven at speeds up to 34 miles per hour. The ROK Army had no tanks and barely any serviceable antitank ammunition and weapons. In fact, just before the war, the chief of the U.S. military advisors had proclaimed Korea too mountainous for tanks. The North Koreans proved him very wrong. The tanks, which maneuvered the terrain quite well, were virtually indestructible and deadly to the South Korean and American troops that first came into contact with them.

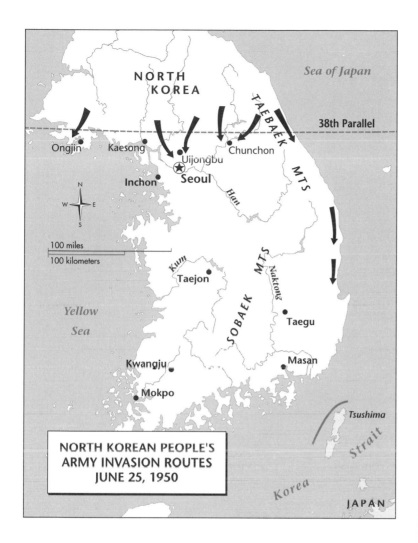

NORTH KOREAN PEOPLE'S
ARMY INVASION ROUTES
JUNE 25, 1950

Many of the South Korean soldiers had never seen a tank before, and the appearance of the tanks on the first day of fighting, when all were reeling from the surprise attack, was overwhelming. While some panicked, there was an amazing show of bravery within First Division commander General Paik Sun Yup's (1920–) troops, as he recalled in his memoirs *From Pusan to Panmunjom:*

> The more courageous soldiers of the 13th Regiment overcame their fear [of the tanks]. Acting without orders from their officers, a number of them broke into suicide teams and charged T-34s clutching explosives and grenades. They clambered up onto the monsters before touching off the charges. Although such desperate acts brought tears to my eyes, the bravery of these men pre-

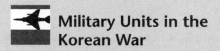

Military Units in the Korean War

Squad: A unit consisting of twelve riflemen (twelve troops).

Platoon: A unit composed of three squads.

Company: A unit composed of three platoons.

Battalion: A unit composed of three companies of riflemen and other companies formed for heavy weaponry.

Regiment: A unit composed of three battalions.

Division: A self-contained tactical unit composed of three regiments (about sixteen thousand troops).

vented NKPA armored units from getting past the 13th all that first day, earning precious time for division troops on leave and pass to return to the 11th Regiment.

An estimated ninety ROK soldiers died in these suicide missions against the tanks on that first day of battle.

Evacuating Americans

It quickly became clear that the ROK Army could not save the city of Seoul. American ambassador to Korea John J. Muccio started procedures for the evacuation of Americans on the first day of the invasion. By the next morning, a Norwegian ship took hundreds of women and children to Japan. Later that day, air transport protected by U.S. fighter planes brought out the remaining American dependents. A portion of the civilian population of the city prepared to flee as well. South Korean president Syngman Rhee (1875–1965) and his government evacuated Seoul late on the night of June 26, heading south for the city of Taejon (pronounced TIE-shon). Muccio closed the U.S. embassy in Seoul on Tuesday afternoon, June 27. By then, chaos reigned in the city, as its people fled south across the Han River by train or on foot with what belongings they could carry on their backs.

During the evening of June 27 the ROK Second and Seventh Divisions gave way to the NKPA forces just north of the capital, and the retreating ROK soldiers were ordered to flee south across the Han River. Seoul was open to the invading North Koreans.

Disaster on the Han River

As the North Korean forces approached Seoul on the night of June 27, the ROK planned to stop their advance by blowing up the bridges on their route. But the order to blow up the three-lane, three-railroad-trestle Han River Bridge that lay just south of Seoul—when at least ten thousand ROK troops remained north of it and would not be able to cross the river with their equipment—caused an uproar at the ROK Army headquarters. Last minute attempts to stop the disaster from happening were unsuccessful. The Han River Bridge blew up at 2:15 A.M. The population of Seoul had been given no warning, and the bridge was flooded with people fleeing south when it exploded. From five hundred to eight hundred civilians and military personnel were killed in this explosion.

After the first three and a half days of fighting, the unprepared ROK Army was in a state of near collapse. Out of the ninety-eight thousand men in the army at the beginning of the war, one week later only fifty-four thousand could be accounted for. The rest—almost one-half the army—had been killed or captured or had deserted. Without support from the United States, the war would have been over very quickly. But the South Korean Army had probably done the very thing needed to foil the stronger and better equipped NKPA. By their resistance, they most likely stopped the North Koreans from swooping down and capturing Seoul within the first twenty-four hours of their invasion. Had the North Koreans taken Seoul before the United States or the United Nations (UN) could respond, they would almost certainly have been the immediate victors of this war.

Early atrocities

During the first few weeks of the war, Rhee's government feared that the leftists within South Korea would join with the invading North Koreans and tip the scale of the war. Therefore tens of thousands of people—men, women, and even children—were jailed on suspicion of being rebels throughout South Korea. When the North Korean People's Army approached South Korean cities and the time for evacuation neared, the political prisoners were often taken out and shot in large groups without trial. There are reports from South Koreans, Western journalists, and the U.S. military showing that at least ten mass executions took place—and there were probably many more than that—killing thousands of civilians.

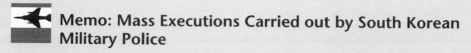

Memo: Mass Executions Carried out by South Korean Military Police

Top Secret Document, Declassified in December 1999
11 August 1950
Subject: Shooting of Prisoners of War by South Korean Military Police
To: 545th Military Police Company

Between the hours of 1500 and 1630, 10 August 1950, while on routine patrol on the highway between Taegu and Waegwan, Korea, a large volume of gunfire was investigated by the undersigned and Pfc. Rant. This gunfire came from a canyon near the top of a mountain that is situated approximately eight miles north of Taegu.

Investigation disclosed that the South Korean Military Police, under command of a Captain of the South Korean Army, were in the process of the killing of a group of Korean Nationals, estimated to be between 200 and 300 persons, including some women and at least one girl. It is the opinion of the undersigned that this child was approximately 12 or 13 years of age.

The methods used by the Koreans in the executions were the placing of about 20 of the condemned persons in a line on the edge of a cliff, and behind each of the victims was placed one Military Policeman with a carbine of American Army current issue. At the command of fire, given by the commanding officer of the group, the military police fired at the head of the prisoner that was in front of him. It was noted in several of the shootings, that due to poor aim of the weapon, the prisoner was not killed instantly, but it was necessary for several other shots to be fired into the body of the victim, and in some cases the mercy shot was not administered, and that about three hours after the executions were completed, some of the condemned persons were still alive and moaning. The cries could be heard coming from somewhere in the mass of bodies piled in the canyon. One man was lying a short way apart from the main mass of bodies,

Meanwhile in the United States

Because of the time difference (it is fourteen hours earlier in Washington, D.C.), when the invasion of South Korea occurred at 4:00 A.M. on Sunday, June 25, in Korea, it was 2:00 P.M. Saturday, June 24, on the U.S. East Coast. News of the attack began to reach key government officials on Saturday evening. Secretary of State Dean Acheson (1893–1971) called President Harry S. Truman (1884–1972) at his home in Independence, Missouri, to tell him the situation in Korea was "serious." Acheson suggested calling an emergency session of and even though unconscious, was noted to be still breathing.

A survey was made by the undersigned of the prisoners that remained on the side of the mountain awaiting their turn to be shot, and it was noted that the hands were tied behind by trussing two of the condemned persons together, and the hands were tied so tightly that there were cries of severe pain coming from the prisoners. One of the women prisoners, a girl of about 19 years, had fallen and in the fall the flesh had been torn from her hands. Extreme cruelty was noted from the Military Policemen to the condemned persons such as striking them on the head with gunbutts, and kicking them on the body for no reason.

The Commanding Officer of the execution group stated that the prisoners were being killed as they were "spies." No other information was given.

The bodies were not properly buried, but were partly covered with dirt and brush, and the cartridge cases were left on the ground. In the event of the fall into the hands of the red army of this area, all of the evidence left by the South Korean Military Police would indicate that the killings were perpetrated by the American Army and not the South Korean Army. The bodies had been stripped of clothing and it would be hard to determine whether the victim was civilian or North Korean Military Personnel.

H. H. Mix
WOJG, USA
/s/ Frank Pearce, Sgt l/c
Division Investigator
1st Cavalry Division
Taegu, Korea

Source: "Bridge at No Gun Ri." Associated Press (AP). [Online] http://wire.ap.org/APpackages/nogunri/executions_doc2.html (accessed on August 14, 2001).

the United Nations Security Council, to which Truman agreed. After receiving the call, Truman was very quiet, recalled his daughter Margaret in her biography, and quoted by Joseph C. Goulden in *Korea; The Untold Story of the War:* "My father made it clear, from the moment he heard the news, that he feared this was the opening round in World War Three."

Like Truman, many Americans jumped to the conclusion that the Soviet Union was responsible for the North Korean attack on the south. The Soviets left behind a panel of military advisors and a sizable arsenal of weapons when their

A U.S. Army photograph, once classified "top secret," of South Korean political prisoners executed by the South Korean military at Taejon over three days in July 1950. They were suspected of being communist sympathizers and possible collaborators. *Reproduced by permission of AP/Wide World Photos.*

troops pulled out of North Korea in 1948. They had also sold vital military equipment to North Korea after the occupation. But many modern historians have concluded that the Soviets were not fully behind the effort. In 1970, memoirs attributed to Soviet Premier Nikita Khrushchev (1894–1971) were published in the West that were thought to be authentic. The memoirs describe a visit that North Korean Premier Kim Il Sung (1912–1994) had made to Moscow, the Soviet capital, in 1949 to try to get support for the planned invasion from Soviet

Premier Joseph Stalin (1879–1953). Stalin was very cautious in his response. Because the Soviets were tied up in other efforts, Stalin's eventual nod of approval to Kim Il Sung's plans for invasion appears to have been just that: moral, but not military or financial, support.

On the first day of fighting, the U.S. Joint Chiefs of Staff met. Created in 1949, the Joint Chiefs of Staff is an agency within the Department of Defense serving to advise the president and the secretary of defense on matters of war. It was then headed by World War II veteran General Omar N. Bradley (1893–1981), who was appointed chairman by the president, and included the chiefs of the army, navy, and air force. When the Joint Chiefs met on June 25, a policy in regard to Korea had already been established: in the event of military conflict in Korea, all Americans, including military advisors, would evacuate, and the United States would not intervene. At the time of the first Joint Chiefs meeting, reports arriving from Seoul seemed positive, and the military leaders had no reason to think the policy would be overturned.

On the afternoon of June 25, the United Nations Security Council met to discuss the invasion. The U.S. representative to the UN proposed a resolution accusing North Korea of "unprovoked aggression." This proposal met with significant opposition from other member nations, but by evening a version had passed condemning the "armed attack on the Republic of Korea" and calling for "the immediate cessation of [end to] hostilities" and withdrawal of NKPA troops to the 38th parallel. Just before the Korean War broke out, the Soviet Union had begun a boycott of the United Nations—they refused to participate in the proceedings—because the UN had failed to recognize the People's Republic of China, headed by Mao Zedong (Mao Tse-tung; 1893–1976). (Ever since 1949, when the Communists defeated the U.S.-backed Nationalists in the Chinese Civil War, the United States and the UN did not recognize Communist China.) Had the Soviets been represented at the UN that day and in the days to come, it is unlikely that the UN resolutions would have passed.

Two Blair House meetings

President Truman arrived back in Washington, D.C., on the evening of June 25 and called the first of his Blair House

Member nations of the United Nations Security Council vote at the emergency session of June 25, 1950, calling for a cease-fire order in Korea.
Reproduced by permission of AP/Wide World Photos.

meetings. (Blair House served as the presidential residence while the White House was being renovated.) Attending were the Joint Chiefs of Staff, Secretary of State Dean Acheson, and other State Department officials. The tone was entirely different than that of the morning meeting. Fears of an expanded Soviet empire became dominant. The issue had changed from interfering in a civil war to stopping the communists from their mission of taking over the world. Everyone agreed that instead of evacuating, the United States should support South Korea.

The Joint Chiefs and Truman agreed to try to limit the American involvement and defer to the United Nations in the major decisions of the action. They assigned to General Douglas MacArthur (1880–1964), commander of the U.S. forces in the Far East whose headquarters were in nearby Japan, the commissions of sending military supplies to the South Koreans and providing air and naval protection for the evacuation of American civilians from Korea. The U.S. Navy's Seventh Fleet, then in the Philippines, was ordered to head for China, where it would be responsible for preventing any hostilities from erupting between the Communists on the mainland and the Nationalists on Taiwan (formerly Formosa).

By the next day, June 26, the situation in South Korea had worsened. At another Blair House meeting, it was agreed that the air force and the navy could fight below the 38th parallel. But all agreed to delay sending ground troops to Korea, heeding Bradley's warning that the United States would not be able to carry out its commitments elsewhere in the world if it were fighting in Korea.

MacArthur goes to Korea

General MacArthur, from his general headquarters in Tokyo, Japan, had the highest confidence in the South Korean Army, so on June 27 he was stunned to learn that Seoul was falling to the NKPA and that Syngman Rhee and his government had fled. Under the orders stemming from the Blair House meetings, he prepared to bomb the North Koreans from the air, thinking that this would be sufficient to end the war. (Bad weather prevented any real results from the air raids the first couple of days.)

Douglas MacArthur is an unusual American hero. A lifetime in the military had brought him a multitude of distinctions, from his days as the heroic brigadier general in World War I (1914–18), through his impressive reign as supreme commander of Allied powers (the United States, the British Commonwealth, the Soviet Union, and other European nations) in Japan after World War II. He was well known for bravery and resourcefulness in combat and was a powerful and charismatic speaker who always managed to seem bigger than life. But MacArthur was also known in military and government circles as someone who believed himself to be above the rules. He had a habit of constantly putting himself into the limelight, taking credit for other people's efforts, and blaming others for his errors. To some who knew him, his legendary bravery often appeared to be staged or just foolhardy. MacArthur was seventy years old when the Korean War brought him back to the world of combat. Although he was a hero to millions (he had accepted the Japanese surrender after World War II), his appointment as commander of the forces in the Korean War worried many leaders in the U.S. military and government.

On June 29, despite bad weather, MacArthur flew into an airport twenty miles south of Seoul and from there drove up to the front. There he impressed his observers as he strode fearlessly in the path of flying bullets. He found Seoul in flames and saw how desperate the situation was. MacArthur's appearance at the front was a welcome relief to the exhausted South Korean Army. General Paik Sun Yup described the effect of the legendary general's visit in *From Pusan to Panmunjom*: "At that time General MacArthur was regarded by Korean soldiers and civilians alike as almost a god. He was the hero of World War II and had accepted the surrender of the emperor of Japan. People today can't imagine the extent of his prestige." After his tour of the front, MacArthur visited Rhee, with whom he already had a warm relationship. Rhee begged for American support. On the way back to Tokyo, MacArthur bragged to Marguerite Higgins, a war correspondent, "Give me two American divisions and I can hold Korea," as quoted in her book, *War in Korea: The Report of a Woman Combat Correspondent*.

U.S. commitment to war

Two days before MacArthur's trip to Korea, the United Nations Security Council met again. The United States proposed a resolution that UN members were to "furnish such assistance to the Republic of Korea as may be necessary to repel the armed attack and to restore international peace and security to the area." The resolution brought about a bitter debate, since, in effect, it meant that all member nations were at war with North Korea. But the resolution did pass, again without the representation of the still-boycotting USSR. The next day, there was another meeting at Blair House, at which new decisions were made: MacArthur's air forces could bomb North Korean targets above the 38th parallel, and he should send in military units as needed to secure the southern part of the peninsula.

The next day MacArthur cabled his own report to Washington, asking that ground forces be committed to Korea immediately: "Unless provision is made for the full utilization of the Army-Navy-Air team in this shattered area our mission will at best be needlessly costly in life, money and prestige. At worst it might even be doomed to failure," as quoted in Clay Blair's *The Forgotten War: America in Korea*. Truman called his advisors together and within a half hour authorized MacArthur to use any of the ground forces he had under his command—way more than he had asked for. The president also approved a naval blockade of North Korea. Although Truman had not brought the decision before the U.S. Congress—only by resolution of the U.S. Congress can the United States declare war on another nation—and he was calling it a "police action under the United Nations," as of June 30 the United States was at war.

Where to Learn More

Alexander, Bevin. *Korea: The First War We Lost.* New York: Hippocrene Books, 1986, revised edition, 2000.

Blair, Clay. *The Forgotten War: America in Korea, 1950–1953.* New York: Times Books, 1987.

Goulden, Joseph C. *Korea: The Untold Story of the War.* New York: Times Books, 1982.

Higgins, Marguerite. *War in Korea: The Report of a Woman Combat Correspondent.* Garden City, NY: Doubleday, 1951.

Paik Sun Yup. *From Pusan to Panmunjom: Wartime Memoirs of the Republic of Korea's First Four-Star General.* Dulles, VA: Brassey's, 1992.

Toland, John. *In Mortal Combat: Korea, 1950–1953.* New York: William Morrow, 1991.

Web sites

Sang-hun Choe, Charles J. Hanley, and Martha Mendoza. "Bridge at No Gun Ri." Associated Press (AP). [Online] http://wire.ap.org/APpackages/nogunri/story.html (accessed on August 14, 2001).

The United States Joins the War: July 1950

5

Though the United States professed to have a strong commitment of support to South Korea in the Korean conflict that was unfolding, it was not backed up by a strong military. Since World War II (1939–45), the administration of President Harry S. Truman (1884–1972) had slashed the budget and trimmed the military to a small fraction of what it had been. In Japan at the time there were four U.S. infantry divisions: the Seventh, First Cavalry, Twenty-fourth, and Twenty-fifth. All were understaffed, undertrained, and short of arms and ammunition. Many of the troops had no combat experience.

The initial job for the first U.S. troops entering Korea was crucial. The North Koreans had broken the defense line at the Han River, south of the capital city of Seoul, on July 3, 1950. From there they were steadily making their way southward. It was necessary for the first U.S. troops to arrive to help the South Korean (ROK) Army stop the North Koreans and hold them in place before they reached the southern tip of the peninsula at Pusan. If they reached Pusan, they would occupy all of South Korea.

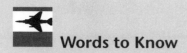

Words to Know

battalion: a military unit usually made up of about three to five companies. Generally one of the companies is the headquarters unit, another the service unit, and the rest are line units. Although the numbers differ greatly, a battalion might consist of about 35 officers and about 750 soldiers.

bazooka: a light and portable rocket launcher or antitank weapon fired from the shoulder that consists of a large tube that launches antitank ammunition.

bug-out: to panic and run away from a battle in confusion; a disorderly retreat without permission.

camouflage: disguise to look like the surrounding plants and environment.

casualties: those who are killed, wounded, missing, or taken prisoner in combat.

evacuation: removal of people from a dangerous area or a military zone.

howitzers: short cannons.

infantry division: a self-sufficient military unit, usually about 15,000 to 16,000 soldiers strong, under the command of a major general. Communist Chinese army divisions were closer to 10,000 soldiers strong.

integration: the act of bringing all the groups of individuals within an organization into the whole as equals; the elimination of separate facilities and structures for different racial groups.

The first group assigned to go from Japan to Korea was General William F. Dean's (1899–1981) Twenty-fourth Division. Dean found that the army did not have the capacity to get all his men to Korea by air, so he arranged for the maximum air transport—a small group of 406 men—to go at once, while the rest of the division would cross by ship. The first group was to begin the defense as the others were arriving. Dean was not worried about sending such a small group to fight without any support. Along with many others, he firmly believed that as soon as the North Koreans saw American uniforms, they would turn around and run back to the 38th parallel. (The 38th degree of north latitude, which bisects the Korean peninsula, was considered the border of North and South Korea.)

missionary: a person who takes on organized religious work with the purpose of converting people to his or her faith.

morale: the way that a person or a group of people feels about the job they are doing or the mission they are working on.

mortar: a muzzle-loading cannon that shoots high in the air.

perimeter defense: fighting the enemy around the outer limits of the area.

POW: prisoner of war.

recoilless rifles: heavy weapons with a high blast.

refugee: someone who is fleeing to a different country to escape danger in his or her own nation.

reunification: the process of bringing back together the separate parts of something that was once a single unit; in Korea, this usually refers to the dream of a single Korea ruled under one government, no longer divided into two nations at the demarcation line.

segregation: the separation of different groups of individuals within an organization or society.

strafe: to fire upon at close range with machine guns from a low-flying plane.

38th parallel: the 38th degree of north latitude as it bisects the Korean Peninsula, chosen by Americans as the dividing line between what was to be Soviet-occupied North Korea and U.S.-occupied South Korea in 1945.

Task Force Smith

The first group of 406 men to arrive in Korea was called Task Force Smith, after its commander, Lieutenant Colonel Charles B. Smith. The men (many were teenage boys) on this team could not have been aware, as they advanced from the town of Taejon (pronounced TIE-shon) to Osan, what a terrifying task they faced. At 3:00 A.M. on July 5, this small force dug themselves into a blocking position near Osan. By 7:00 A.M. they could see the North Korean tank column approaching, and at 8:15 A.M. they began to fire on the tanks with howitzers (short cannons). Their fire had no effect. As the tanks got closer Task Force Smith fired recoilless rifles (heavy weapons with a high blast) at them. The tanks kept moving without even slowing down. Task Force Smith then began to shoot at

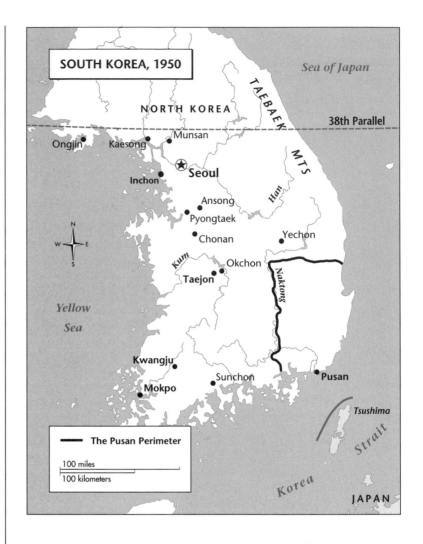

SOUTH KOREA, 1950

the rear of the tanks—their weakest point—with 2.36-inch bazookas (rocket launchers or antitank weapons of World War II vintage). Still, the tanks moved steadily on without damage. Finally two tanks were struck by howitzers using the task force's limited supply of high explosive antitank ammunition (HEAT). It was the only thing that had the power to stop them. Four tanks were taken out that morning, but the other thirty-one tanks rolled right on past, leaving thirty Americans dead behind them.

The survivors in Task Force Smith barely had time to catch their breath when, about a half hour later, two North Korean People's Army (NKPA) regiments—forming a six-mile-

A gunner with the Thirty-first Regimental Combat Team (crouching forward), with the assistance of his gun crew, fires a seventy-five-millimeter recoilless rifle near Oetlook-tong, Korea, in support of the infantry units directly across the valley, June 9, 1951. *Reproduced by permission of Double Delta Industries, Inc.*

long line of trucks and soldiers, about five thousand men— appeared, clearly not suspecting the American presence. With incredible courage, the task force held its position until the enemy was within a thousand yards and then let them have it with everything they had: rifles, mortars (muzzle-loading cannons that shoot high in the air), and machine guns. Within a couple of hours about one hundred Task Force Smith personnel were dead and the North Koreans had almost completely

Military Women in the Korean War

American women were not permitted to serve in combat during the Korean War, and in 1950 men and women in the military were not integrated. Nevertheless, thousands of American military women served in the war. Just four days after Task Force Smith arrived in Korea, a group of fifty-seven army nurses (all women) coming from Japan arrived at Pusan to help set up the first U.S. Army hospital. On July 8, 1950, twelve nurses went to the battlefront at Taejon to set up a Mobile Army Surgical Hospital (MASH).

When the war started, there were about twenty-two thousand women in American military service. About one-third were in health care positions, and the rest worked in the Women's Army Corp (WAC), Women in the Air Force (WAF), Women Accepted for Volunteer Emergency Service, or Navy Women's Reserve (WAVES) and Women Marines. Only a few women in non-health care positions served in Korea, but many military women served at the Far East Command headquarters in Tokyo, Japan, in administration, communication, personnel, supply, and food service. In Japan, some of the women became senior noncommissioned officers or served in supervisory positions normally held by men.

An army nurse at a MASH unit examines a wounded soldier. *Reproduced by permission of the Corbis Corporation.*

The army, air force, and navy nurses who served in Korea worked in the same extreme conditions as the soldiers fighting the war, wearing fatigues and living in tents near the front. No American military women were killed by the enemy during the war, but one army nurse was killed in a plane crash on her way to duty in Korea, and two air force nurses were killed in another aircraft accident.

surrounded the survivors. When the order was given to withdraw, a mad scramble amid enemy machine gun fire ensued. The wounded had to be left behind. The rest of Smith's scattered crew eventually regrouped and marched on to Ansong.

At this time, other elements of the Twenty-fourth Division had arrived and were getting into defensive positions in the area. News of what had happened to Task Force Smith spread like wildfire, and the morale of the incoming American troops dropped as they realized the mission in Korea was not the easy task they had been led to believe.

For ROK troops still fighting the North Korean People's Army (NKPA), morale was dropping for another reason. As the weather cleared, the U.S. Air Force started its bombing mission. The fighter pilots had no training and no coordination systems with the ground troops, and the errors in the first few days were disastrous. In one day, July 3, U.S. planes bombed and strafed (attacked with a machine gun or cannon from a low-flying aircraft) the ROK forces at Pyongtaek and Suwon, destroying an ammunition train and the Pyongtaek depot and a large part of the town itself, as well as the Suwon depot and thirty ROK trucks. An estimated two hundred ROK soldiers were killed by these mistaken raids, and no one knows how many civilians casualties there were.

Bug-out

From July 6 through July 12, elements of the Twenty-fourth Division were stuck in a pattern of setting themselves up in defensive positions in the line of NKPA movement and then retreating from the stronger, better-armed enemy. Over and over, as the Americans met the North Korean forces, they "bugged-out," or panicked and ran away in confusion, leaving behind them weapons that the NKPA would soon be using against them. The bloodshed was overwhelming. Because the men were not standing their ground, the leaders were often killed trying to do the soldiers' work; leaderless troops with little or no combat experience added greatly to the confusion. Marguerite Higgins (1920–1966), the only female American war correspondent in Korea, was on the scene of these battles and later described the prevailing mood of the troops in her book *War in Korea: The Report of a Woman Combat Correspondent:* "In the coming days I saw young Americans turn and bolt in battle, or throw down their arms cursing their government for what they thought was embroilment in a hopeless cause. . . . It was routine to hear comments like 'Just give me a jeep and I know what direction to go in. This mama's boy ain't cut out to be no hero.'"

As the first week of American fighting ended in Korea, the North Koreans had advanced fifty miles, delayed by the Americans in their southward progress by about two to three days. About three thousand Americans were dead, missing, wounded, or captured, and much of the weapons and ammunition had been lost in the bug-outs.

The air force regroups

The air force, trying to make up for its dismal mistakes of July 3, set up a vital communications process between the fighting aircraft and ground troops. On July 9, an American battalion spotted NKPA tanks and troops and radioed for an air strike. By dusk that evening, the air support had destroyed about one hundred North Korean vehicles, including five tanks. On July 10, air force jet fighters happened to discover a huge NKPA convoy brought to a standstill by a bombed bridge. Gathering more air support, the air fighters destroyed as many as thirty-eight tanks and more than one hundred trucks, killing many NKPA soldiers in the process. This raid drastically changed the North Koreans' patterns. From that day on, the North Koreans were forced to use camouflage (disguises designed to look like the environment) and move their tank columns only at night or in bad weather.

Troops of the ROK Eighth Division dressed in camouflage and waiting in a trench for the enemy, on the east-central Korean front, June 1953. *Reproduced by permission of AP/Wide World Photos.*

North Koreans begin their occupation

As the North Koreans captured Seoul and then other South Korean cities in battle, they proceeded to move in as occupiers. They began by distributing anti-United States and anti-Syngman Rhee pamphlets. (Rhee [1875–1965] was president of South Korea at the time.) Loudspeakers were installed in every occupied town so that the North Koreans could broadcast their messages. Posters were plastered everywhere. The North Koreans let it be known that they were coming in to liberate South Korea and to reunify the country.

Just prior to the war, in May 1950 there had been an election in South Korea. The original National Assembly had been replaced by moderates and liberals, showing growing dissatisfaction with Rhee's tyrannical (authoritarian or oppressive) government. Some South Koreans, particularly the students and the poor, welcomed the North Koreans, hoping they would bring about a just government and the reunification of Korea. Soon after they arrived, the North Koreans established a People's Committee in Seoul comprised of South Korean communists. (People's Committees were originally formed as local branches of the Committee for the Preparation of Korean Independence [CPKI], the first organized effort after World War II for Korean independence. In many places they served effectively as the local government. North Korea had a communist government in power, one that advocated the elimination of private property.)

But even among those who welcomed the North Koreans, relations became strained for a number of reasons. The North Koreans quickly began trials and executions of South Koreans involved in Rhee's government or the ROK Army. The North Koreans also started gathering young men and boys in South Korea to serve in the military. At first many volunteered to join, but the draft took more than the population could tolerate. Another factor that turned many South Koreans against the North Koreans was that the soldiers came in to occupy cities with no food or supplies. Compelled to get their food from the people in the city, they often went door-to-door demanding rice. The burden became too great to bear for many of the impoverished of South Korea, who did not have enough to feed their own families. The North Koreans—who, as communists, did not acknowledge organized religion—were also unpopular among the many Christians in South Korea, who watched as the North Korean soldiers arrested missionaries (people who conduct religious or charitable work in a territory or foreign country), some of them elderly men and women, and marched them off to prisoner of war (POW) camps.

The Far East Air Forces

The United States Air Force (USAF) was only three years old when the Korean War started in 1950, having formerly been a branch of the army. The United States's Far East Air Force (FEAF), based in Japan, was responsible for combat in Korea. At the beginning of the war the FEAF was composed of 33,625 personnel and 657 aircraft. One year later it had 1,441 aircraft, and by the end of the war there were 112,200 personnel in the FEAF.

In the early days of the war, it became apparent that the aircraft the United States had used in World War II (1939–45) was not sufficient to take on the planes being used by the North Koreans, Russian-made MiG-15s, that had been produced in 1947. The MiG-15 was heavily armed and could climb to high altitudes more quickly than any of the jets the Americans were using. The United States then acquired new models for the war. Aircraft used by the United Nations Command in Korea (of which the United States was a part) were:

- **F-86A "Sabre":** This single-pilot fighter aircraft, introduced in December 1950, became the standard in the war. Although a more stable plane than the Soviet MiG-15, the F-86A could not climb at as rapid a rate until later improvements were added.

- **B-29A "Superfortress":** The largest aircraft used during the war by either side, the B-29 was used against stable land targets, such as buildings and factories, or against whole units of advancing enemy troops. With a wingspan of 141 feet and a length of 99 feet, this bomber was armed with a 20-millimeter cannon and ten .50-caliber machine guns. It could carry 20,000 pounds of bombs.

- **F-4U1D "Corsair":** Updated from the famous World War II Corsairs, the Corsair was a single-pilot fighter plane used by the navy and the marines. Launched from aircraft carriers off the coasts of Korea, the Corsairs were armed for battle with six .50-caliber machine guns

America gears up for war

Commander of the U.S. forces in the Far East General Douglas MacArthur (1880–1964) realized by early July that the enemy was showing discipline, skill, and strategy and that it was well armed. In his report to the Joint Chiefs of Staff, he demanded a huge force of troops. (Created in 1949, the Joint Chiefs of Staff is an agency within the Department of Defense serving to advise the president and the secretary of defense on matters of war.) On

An F-86 Sabre flying over North Korea, circa 1951. *Reproduced by permission of Double Delta Industries, Inc.*

and could carry up to 2,000 pounds of bombs.

According to Michael J. Varhola in *Fire and Ice: The Korean War, 1950–1953,* during the war the FEAF claimed the following accomplishments:

- It dropped or fired 476,000 tons of bombs, rockets, and ammunition in 720,980 sorties (air missions).

- It destroyed 900 enemy aircraft in the air and many more on the ground.

- It destroyed 1,100 tanks, 800 bridges, 800 locomotives, 9,000 railroad cars, 70,000 motor vehicles, and 80,000 buildings.

- It inflicted nearly 150,000 North Korean and Chinese casualties.

During the Korean War, 1,466 FEAF aircraft were lost, 1,180 air force personnel were killed in action, 368 personnel were wounded in action, and 5,884 died from illness or wounds. Thousands of air force personnel from the Korean War are still missing in action.

As the war progressed, other nations besides the United States provided air power in Korea, particularly South Korea, South Africa, Australia, Britain, and Canada.

July 10, the Security Council of the United Nations (UN) agreed to create a unified Korean Command with MacArthur to serve as the commander in chief of the UN Forces. Rhee then placed the South Korean Army in the service of MacArthur. An emergency airlift began transporting much-needed supplies, weapons, and men from the United States to Korea.

On July 7, Walton H. "Johnnie" Walker (1889–1950), commander of the Eighth Army (all the divisions then avail-

Task Force Smith arrives at the rail station at Taejon, South Korea, en route to the front, July 5, 1950.
Reproduced by permission of AP/Wide World Photos.

able in the Far East), arrived in Taejon to meet with General Dean, commander of the Twenty-fourth Division. The two generals, seeing how desperate the situation was, decided that the remaining elements of the Twenty-fourth should consolidate in a defensive line along the Kum River and that an all-out effort should be made to hold the city of Taejon until more troops arrived.

Defense of the Kum River

On July 14, the North Koreans advanced on the Kum River at Kongju. In two attacks, the North Koreans shattered the two regiments of Dean's Twenty-fourth Division. As they fled from the Kum River line, the men of the Nineteenth Regiment gathered into small, unorganized bands to fight for their own survival. The North Koreans had circled around from behind and enveloped them. There were NKPA roadblocks stopping all vehicles of fleeing Americans. The wounded that had made it onto trucks for the flight ended up taking more bullets where they lay. There were nine hundred men of the Nineteenth Regiment on the Kum River on July 16. When the defense line collapsed, more than half of them were missing, either dead or captured.

The fall of Taejon

After the fall of the Kum River line, General Dean took stock of the badly damaged Twenty-fourth Division and knew he did not have the power to hold the city of Taejon. Even so, when General Walker asked him to hold on to Taejon for a couple more days, Dean committed his Thirty-fourth Regiment to the task. Some observers have said he was, by that time, too exhausted to think straight.

The NKPA attacked at Taejon on July 19, striking with their usual force. The battalions of the Thirty-fourth Regiment were dug into position and waiting for them. But a second NKPA division began immediately traveling south and then circling east, enveloping the Thirty-fourth Regiment and then attacking with full strength. The Thirty-fourth called for help, and General Dean himself appeared with a unit from the Nineteenth Regiment. By nightfall, both the Thirty-fourth and the added unit were surrounded. During the night, the North Korean tanks entered the city, and an NKPA roadblock was in place just outside the city, impeding the route of retreat. In the morning, the North Koreans attacked in force and shattered the Thirty-fourth and Nineteenth Regiments, completely eliminating organized fighting for the Americans. Leaders were dead; communication lines were gone. By the time retreats were ordered, the troops had already fled.

General Dean, who was still in the city, grabbed two bazooka teams and took off on foot to try to destroy the enemy tanks. He finally did manage to blow one up. By 6:00 that evening, the city of Taejon was on fire and littered with dead bodies. Dean and the other remaining commanders got in their jeeps and tried to leave the city but were stopped by the NKPA roadblock. Abandoning his jeep, Dean took to the hills. He spent the next thirty-six days trying to get back to his troops while avoiding North Korean soldiers. In the end, South Korean civilians turned him over to the North Koreans, and he spent the next three years as the highest ranking POW in Korea.

A Soldier's Experience of the Fall of Taejon

William Caldwell, a platoon leader in the First Battalion of the Thirty-fourth Regiment (Twenty-fourth Division), remembers the chaos that followed the fall of the city of Taejon on July 20, 1950:

> The first battalion was decimated. I ended up on the high ground south of Taejon with Marks and three other officers and about two hundred men, many of them wounded. We had no maps, no communications, no ammo, except that on our backs, no food, no water, no vehicles. We headed south, then west, moving rather ponderously because of the injured and wounded. On the third day without food, men went into the fields and dug up potatoes and vegetables and ate them raw, a distressing sight.
>
> On the third or fourth night Marks and I, who were in superb condition, were elected to go ahead of the main party and try to find friendly forces and get help—transportation. We finally managed to reach a ROK headquarters, where we were refused help until Marks threatened to create an "international incident". The ROKs relinquished three trucks, and we shuttled the men to the [ROK] headquarters. The ROKs would do nothing more for us, nor would the [American] Army command in Pusan, which we raised by landline. We then commandeered a train and went due south to Yosu on the coast, cooking our first edible food—eggs—in the engine boiler and washing them down with sips of sake and beer, the first purified liquid we'd had since Taejon. At Yosu we commandeered a boat, loaded our troops, and sailed for Pusan, where we were issued new gear and sent back into the line—every soldier in that group now a fighter.

Source: Clay Blair. The Forgotten War: America in Korea, 1950–1953. *New York: Times Books, 1987.*

In the attempt to hold Taejon for two days, 4,000 American soldiers were deployed. Of these, 1,150 were killed, wounded, or missing and presumed dead. At the end of the second week of American fighting, of the 15,965 troops in the Twenty-fourth Division, only 8,660 could be accounted for. The North Koreans had advanced another twenty-five miles on the central front.

In the week after the fall of Taejon, the North Koreans attacked the First Cavalry Division, which was trying to protect the village of Yongdong. Three of the First Cavalry's battalions were destroyed and its efforts to save Yongdong failed. The two remaining regiments of the horribly battered Twenty-fourth Division, under the command of General John H.

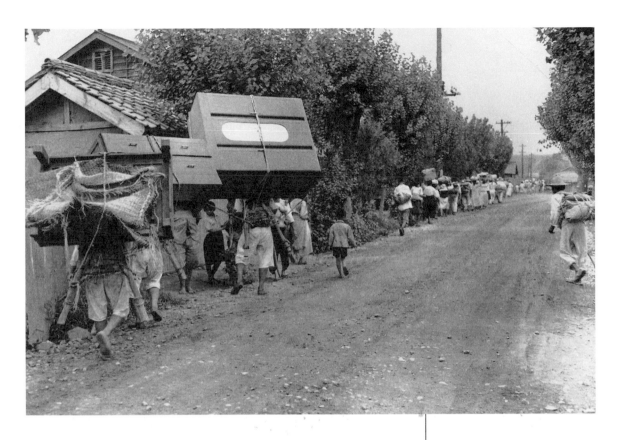

One Korean family in a long line of refugees fleeing Yongdong, South Korea, tries to save some furniture, July 26, 1950. *Reproduced by permission of AP/Wide World Photos.*

Church since Dean's disappearance, were enlisted to attack Hadong, a North Korean-occupied town to the west, with help from two battalions from the Twenty-ninth Regiment. The troops walked right into an enemy ambush near Hadong. The two forward companies were slaughtered, their leaders killed, and once again the survivors fled, fighting to save themselves. In this battle, 313 were killed and 100 were captured.

No Gun Ri Massacre

On July 23, American soldiers entered two villages in North Chungchong Province in South Korea, warning civilians to evacuate their homes immediately. The people evacuated to the nearby village, Im Ke Ri. On July 25, the American soldiers arrived at Im Ke Ri and gathered the refugees, promising to take them to safety in the city of Pusan, in the south of the peninsula. The soldiers brought the villagers to Ha Ga Ri and abandoned them there. The next day the villagers began the trip south on their own. When they arrived at No Gun Ri on July 26, American soldiers ordered them to stop. The soldiers inspected them for weapons and found none. Suddenly, an air attack was launched upon the unarmed people.

Many of the refugees were killed in the attack, but the majority escaped into a water tunnel. There they were pursued by U.S. soldiers, who were later identified as members of the H Company, Second Battalion of the Seventh Regiment, First Cavalry Division, who had arrived in Korea only three days before. These troops were young and untrained and knew little or nothing about Korea or its war. For three days the soldiers stood at the ends of the tunnels and fired at the helpless villagers. Those inside who survived had no food or water and were forced to use the bodies of their families and neighbors as shields against the American gunfire. "The American soldiers played with our lives like boys playing with flies," said a South Korean woman named Chun Choon-ja, who was twelve years old at the time, according to an Associated Press article. On July 29, the U.S. soldiers disappeared, evidently due to the arrival of the North Korean People's Army.

It is estimated that three hundred people were killed at the No Gun Ri Bridge and that another one hundred were killed in the air attack. The story only came to light in the United States in the mid-1990s, when a group of survivors petitioned the United States for an apology and compensation, resulting in an investigation by the Associated Press news agency that unearthed convincing evidence. In 2001, President Bill Clinton (1948–) replied to the petition, acknowledging that innocent people at No Gun Ri had died at the hands of U.S. troops.

"Johnnie" Walker's plan

Although in the first month of war the North Koreans had outnumbered the Americans and South Koreans by about four to one, the massive buildup of UN troops had evened things. Along with the three U.S. divisions already in Korea, the battered Twenty-fourth, the First Cavalry, and the Twenty-fifth, there were now a British brigade and a U.S. Marines brigade. Furthermore, the ROK had started a draft and enrolled another forty-five thousand men. New equipment was coming in daily.

General Walker wanted to consolidate all the UN forces in one place. He planned to withdraw the entire Eight Army behind the Naktong River and hold on to a one-hundred-mile long, fifty-mile wide area. The area, called the Pusan Perimeter, was bordered by the Naktong River on the west, the Sea of Japan on the east, mountains at the north, and the Korean Strait at the south. There the United States and ROK armies could build a solid perimeter defense (fight the enemy around the outer limits of the area) and turn the war around.

Walker phoned MacArthur's headquarters to get permission to establish the new line. Instead of giving an answer, the next day MacArthur publicly announced that there would be no "Korean Dunkirk." (Dunkirk is a port in Northern France famous for a massive evacuation during World War II.) In other words, MacArthur was saying "no" to the idea of a massive retreat.

"Stand or Die"

On July 29, General Walker gave his famous "Stand or Die" speech, leading his troops to believe they would not be retreating any time soon. The speech was recorded in an attending officer's notes, so the words that most historians quote from the Army historian Roy E. Appleman's records are not exact, but Walker's point is clear:

> We are fighting a battle against time. There will be no more retreating, withdrawal, or readjustment of the lines or any other term you choose. There is no line behind us to which we can retreat. Every unit must counterattack to keep the enemy in a state of confusion and off balance. There will be no Dunkirk . . .; a retreat to Pusan would be one of the greatest butcheries in history. We must fight until the end. Capture by these people is worse than death itself. We will fight as a team. If some of us must die, we will die fighting together. Any man who gives ground may be personally responsible for the death of thousands of his comrades. I want you to put this out to all men in the division. I want everybody to understand that we are going to hold this line. We are going to win.

The planned retreat

Despite Walker's speech, the withdrawals continued, and the general carried out his original strategy to build a fortified line of defense beyond the Naktong River. Soon the whole Eighth Army was behind the line.

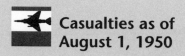

Casualties as of August 1, 1950

United States	6,003
	1,884 dead
	2,695 wounded
	523 missing
	901 POWs
ROK	70,000
NKPA	58,000

After getting across the river, the First Cavalry was instructed to blow up the bridges across the Naktong. A flood of panicking refugees—people who had been forced south in their attempt to stay within United Nations territory—kept following the soldiers across the bridge, making it impossible to destroy it. In the end, the commander of the First Cavalry gave the order to blow up the bridge with civilians on it; many were killed. It was a nightmarish end to a dismal chapter in the war in Korea.

Where to Learn More

Alexander, Bevin. *Korea: The First War We Lost.* New York: Hippocrene Books, 1986, revised edition, 2000.

Appleman, Roy E. *South to the Naktong, North to the Yalu: United States Army in the Korean War.* Office of the Chief of Military History. Washington, DC: U.S. Government Printing Office, 1961.

Blair, Clay. *The Forgotten War: America in Korea, 1950–1953.* New York: Times Books, 1987.

Higgins, Marguerite. *War in Korea: The Report of a Woman Combat Correspondent.* Garden City, NY: Doubleday, 1951.

Summers, Harry G., Jr. *Korean War Almanac.* New York: Facts on File, 1990.

Toland, John. *In Mortal Combat: Korea, 1950–1953.* New York: William Morrow, 1991.

Varhola, Michael J. *Fire and Ice: The Korean War, 1950–1953.* Mason City, IA: Savas Publishing, 2000.

Web sites

"Bridge at No Gun Ri." Associated Press (AP). [Online] http://wire.ap.org/APpackages/nogunri/ (accessed on August 14, 2001).

Feldman, Ruth Tenzer. "Women in the War." Cobblestone: Korean War Fiftieth Anniversary Issue. [Online] http://korea50.army.mil/cobblestone/29.html (accessed on August 14, 2001).

United States Army. "Women in the Korean War." Fiftieth Anniversary of the Korean War Commemoration Site. [Online] http://korea50.army.mil/history/factsheets/women.html (accessed on August 14, 2001).

Turning the Tide: The Pusan Perimeter

6

During the two-hundred-mile retreat of the Eighth Army (which included both U.S. and South Korean troops) down the Korean peninsula between the onset of the Korean War on June 25, 1950, and the withdrawal to the Pusan Perimeter that took place between August 1 and 3, 1950, the North Koreans had been fighting in their element. U.S. troops fought best on roads, in formation, and with heavy equipment. The North Koreans, many having learned to fight in guerrilla warfare against the Japanese when Korea was under Japanese occupation from 1910 to 1945, were mobile fighters, skilled at nighttime attacks, fighting in the mountains, and hand-to-hand combat. The North Korean People's Army (NKPA) relied heavily on the battle technique of infiltrating (passing through gaps in the enemy defense line) and mixing themselves right into the ranks of the enemy, where they were able to kill at close range. They also had developed an effective method of sending troops around and to the rear of the enemy while the main forces were fighting at the front. Enveloping the enemy troops, they were often able to cut them off from help and to inflict terrible casualties.

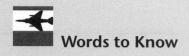

Words to Know

amphibious attack: an invasion that uses the coordinated efforts of land, sea, and air forces.

bazooka: a light and portable rocket launcher or antitank weapon fired from the shoulder that consists of a large tube that launches antitank ammunition.

Corsair: a single-pilot fighter plane used by navy and marine forces.

division (or infantry division): a self-sufficient military unit, usually about 15,000 to 16,000 strong, under the command of a major general. Communist Chinese army divisions were closer to 10,000 soldiers strong.

heat exhaustion: also called heat prostration; the symptoms that arise when one physically exerts oneself in hot weather, including dizziness, nausea, weakness, and sweating.

infantry: the branch of an army that is composed of soldiers trained to fight on foot.

machine-gun emplacement: a prepared position for a powerful automatic weapon.

mortar: a muzzle-loading cannon that shoots high in the air.

perimeter: the outside limits of a geographical area.

regiment: a military unit composed of three battalions.

reunification: the process of bringing back together the separate parts of something that was once a single unit; in Korea, this usually refers to the dream of a single Korea ruled under one government, no longer divided into two nations at the demarcation line.

stalemate: deadlock; the state in which the efforts of each party in a conflict cancels out the efforts of the other party so that no one makes any headway.

strafe: to fire upon at close range with machine guns from a low-flying plane.

Because the North Koreans kept attacking, relentlessly pushing U.S. troops farther south, most observers thought they greatly outnumbered the South Korean and American forces. Indeed, the North Koreans were characterized by the American media as unstoppable "waves" of soldiers. This was not true. By August 4, 1950, with new troops arriving, the Eighth Army in Korea numbered around ninety-two thousand, and the North Korean People's Army (NKPA) numbered

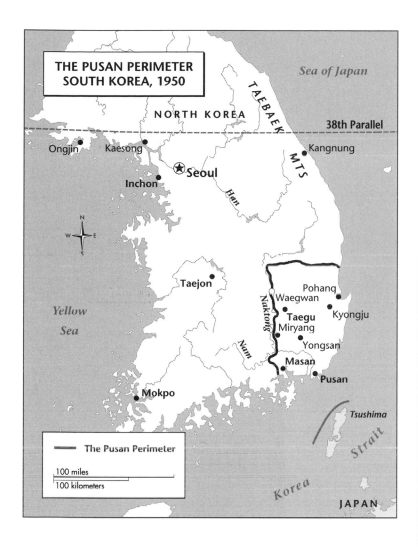

The Pusan Perimeter
South Korea, 1950

around seventy thousand. The North Koreans were exhausted and far away from their home base and supplies. They had a serious shortage of food and equipment. To make up for their battle losses, they were recruiting soldiers from the newly occupied South Korean cities. Many of these young men had no training and were not even given weapons. The North Koreans continued to distinguish themselves, however, motivated by the confidence of their many victories and their mission of reunifying Korea. But by August, they knew that time was running out. If members of the United Nations (UN) kept pouring more troops and weapons toward the defense of South Korea, the North Koreans would not have a chance against

Weary from long duty, a U.S. soldier rests alongside his machine gun dugout while allied forces guard the Pusan Perimeter, South Korea, August 9, 1950. *Reproduced by permission of AP/Wide World Photos.*

them. North Korean premier Kim Il Sung (1912–1994) promoted the mission to "take Pusan by Liberation Day," which was August 15, the anniversary of Korean liberation from Japanese rule following World War II (1939–45). When it became clear that the NKPA was not going to capture Pusan on time, Kim changed the mission to "Taegu by Liberation Day."

The U.S. and South Korean (ROK) forces were all in place behind the Naktong River by August 3. American general Walton H. "Johnnie" Walker (1889–1950) knew that they would finally be in their own element here, where they could form a more secure defense line with all units in a structured formation. There, the heavy weaponry (being airlifted in daily) could be set up to fire at all possible avenues of approach. There was even a railroad loop—Pusan-Kyongju-Taegu-Pusan—that could deliver supplies and troops throughout the perimeter as needed.

However, defending the Pusan Perimeter was no simple task, even with new troops and supplies. The area was too large for a dense defense line, and the troops who were arriving had little combat experience and no familiarity with Korea. Walker carefully planned the positions of every unit assigned to Korea for the defense of the huge area. The five divisions of the South Korean Army defended a large line in the north and northwest; the First Cavalry defended an eighteen-mile line from Waegwan south along the Naktong River; the Twenty-fourth Division defended a twenty-five-mile line extending to the meeting of the Naktong and Nam Rivers; and a reinforced Twenty-fifth Division defended the line south to the Korean Strait. The Twenty-fifth had recently been built up significantly with newly arrived battalions and ROK survivors. In addition, two regiments of the Second Infantry Division had arrived. Along with other weapons, Sherman tanks were arriving from Japan that could destroy the dreaded T-34 tanks the North Koreans were using. With more troops and supplies, and a more defensible station, it seemed as though the Eighth Army could quickly defeat the NKPA. However, it was not so easy.

A weak start

The first order of business after setting up the defensive line in the perimeter was to stop the North Korean drive down the western roads leading to Masan. Walker sent the Twenty-fifth Division, under General William Kean (1897–1981). Task Force Kean began a counterattack on August 7. The counterattack ultimately failed despite the fact that the Americans outnumbered the NKPA twenty thousand to seventy-five hundred and seemed to have all the advantages. Several things contributed to the loss. It was very hot, with temperatures reaching 105 degrees Fahrenheit. Many soldiers dropped from heat exhaustion. On their way to battle, the Fifth Regimental Combat Team took a wrong road, allowing the North Koreans time to get control in the hills.

The U.S. Marines, in their first highly publicized fight in Korea, did extremely well, twice bailing out the Twenty-fifth Division. The marines were not only combat experienced, but brought with them their own air support and good weapons and ammunition. But even their support was not enough. From the hills, the North Koreans achieved the advantage, engaging the Americans in a vicious battle later known as Bloody Gulch. At the end of August, the Masan front was in a stalemate.

United Nations Forces in Korea

AUSTRALIA

Infantry: 3 battalions
Naval forces: 1 aircraft carrier,
2 destroyers, 1 frigate
Air forces: 1 fighter squadron,
1 air transport squadron
Casualties: 1,200 wounded,
339 killed

BELGIUM AND LUXEMBOURG

Infantry: 1 battalion
Nonmilitary: DC-4 transportation
aircraft and 2 nurses
Troops throughout war: 3,498
Casualties: 101 killed, 350 wounded,
5 missing, 1 died in captivity

CANADA

Infantry: 1 army brigade
Naval forces: 3 destroyers
Air forces: 1 air transport squadron
Troops throughout war: 21,900
Casualties: 300 killed, 1,200 wounded,
32 captured

COLOMBIA

Infantry: 4 battalions, one at a time
Naval forces: 1 frigate
Casualties: 600

DENMARK

Nonmilitary: 100-member medical
detachment; hospital ship

ETHIOPIA

Infantry: 1 battalion
Nonmilitary: Nurses
Troops throughout war: 3,158
Casualties: 121 killed, 536 wounded

FRANCE

Infantry: 1 battalion
Naval forces: 1 warship
Troops throughout war: 3,421
Casualties: 287 killed, 1,350 wounded,
7 missing, 12 POWs

GREAT BRITAIN

Infantry: 3 army brigades,
2 field artillery regiments,
1 armored regiment
Naval forces: 1 aircraft carrier,
2 cruisers, 8 destroyers,
marine units
Troops throughout war: 14,000
Casualties: 700 killed, 4,000 wounded
or POW

Attack at Naktong Bulge

The North Koreans began an attack on August 5 in an area called the Naktong Bulge, about seven miles north of the meeting of the Nam and Naktong Rivers. The Americans were using the river as a part of their defense, but the North Koreans by the hundreds managed to cross it during the night.

GREECE

Infantry: 1 battalion
Air forces: 1 air transport squadron
Troops throughout war: 397
Casualties: 12 killed

INDIA

Nonmilitary: 1 unit Indian Medical Corps; parachute field ambulance unit

THE NETHERLANDS

Infantry: 1 battalion
Naval forces: 1 destroyer
Troops throughout war: 3,148
Casualties: 120 killed, 645 wounded

NEW ZEALAND

Infantry: 1 artillery regiment
Naval forces: 6 frigates
Troops throughout war: 6,000
Casualties: 46 killed, 79 wounded, 1 POW

NORWAY

Nonmilitary: 105-member mobile surgical hospital (NorMASH)

THE PHILIPPINES

Infantry: 4 motorized battalion combat teams (1 at a time)

Troops throughout war: 7,420
Casualties: 112 killed, 299 wounded, 16 missing, 41 POWs

SOUTH Africa

Air forces: 1 fighter aircraft squadron ("Flying Cheetahs")
Casualties: 36 killed, 9 POWs

SWEDEN

Nonmilitary: 154-member medical team

THAILAND

Infantry: 1 regimental combat team
Naval forces: 4 frigates, 1 cargo ship
Air forces: 1 air transportation squadron
Nonmilitary: 3 medical service detachments

TURKEY

Infantry: 1 army brigade
Troops throughout war: 14,396
Casualties: 741 killed, 2,068 wounded, 163 missing, 244 POWs

They took their heavy equipment across the river on underwater bridges made up of sandbags, rocks, logs, and barrels built up from the river bottom to about a foot below the river's surface. The North Koreans then infiltrated the very weak Thirty-fourth and Nineteenth Regiments of the Twenty-fourth Division that defended this line. For several days, despite fierce

combat, the NKPA continued on their drive into the perimeter, getting as far as Yongsan, a village eight miles east of the Nak-tong. They also set up a powerful roadblock on the road to Miryang. More American units arrived but counterattacks, though heavy in casualties, failed to drive the North Koreans from the bulge.

Then the marines were called in, along with several new army regiments. On August 17, the marines struck the ridgeline within the Naktong Bulge called Obnong-ni, where the savage fighting had been taking place. The marines first came in with their Corsairs (fighter planes), strafing the North Koreans, attacking them with machine gun or cannon from the low-flying aircraft. Then the infantry climbed the hills under heavy enemy fire. After being repulsed, the marines made a combined effort with the army regiments and shattered the North Koreans. When, as a last resort, the North Koreans pulled out their T-34 tanks, three U.S. M26 Pershings (heavily armed forty-six-ton tanks) met the T-34s and quickly destroyed them. After a full day of fierce battle, at great cost in American and North Korean lives, the marines had shattered the enemy. The next morning, after a Corsair bombing had destroyed a machine-gun emplacement, the surviving North Koreans ran back to the Naktong River. The North Koreans were facing a new enemy and fighting a different kind of war.

The battle for Taegu

Taegu was the headquarters for the Eighth Army and the seat of the South Korean government during this phase of the war. It was defended by the First Cavalry and the ROK First and Sixth Divisions. In mid-August, the U.S. Army had learned through decoded North Korean radio messages that the NKPA was approaching on the roads leading to Taegu, ready to attack. U.S. and ROK troops were ready when the strike came on the night of August 9. They lit the sky with flares and started heavy fire on the North Koreans, killing thousands. On August 12, another NKPA division struck at Yongpo and was virtually slaughtered. But the attack on Taegu was a desperate one for the North Koreans: four full divisions were committed to it. The NKPA kept attacking until their enemy was exhausted. The ROK First, short on weapons and outnumbered by the NKPA, fought well for days but finally collapsed. By August 15, the North Koreans had pushed past them and gone on to Tabu, fifteen miles north of Taegu. Another NKPA division slipped behind the ROK Third and captured the town of Pohang, threatening Taegu from behind.

A massive bombing

In what many consider to be a large-scale blunder, General Douglas MacArthur (1880–1964; commander of the UN Command in Korea) decided to bomb a twenty-six-square-mile area north of Waegwan in the belief that the North Korean troops were gathering there. U.S. Air Force officers explained to him that the area he wished to bomb was too large and mountainous for this kind of bombing, but he went ahead with his plans. On August 16, twelve B-29 squadrons released 3,084 five-hundred-pound bombs and 150 one-thousand-pound bombs over the area in question. Apparently no North Korean troops were killed in the bombing, and in fact there is evidence that they were elsewhere at the time. According to

American soldiers plotting their next move against the North Korean enemy, September 1950.
Reproduced by permission of Archive Photos, Inc.

the commander of the First Division, General Paik Sun Yup (1920–), the bombing did have the positive effect of raising the ROK morale and badly wounding NKPA morale.

The Bowling Alley

The NKPA kept fighting to reach Taegu. A few North Koreans got close enough to Taegu to fire mortar (small cannon) rounds in the city, creating general panic. The civilian population and Syngman Rhee's government prepared once more to evacuate. (Rhee [1875–1965] was president of South Korea at the time.) Walker, unwilling to allow any kind of withdrawal, sent the highly successful Twenty-seventh Regiment, called the Wolfhounds, led by Lieutenant Colonel John "Mike" Michaelis, to join General Paik Sun Yup's First Division just north of Tabu. There a seven-night battle raged in a place called the "Bowling Alley," a two-mile stretch of road with mountains rising on either side. Paik's troops held the mountains, while the Twenty-seventh held the roads.

Each night during this battle, the North Korean tanks would begin the attack by firing down the road at the Americans. The Twenty-seventh's bazookas would destroy the first couple of tanks in line, and the rest would eventually turn around, only to come back the next night. As the North Koreans fired, red balls flew down the road. General Paik recalled these battles in his memoirs *From Pusan to Panmunjom*: "The NKPA attackers not only gave the impression of bowlers approaching a lane, but also the sharp cracks of exploding shells reminded observers of the sharp 'crack crack' sounds of flying bowling pins." Paik, who probably got along with American officers better than any of the other ROK generals, was a little offended at the Americans' comparison, however. "I must say, at the time I found it difficult to understand the Americans' humor when they referred to a grisly battlefield with such a lighthearted term."

The ROK and U.S. forces were able to inflict heavy damages on the North Koreans in the night battles by illuminating the sky with flares and then firing continuously on the enemy. By day, the air support strafed the enemy. Unable to penetrate the UN positions, the North Koreans traveled around them in the hills and very successfully attacked the

John "Mike" Michaelis, commander of the famed Wolfhounds, inspects a telescopic sight captured from a North Korean T-34 tank in the Taegu-Waegwan sector of South Korea, August 1950. *Reproduced by permission of AP/Wide World Photos.*

Weapons Most Frequently Used in the Korean War

Small Arms

- **M-1911A1 .45 Caliber Pistol:** The standard U.S. sidearm in the Korean War, a semiautomatic weapon that carried seven rounds. Weighing three pounds, it had a maximum range of thirty yards.

- **M-1 "Garand" .30 Caliber Rifle:** The primary rifle used by Americans and South Koreans, a gas-operated semiautomatic weapon with an eight-round clip. Weighing 9.5 pounds, its range was about 550 meters and it had a rate of fire of about thirty rounds per minute.

- **M-1918A2 Browning Automatic Rifle (BAR):** At least one BAR was issued to every rifle squad in the U.S. infantry and it became the basic automatic support weapon. The BAR could fire either automatically or semiautomatically. It had a twenty-round detachable box magazine. Weighing 19.5 pounds, it had a range of about eight hundred meters and a rate of fire of about three hundred to six hundred rounds per minute. It could be fired from the shoulder or from a bipod.

- **Bayonets:** Knives that are attached to the end of rifles so that in hand-to-hand combat they can be used as spears.

Grenades

Grenades are small bombs that are filled with explosives, gas, or chemicals. They can be thrown by hand or shot from a launcher. A grenade is usually activated by pulling a pin and then holding down a safety lever until the user is ready to throw it. Within seconds of the release of the safety lever, the grenade explodes.

Heavy Weapons (usually require more than one soldier to fire)

- **.30 Caliber Machine Guns:** Air-cooled or water-cooled, these guns were used heavily in Korea. They used the same ammunition as the BAR and shot at a rate of four hundred to six hundred rounds per minute.

- **.50 Caliber Machine Guns:** A heavy weapon mounted on armored vehicles and trucks and used to support the infantry. It fired about 575 rounds per minute and had a range of about two thousand yards.

- **3.5-inch Rocket Launcher or "Super-Bazooka":** Bazookas are rocket launchers that fire antitank ammunition. The 3.5-inch bazooka was sent to Korea in a hurry when the troops found that the 2.35-inch bazooka from World War II was ineffective against the Soviet-made tanks used by the North Koreans. The "super bazooka" was a twenty-five-inch tube with a range of about sixty-five meters. It could penetrate up to 280 millimeters of tank armor.

Tanks

When the Korean War began, the United States had no tanks in Korea, due to a belief that tanks would not be able to maneuver in the mountainous terrain. When the North Koreans successfully used the Soviet T-34 tanks, the United States saw their error. Tanks were especially necessary as antitank weapons. Three types of tanks were used by the United States:

- **M-4 "Sherman" Medium Tank:** The most successful tank in the Korean terrain, the Sherman was a thirty-five-ton vehicle armed with a high velocity seventy-six-millimeter main gun and two machine guns. The hull, tank, sides, and turret of the tank were protected by varying thicknesses of armor. It could move up to twenty-four miles an hour.

- **M-26 "Pershing" Heavy Tank:** A more advanced tank than the Sherman, the Pershing weighed forty-five tons and was run by a five-member crew. It was armed with a ninety-millimeter main gun and two machine guns and could reach speeds of up to twenty-five miles an hour.

- **M-24 "Chaffee" Light Tank:** With less armor and fewer arms, this tank could move more quickly than the heavier tanks and could be run by a crew of four. It weighed eighteen tons.

Artillery

- **M1 eight-inch (203.2mm) Howitzer:** Howitzers are cannons that shoot high. The eight-inch howitzer weighed about fifteen tons and was mounted on a four-wheel carriage, to be towed by a ten-ton truck or tracked utility vehicle. The weapon was about thirty-six feet long, had a range of about ten miles, and had a rate of fire of about thirty rounds an hour. The eight-inch howitzer was operated by a crew of about fourteen and took twenty minutes to set up.

- **M-114 155-millimeter Howitzer:** A medium-sized howitzer, weighing 6.5 tons and measuring twenty-four feet long. It fired at a range of about ten miles, at a rate of fire of about one hundred rounds per hour, and was operated by a crew of eleven.

- **M-101A1 105-millimeter Howitzer:** This lighter howitzer had a range of about seven miles and a rate of fire of about one hundred rounds per hour. It needed a crew of eight and could be set up in about three minutes.

Source: Michael J. Varhola. Fire and Ice: The Korean War, 1950–1953. *Mason City, IA: Savas Publishing, 2000.*

Twenty-third Regiment of the Second Division, but the air support again bombed them relentlessly, stopping their drive for Taegu.

Now or never

There was a lull in the fighting in the last few days of August. The North Koreans were too weak to continue but unwilling to give up. General MacArthur was finalizing his plans for an amphibious (using land, sea, and air forces) attack at the port city of Inchon, near the capital city of Seoul. Though it should have been top secret, his boasts to the media made the plan common knowledge, even if the place for the landing was unknown. The North Koreans were more aware than ever that they had to capture the Pusan Perimeter soon. They rapidly overhauled their army, filling it up with about thirty thousand new recruits and lumping together survivors of vanquished divisions into reformulated units. Once again, in the first days of September, they struck savagely on five different fronts. And once again, although outnumbered and without food and supplies, the North Koreans were successful: they penetrated the Naktong Bulge and the towns of Pohang, Tabu, and Ka-san. They moved in force into many mountains just north of Taegu.

General Walker deployed all his forces to the trouble spots in these critical days. He was most worried about the Naktong Bulge, where the penetration was deepest. Although he was aware that the marines were being moved to Pusan to embark for the attack at Inchon, in desperation he called for their help. MacArthur allowed him the use of the marines for three days. In those three days, the marines counterattacked, reaching the ridge at Obong-ni for a second time by the third day. There they engaged in fierce battle. But just after midnight on September 6, they pulled out, under orders from MacArthur. As the marines got ready for the attack at Inchon, Walker was faced with a continuing North Korean penetration at the Pusan Perimeter. The loss of the marines was devastating, as they were the only force that had been able to stop the NKPA so far. He knew that another withdrawal was the only way to ensure the safety of his troops. But he decided to hold the line.

Where to Learn More

Alexander, Bevin. *Korea: The First War We Lost.* New York: Hippocrene Books, 1986, revised edition, 2000.

Blair, Clay. *The Forgotten War: America in Korea, 1950–1953.* New York: Times Books, 1987.

Paik Sun Yup. *From Pusan to Panmunjom: Wartime Memoirs of the Republic of Korea's First Four-Star General.* Dulles, VA: Brassey's, 1992.

Toland, John. *In Mortal Combat: Korea, 1950–1953.* New York: William Morrow, 1991.

Varhola, Michael J. *Fire and Ice: the Korean War, 1950–1953.* Mason City, IA: Savas Publishing, 2000.

From Inchon to the Chinese Border

A lmost as soon as the United States joined the fighting in Korea in mid-1950, General Douglas MacArthur (1880–1964), commander of the United Nations (UN) forces in Korea, had developed a plan for an amphibious attack, using land, sea, and air forces. MacArthur's plan was simple. While the North Korean People's Army (NKPA) was using most of its forces to drive the South Korean (ROK) and UN troops south, a separate UN force would enter the country to the north at the rear of the enemy, coming in from the sea and strongly backed by air and naval support. Once troops had entered, the UN troops holding the Pusan Perimeter could break out and drive north to meet up with the new offensive. (The area called the Pusan Perimeter was bordered by the Naktong River on the west, the Sea of Japan on the east, mountains at the north, and the Korean Strait at the south. See Chapter 6.) The city of Inchon, the port nearest the South Korean capital of Seoul, was MacArthur's choice site for this amphibious attack. Unfortunately, Inchon had very unfavorable naval conditions, with dangerous tides and weather and enemy-held islands surrounding it. The poor conditions gave MacArthur the edge he

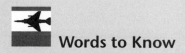

Words to Know

airborne operation: a military action involving movement of troops into a combat area by aircraft, often referring to a mission using parachutes.

aircraft carrier: a warship with a huge deck on which planes take off and land.

amphibious attack: an invasion that uses the coordinated efforts of land, sea, and air forces.

artillery: large weapons, such as howitzers, rockets, and 155-millimeter guns, that shoot missiles and generally take a crew to operate.

battleships: huge combat ships used in Korea primarily for their big guns as support to the ground forces.

Corsair: a single-pilot fighter plane used by navy and marine forces.

cruiser: a fast, lightly armored warship, smaller and with less armor but faster than a battleship.

destroyers: small, fast battleships with guns, depth charges, and torpedoes, used to support the main battleship.

Joint Chiefs of Staff: an agency within the Department of Defense serving to advise the president and the secretary of defense on matters of war. The Joint Chiefs of Staff consists of a chairman, a vice chairman, the chief of staff of the army, the chief of naval operations, the chief of staff of the air force, and the commandant of the marine corps.

wanted. According to him, no one would suspect the UN forces to strike at Inchon precisely because of these dangers.

Doubting MacArthur

The Joint Chiefs of Staff had growing concerns about MacArthur's ability to stay within his realm of authority. (Created in 1949, the Joint Chiefs of Staff is an agency within the Department of Defense serving to advise the president and the secretary of defense on matters of war.) In July 1950, on hearing a rumor that the Communist Chinese Army (the People's Liberation Army or PLA) was about to attack Taiwan (formerly Formosa), the Joint Chiefs had authorized MacArthur to go to Taiwan to survey the situation. (Communist Chinese leader Mao Zedong [Mao Tse-tung; 1893–1976] had driven the Amer-

logistics: the military science of tending to the acquisition, upkeep, and transportation of military equipment, goods, and personnel.

mine: a buried explosive set to go off if it is disturbed.

minesweeper: a warship that drags the bottom of the sea to remove or deactivate mines.

mop up: the clearing of an area of all enemy troops or resistance.

napalm: a jellylike material that turns to flame as it is shot from bombs and flame throwers; napalm is known for sticking to its targets as it burns them.

paratroopers: soldiers who are trained to jump from airplanes with parachutes.

reunification: the process of bringing back together the separate parts of something that was once a single unit; in Korea, it connotes the dream of a single Korea ruled under one government, no longer divided into two nations at the demarcation line.

satellite: a state or nation that is controlled by a stronger nation.

strafe: to fire upon at close range with machine guns from a low-flying plane.

38th parallel: the 38th degree of north latitude as it bisects the Korean Peninsula, chosen by Americans as the dividing line between what was to be Soviet-occupied North Korea and U.S.-occupied South Korea in 1945.

ican-backed Chinese Nationalist leader Chiang Kai-shek [1887–1975] and his forces to the island of Taiwan in October 1949 following a bloody civil war [see Chapter 3].) When he got there on July 31, although he found nothing to support the rumor, MacArthur staged a ceremonious two-day visit with Chiang that made it appear to the world that there was a U.S. alliance with the Nationalists on Taiwan. Since President Harry S. Truman (1884–1972) had announced a hands-off policy in China, MacArthur's display of alliance with Chiang was highly inappropriate. Later in August, in a message he provided to the Veterans of Foreign Wars, MacArthur again emphasized Taiwan's importance to the United States—as he had done before—but added a strong paragraph that was insulting to President Truman and probably very threatening to the Chinese. Offhandedly condemning the ignorance of those people

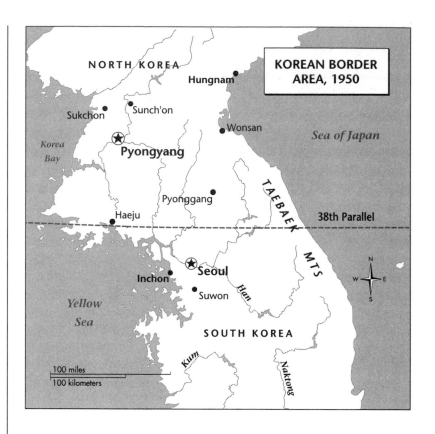

KOREAN BORDER AREA, 1950

NORTH KOREA

Hungnam

Sukchon

Sunch'on

Wonsan

Sea of Japan

Korea
Bay

Pyongyang

TAEBAEK MTS

Pyonggang

38th Parallel

Haeju

Seoul

N

Inchon

W E

Suwon

Han

S

Yellow
Sea

SOUTH KOREA

Kum

Naktong

100 miles

100 kilometers

(Truman and his administration) who were attempting to keep peace with the Communist Chinese, MacArthur made it clear that he believed the United States should set up a military base in Taiwan and use its position there to keep the Asian communist countries in line.

Representatives from the Joint Chiefs had met with MacArthur in Tokyo, Japan, in July to address these policy issues. MacArthur was, as always, impressive and clear about his intentions. During the course of the meeting he announced that his intentions were to destroy the North Korean forces and to possibly occupy all of North Korea. Nowhere in any policy statement had the Truman administration ever suggested that it intended to dismantle the North Korean government. Yet the Joint Chiefs did not contradict the general.

Later when the U.S. diplomat Averell Harriman (1891–1986) and a group of Washington military and political officials went to Tokyo to see MacArthur, he was quite con-

vincing about his Inchon plan, and many came back in favor of it. Truman himself, although annoyed with MacArthur, was enthusiastic about Inchon. The Joint Chiefs of Staff and the navy and marines leaders still had great objections to the logistics of the amphibious landing and went through them all with MacArthur. They got nowhere. In the end, MacArthur received the full support and authorization of the Joint Chiefs and the State Department for a September 15 attack.

The beach landing at Inchon, South Korea, September 15, 1950. Soldiers and equipment are unloaded from tank landing ships (LSTs). Reproduced by permission of Double Delta Industries, Inc.

The landing at Inchon

The mission at Inchon was given to the new X Corps (the First Marine Division, the Third and Seventh Infantry divisions, and ROK I Corps) under the command of MacArthur's chief of staff, Major General Edward M. Almond (1892–1979). Joint Task Force 7 provided naval support for the Inchon landing. Combining the resources of nine nations, the task force consisted of 230 battleships (huge combat ships used

The South Korean victim of a napalm bombing raid near Suwon, South Korea, in January 1951. *Reproduced by permission of AP/Wide World Photos.*

in Korea primarily for their big guns as support to the ground forces), 21 aircraft squadrons, and many specialty teams. As many as 75,000 troops participated in the attack.

Preparing the entryway

Prior to landing at Inchon, the UN forces needed to clear enemy-held Wolmi Island, which was in the line of approach to the port city. On September 10, Corsairs (single-pilot fighter planes used by navy and marine forces) dropped on the island ninety-five tanks of napalm, a jellylike material that turns to flame as it is shot from bombs and flame throwers (napalm is known for sticking to its targets as it burns). But the UN forces soon learned that, despite their bombings, an enemy gun emplacement was located somewhere on Wolmi Island. Cruisers (fast, lightly armored battleships) and destroyers (small, fast battleships with guns, depth charges [explosive projectiles for use underwater], and torpedoes, used to support the main battleship) were sent in on the morning of September 13. They destroyed the North Korean artillery and then fired on Wolmi all that day and the next, taking turns with naval aircraft. When they were done on the afternoon of September 14, the island of Wolmi was almost completely burned.

On the morning of September 15, the Corsairs once again bombed Wolmi Island. In the morning, a group of marines landed on Wolmi's beaches and secured the island. All day, aircraft covered the roads into Inchon to make sure that no new enemy troops could enter. In the afternoon, when the tide again allowed movement into the channels, two groups of marines, the First and the Fifth, got into landing craft as rockets were fired onto the beaches of Inchon. There they faced another of the problems of an Inchon landing: there were tall seawalls all around the city. The marines had to bomb the walls or find holes through which to enter.

The Fifth Marines struck at Red Beach. On the other side of the seawall they penetrated was the heart of the city of Inchon, where NKPA troops were waiting for them. After vicious fighting, the North Koreans were eliminated; eight marines were killed and nearly thirty were injured. The Fifth Marine units then moved on to secure two hills determined to be strategically important. The First Marines ran into less resistance; with one man killed and nineteen wounded, they reached their goal of the Seoul-Inchon Highway by midnight. The next morning the two groups met, sealing off the city of Inchon. MacArthur's plan was a success.

Although many of the city's 250,000 citizens had fled in terror when the attack began, there was no fleeing once the troops enveloped Inchon. The South Korean marines began to "mop up" the city. In the process, the remaining troops of the sixteen-hundred-man North Korean garrison and many civilians were killed.

On from Inchon

The UN and ROK marines quickly went on to capture Kimpo Airport, just outside of Seoul. They reached the Han River on the night of September 18. By then, the NKPA had brought in twenty thousand troops to defend the capital city. From September 22 to September 25, the UN forces and the

A War Correspondent's View of the Recapture of Seoul

United Press war correspondent Rutherford Poats was just one of the news reporters following the marines into the battle for Seoul. Although the recapture of the city was a major victory for the United Nations forces, the gruesome combat in the city streets turned the once-bustling capital city into a nightmarish burning landscape. Poats captured the aftermath in this often-quoted description from his book *Decision in Korea*:

> I followed the 1st Marines through the smoldering rubble of central Seoul the day after its premature "liberation." The last desperate Communist counterattack had been hurled back during an eerie 2 A.M. battle of tanks firing at point blank range, American artillery crashing less than a city block ahead of Marine lines, the echoed and re-echoed rattle of machine guns—all against the background of flaming buildings and darting shadows.

> Now it was almost quiet. The angry chatter of a machine gun up ahead now and then punctuated the long pauses between mortar and artillery strikes. But on this street corner was condensed the full horror of war, stripped of the vital challenge and excitement which make it bearable to the men who must fight wars.

> Telephone and power lines festooned the streets or hung from shattered poles which resembled grotesque Christmas trees. Bluish smoke curled from the corner of a clapboard shack—the only building even partially spared destruction along the left side of the street. A young woman poked among a pile of roof tiles and charred timbers for her possessions, or perhaps for her child. A lump of flesh and bones in a mustard-colored Communist uniform sprawled across the curb up ahead, and the white-robed body of an old man lay on a rice-straw mat nearer the street corner. Marine ammunition and mess trucks churned the plaster and adobe rubble into dust as they shuttled back and forth from the front, six blocks north. Southbound ambulance jeeps, almost always fully loaded with four stretcher cases on their racks, told the story of the pre-dawn battle.

> A tiny figure wrapped in a Marine's wool shirt stumbled down the street. Her face, arms, and legs were burned and almost eaten away by fragments of an American white phosphorous artillery shell. She was blind, but somehow alive. She was about the size of my little girl. Three other Korean children, luckier than she, watched as the child reached the curbing, stumbled, and twice failed to climb up on the sidewalk. The kids laughed.

Source: Rutherford M. Poats. Decision in Korea. *New York: McBride, 1954.*

North Koreans battled savagely at the western approaches to Seoul with heavy losses on both sides. On September 25, the North Koreans, having lost as many as thirty-five hundred men and facing the far superior naval and air forces of the UN troops, panicked and began to withdraw. General Almond

United Nations troops
taking back the streets of
Seoul, South Korea,
September 1950.
*Reproduced by permission of
Double Delta Industries, Inc.*

announced that Seoul had been recaptured, but in fact much of the city was still in North Korean control. Gruesome street fighting continued until September 27.

On September 28 the South Korean flag was raised once again at the government building in Seoul. The centuries-old city had been virtually destroyed. Many civilians were killed, historical treasures and priceless artworks were looted, and buildings were burning everywhere. With the streets ablaze and the city population terrorized, MacArthur brought South Korean president Syngman Rhee (1875–1965) back to Seoul on September 29. In the celebration commemorating the return of the capital to the ROK government, Rhee spoke with tears in his eyes, telling MacArthur, as quoted in Joseph C. Goulden's *Korea: The Untold Story of the War,* "We love you as the savior of our race."

MacArthur went back to his headquarters in Tokyo after delivering Rhee to the South Korean capital. The whole

Seoul, the capital of South Korea, in October 1950, demolished after months of bitter fighting but once again in the hands of the South Koreans. *Reproduced by permission of the Corbis Corporation.*

world seemed to be in awe of the general who had so dramatically turned the war around.

Breakout from the Pusan Perimeter

General Walton H. "Johnnie" Walker's (1889–1950) Eighth Army had continued its fight in the Pusan Perimeter while the Inchon landing was carried out. The Eighth Army was now made up of two new corps: I Corps ("eye" corps), with the Twenty-fourth, First Cavalry, and ROK First Divisions; and IX Corps ("nine" corps), with the Second and Twenty-fifth Divisions. The troops, happy to learn that the attack at Inchon had gone well, eagerly got ready to break out of the defensive positions they had been struggling to hold.

But no one told the NKPA troops fighting in the Pusan Perimeter about Inchon: their commanders wisely kept the news of the attack to themselves. Had the troops known that a powerful enemy force was at their back, they probably would have headed north immediately to avoid being cut off from their army. Ignorant of the event, the North Koreans fought as relentlessly as they had always fought. At first the Eighth Army's plans to drive north were in jeopardy; for every minor advance there were many casualties. Finally, on September 19, the weather cleared up, allowing the use of air support. The North Koreans fell at some key points and the Eighth Army moved forward. By September 23, the word was out about Inchon among the North Koreans, and there was a general North Korean flight.

Walker's Eighth Army troops were under instructions to advance as quickly as possible to join the X Corps near Seoul. However, they faced an unpredictable enemy. The NKPA military units had fallen apart, so the surviving North Koreans were traveling and fighting in small groups or by themselves. Some withdrew northward in good order, while others ran away into the mountains to make the difficult journey home. Still others surrendered without a fight. Many were killed by the ground troops and many more by the strafing (machine gun fire at close range from low-flying aircraft) and napalm bombs of the air force.

Once they had broken out from the Pusan Perimeter, Eighth Army units moved quickly, some units making the trip up the peninsula in three days. On September 27, a task force from the First Cavalry met up with a regiment of the Seventh Division near Suwon—that is, an Eighth Army unit met an X Corps unit. The ROK troops were heading up the east coast. This completed the incredibly successful Inchon attack.

Now what?

Perhaps due to the controversy about striking at Inchon in the first place, there was no plan for making the

After the American invasion and bombardment of Inchon, South Korea, a civilian casualty receives treatment from a U.S. medic. *Reproduced by permission of Archive Photos, Inc.*

most out of this success when it occurred. Because of this, many of the routes to the north were left clear, allowing North Korean soldiers to return to their army.

Key questions about what the UN forces were doing in Korea remained. Did the United States want to occupy North Korea and force a reunification under Syngman Rhee or only stop the North Korean invasion of South Korea? Should the border between North Korea and South Korea at the 38th parallel be strengthened to protect South Korea or should it be smashed for reunification? The initial UN resolution empowered the troops to stop an invasion, not to destroy a nation.

Back in the United States, the Joint Chiefs of Staff cabled MacArthur (JCS 92801 to Far East Commander MarcArthur, quoted in Goulden) on September 27 with instructions:

> Your military objective is the destruction of the North Korean armed forces. In attaining this objective you are authorized to conduct military operations . . . north of the 38th Parallel in Korea, provided that at the time of such operation there has been no entry into

North Korea by major Soviet or Chinese Communist Forces. . . . Under no circumstances, however, will your forces cross the Manchurian or USSR borders of Korea, and as a matter of policy, no non-Korean ground forces will be used in the northeast provinces bordering the Soviet Union or in the area along the Manchurian border.

The Joint Chiefs and the State Department then sent MacArthur some very ambiguous messages. They knew he wanted to cross the 38th parallel and wipe out the North Koreans, and they thought if he did it quickly enough they could present it to the United Nations as a "done deal." In their messages, the Joint Chiefs told MacArthur (JCS 92985, September 29, 1950) he should "feel unhampered tactically and strategically" by the 38th parallel, but that he should avoid making any public statements about crossing it. Further, the military leaders advised against using any non-Korean troops in the border zones of Russia and China. Beyond these orders, they left a great deal up to MacArthur.

By nearly all accounts, these decisions should have been made long before the Inchon attack, and they should have been made by President Truman and his administration. Policymaking is not typically the job of the commander of the forces. But MacArthur carried more sway than other military leaders, particularly after Inchon. In his book *Korea: The Untold Story of the War,* Goulden quoted General Matthew B. Ridgway (1895–1993), deputy to the army chief of staff and later commander of the Eighth Army, explaining the lack of direction from Washington to MacArthur: "A more subtle result of the Inchon triumph was the development of an almost superstitious regard for General MacArthur's infallibility. Even his superiors, it seemed, began to doubt if they should question *any* of MacArthur's decisions."

On September 30, the British representative to the United Nations introduced a resolution that "appropriate steps be taken to ensure conditions of stability throughout Korea" and that all of Korea—North and South—should be invited to participate in a UN-sponsored election for the establishment of a unified government. This resolution did not directly say whether force should be used.

The People's Republic of China responds

As decisions on how to proceed in Korea after Inchon were being discussed, there was great concern about how the

Soviet Union and China would react to UN forces crossing the 38th parallel. It was determined that the Soviet Union was not likely to enter the war. (The Soviet Union was the first communist country and was made up of fifteen republics, including Russia. It existed as a unified country from 1922 to 1991.) The United States, gravely underestimating China as only a satellite (a dependent nation) of the Soviet Union, failed to understand that it would act as an independent and powerful agent on its own if threatened with having a hostile world power such as the United States approaching its border.

In fact, since August, China had been warning the United States and the world that it would intervene in the war if necessary. After a fiery speech on August 17 from U.S. ambassador to the United Nations Warren Austin about the necessity of unifying Korea, the People's Republic of China Premier and Foreign Minister Zhou Enlai (Chou En-lai; 1898–1976) cabled the United Nations with this message, as quoted in Allen S. Whiting's *China Crosses the Yalu: The Decision to Enter the Korean War*: "Since Korea is China's neighbor, the Chinese people cannot but be especially concerned about solution of the Korean question, which must and can be settled peacefully." On September 24, China again cabled the United Nations to protest the strafing of sites in Manchuria (an area in northern China just north of the Korean border) by U.S. aircraft (some apparently accidents). On October 1, Zhou delivered a speech in the Chinese capital of Beijing (Peking) saying that the People's Republic of China considered the crossing of the 38th parallel by UN troops to be "a possible cause for war." Two nights later, Chou told the ambassador of the neutral nation of India that the People's Republic of China *would* intervene in the war if American troops crossed the 38th parallel. He said China would not intervene if the South Korean troops crossed the parallel on their own. The Indian ambassador's message was dismissed by Truman and his administration, who believed it was a bluff.

The United States knew that Chinese troops were building up in Manchuria just across the border at the Yalu River. According to the Far East Command's intelligence reports, there had been 189,000 People's Liberation Army (PLA) regulars in Manchuria in July, approximately 246,000 at the end of August, and 450,000 troops there on September 1.

Naval Operations in the Korean War

Although the United States cut down the size of all of its military branches after World War II (1939–45), the U.S. Navy emerged in those years as the primary world naval power, taking the place of Great Britain's once powerful navy. When the war in Korea started, President Harry S. Truman hoped to prevent sending ground troops to the distant land. His first efforts to stop the enemy were with air and naval forces.

The day the war started, June 25, 1950, the U.S. Navy's Seventh Fleet was ordered to the Straits of Taiwan, where it was to ensure that no conflicts erupted between the Chinese Communists on mainland China and the Chinese Nationalists on Taiwan (formerly Formosa). The Seventh Fleet then joined with Australian, Canadian, and New Zealand warships, forming Task Force 77, which set up a naval blockade to impede North Korea's access to the sea. Within the first few months of the war, the UN forces had destroyed North Korea's small navy and for the rest of the war remained unopposed in the waters around the Korean peninsula. There were no battles at sea after this, and the navy served as support to the ground effort.

UN ships carried supplies and troops to and from battlegrounds. Aircraft carriers brought in fighter planes, and minesweepers cleared out the mines (buried explosives that are set to go off if disturbed) planted in the waters off of the port cities by the enemy. The most heavily used large ships in the war were aircraft carriers, battleships, cruisers, destroyers, and minesweepers.

Truman was concerned and decided to pay a visit to MacArthur himself. The two met on October 15, 1950, in Wake Island, a U.S.-owned atoll (a ringlike coral island) in the Pacific Ocean. They had a private one-hour conference and then met with a group of statespeople to discuss the war. MacArthur predicted that the North Koreans would completely cede by Thanksgiving and also expressed his belief that the Chinese would not at this point interfere in Korea.

MacArthur's plan

After his successful assault at Inchon, MacArthur broadcast to the North Koreans two orders to surrender on October 1

The battleship U.S.S. *Missouri* fires its weapons on Chongjin, North Korea.
Reproduced by permission of Double Delta Industries, Inc.

and October 9. No answer to the broadcasts was expected, and none was received. On October 10, North Korean Premier Kim Il Sung (1912–1994) broadcast a message to his troops telling them to continue to fight to the end. In the meantime, the UN forces got ready to attack north of the 38th parallel.

MacArthur started by sending the X Corps by sea around the Korean peninsula to the port of Wonsan. He would send the Eighth Army by land to the north to capture the North Korean capital of Pyongyang. Then the X Corps would drive west to meet the Eighth Army, and the two forces would form a line across North Korea about one-hundred miles north of the 38th parallel. In these initial plans, only the ROK troops would fight above that line.

MacArthur's plan had two immense flaws. Pulling the marines out of the fighting and getting them out to sea caused innumerable delays just when the forces should have been pursuing the North Korean survivors. Splitting the command of the two corps, the X Corps under Almond's command and the Eighth Army under Walker, would have grave consequences.

The drive north

Rhee had already summoned the ROK commanders and instructed them to cross the 38th parallel and head up to the Yalu River, Korea's northern border with Manchuria, no matter what the United Nations instructed. The ROK Third Division crossed the 38th parallel on the east coast on September 30. Ten days later the ROK Third and Capital Divisions had secured the port of Wonsan, before the X Corps had even gotten out to sea.

In the meantime, the Eighth Army pushed on into North Korea, where the First Cavalry Division fought the desperate North Koreans in a series of brutal fights. As the UN and ROK forces approached, Premier Kim Il Sung and his government fled to the border city of Sinuiju on the Yalu River. On October 19, the First Cavalry reached the North Korean capital of Pyongyang, followed quickly by the four ROK divisions, the U.S. Twenty-fourth Division, the Twenty-seventh British Commonwealth Brigade, and a battalion of the Royal Australian Regiment. The North Korean People's Army had evacuated the capital. There was little resistance and massive surrender. The city, unlike Seoul, was temporarily saved from complete destruction.

On October 21, MacArthur flew to Pyongyang to address the troops there. A new governing council was created to replace Kim Il Sung's government, comprised of noncommunist citizens of the city. Kim Il Sung in the meantime moved again, this time to north central Korea. Small bands of

A woman and her grandchild wander among the debris following an American air raid over Pyongyang, the fallen North Korean capital, October 30, 1950.
Reproduced by permission of Archive Photos, Inc.

soldiers from the NKPA continued to attack throughout the country. The North Korean People's Army was not beaten, but it was too spent to be a real threat for some time to come. Everywhere in Korea the UN soldiers began to plan their trips home. Everyone thought the war was over.

MacArthur urges UN forces to the border

Changing his plans in an attempt to hasten the end of the war, MacArthur ordered the X Corps to travel north to the Yalu on the eastern side of the mountains that ran up and down North Korea. The Eighth Army was to continue its drive on the western side of the mountains. The mountains allowed no communication or contact between the two armies. MacArthur then ordered all troops, not just Koreans, to a point north of the original objective line. On October 20, he ordered all units to be prepared to advance rapidly to the border. MacArthur then authorized both the Eighth Army and the X Corps "to use any and all ground forces . . . as necessary to secure all of North Korea," as quoted by the Army historian Roy E. Appleman, violating the intent of the September 27 directive that recommended placing only Korean troops near the border in order to avoid a direct confrontation between U.S. troops and the Chinese. The Joint Chiefs demanded to know what he was planning. MacArthur's response to them was long but not very satisfactory and he did not change his tactics.

On October 20, the Eighth Army began its advance north to the Chongchon River, which is about sixty miles south of the Yalu. The Eighth Army's drive started out with a massive airdrop twenty-six miles north of Pyongyang. In this first airborne operation of the war, 2,860 paratroopers of the 187th Airborne Regimental Combat Team as well as their vehicles, guns, and other heavy equipment were dropped by parachute into Sukchon and Sunch'on. Their mission was to rescue some American prisoners of war who were being transported by the enemy troops. Although they did not find the train transporting the prisoners, one of the drops was right behind an NKPA Regiment that had stayed behind to delay the UN forces. During the next couple of days the paratroopers and a battalion of the Royal Australian Regiment fought a hard battle and almost completely eliminated the North Koreans. By October 23, the Eighth Army had pressed through to the Chongchon River.

The area between the Chongchon and the Yalu is made up of a ridge with valleys. Three villages—Taechon, Unsan, and Onjong—lie at the entrance to the valleys. Control of the Yalu River crossings required control of the divide. The Chinese, with troops amassed on the other side of the river, were watching and ready.

Where to Learn More

Alexander, Bevin. *Korea: The First War We Lost.* New York: Hippocrene Books, 1986, revised edition, 2000.

Appleman, Roy E. *South to the Naktong, North to the Yalu: United States Army in the Korean War.* Office of the Chief of Military History. Washington, DC: U.S. Government Printing Office, 1961.

Goulden, Joseph C. *Korea: The Untold Story of the War.* New York: Times Books, 1982.

Poats, Rutherford M. *Decision in Korea.* New York: McBride, 1954.

Varhola, Michael J. *Fire and Ice: The Korean War, 1950–1953.* Mason City, IA: Savas Publishing, 2000.

Whiting, Allen S. *China Crosses the Yalu: The Decision to Enter the Korean War.* Stanford, CA: Stanford University Press, 1960.

China Enters the War

O f all the errors leading to the Korean War, the Americans' underestimation of the Chinese was one of the gravest. An accurate view of China had become virtually impossible in the United States during the cold war, a period of political tension and military rivalry between the United States and the Soviet Union and other communist countries that began following World War II (1939–45) and continued until the breakup of the Soviet Union in 1991. The reasons for American blindness had deep roots in the past.

In the nineteenth century, China had become prey to trade exploitation at the hands of the British, and later the French, Russians, and Americans. After two small wars, the European nations forced China to open more ports, legalize opium (an addictive narcotic drug made from the opium poppy), and welcome Christian missionaries (people who conduct religious or charitable work in a territory or foreign country). Westerners then carved up China among themselves, setting up areas in which the different nations predominated.

During the next generations, many Christian missionaries served in China and returned to the United States with a

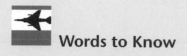

Words to Know

artillery: large weapons, such as howitzers, rockets, and 155-millimeter guns, that shoot missiles and generally take a crew to operate.

atomic bomb: a powerful bomb created by splitting the nuclei of a heavy chemical, such as plutonium or uranium, in a rapid chain reaction, resulting in a violent and destructive shock wave as well as radiation.

battalion: a military unit usually made up of about three to five companies. Generally one of the companies is the headquarters unit, another the service unit, and the rest are line units. Although the numbers differ greatly, a battalion might consist of about 35 officers and about 750 soldiers.

buffer zone: a neutral area between the territories of opposing forces.

casualties: those who are killed, wounded, missing, or taken prisoner in combat.

China Lobby: a group of Americans during the late 1940s and early 1950s who fervently supported Chinese Nationalist leader Chiang Kai-shek in his struggles against the Communist Chinese, and who held a romanticized and sometime patronizing view of the Chinese people and their relations with Americans.

one-sided view of the Chinese people as a submissive, colonialized people who were grateful and devoted to Americans. *Time* magazine publisher Henry Luce (1898–1967), who had been born in China as the son of missionaries, promoted this stereotypical view of the Chinese people in his publications, as did other prominent politicians and writers.

The China Lobby

By the mid-twentieth century, a romanticized view of American friendship with the Chinese people prevailed. Chinese Nationalist leader Chiang Kai-shek (1887–1975) was held up as a heroic anticommunist figure. Churches and social groups set up charity drives for China. The large group of Americans who participated in this effort came to be known as the "China Lobby." Although the movement was quite strong, very few people had any idea what was actually happening in China, where Chiang was losing the popular support due to

delegate: a person who represents another person, a group, or a nation.

demilitarized zone (DMZ): an area in which military presence and activity are forbidden.

egalitarian: promoting equality; allowing each person in a group more or less equal powers.

guerrilla warfare: an irregular form of combat; in Korea it usually involved small groups of warriors who hid in mountains, enlisted the help of the local population, and used ambushes and surprise attacks to harass or even destroy much larger armies.

infantry: the branch of an army that is composed of soldiers trained to fight on foot.

hierarchy: organization by rank; in most hierarchies, the higher the rank, the greater the individual's power and authority.

mortar: a muzzle loading cannon that shoots high in the air.

tactician: a person who plans how to use the military forces in combat.

warlord: a leader with his own military whose powers are usually limited to a small area that, in most cases, he took by force.

his corrupt government. Therefore, the American public was truly shocked when the Chinese Nationalists lost power to Mao Zedong (Mao Tse-tung; 1893–1976) and the Chinese Communists in 1949.

The rise of the Communists in China should not have surprised Americans. Communism is a political belief system that advocates the elimination of private property, a system in which goods are owned by the community as a whole rather than by specific individuals and are available to all as needed. At its heart it is at odds with the American economic system, capitalism, in which individuals, rather than the state, own the property and businesses, and the cost and distribution of goods are determined by the free market. In the 1940s, professional American diplomats who understood the political factions and issues facing China urged the U.S. government to take the Communists seriously. They knew that the Chinese Communists were of a different breed than the Soviet Communists. In the early days, many of the new leaders were open to a range of economic and social ideas; the Chinese Communists had a history of tensions with the Soviets and were also open to alliances with other nations. The diplomats also knew that Chiang Kai-shek was on his way out. The country, ruled by warlords (often military leaders who control parts of a country, particularly when the central government is not in control) and other local leaders, as well as the Nationalist government, did not support Chiang. The diplomats, who had kept open communications with the Communist Chinese, were harassed by the China Lobby and accused of being communist sympathizers or even spies for the Soviets. They finally withdrew from their posts in China. Consequently, when the United States went to war in Korea, there was no adequate source of information on the Chinese. The United States did not know its enemy.

China

China is one of the oldest cultures in the world and has been the "Middle Kingdom," the center and leader of Asian countries, for centuries. At the time the Korean War started in 1950, China had the largest army in the world, with over five million men and 253 divisions. Because of the civil war between the Nationalists and the Communists and the long-term war against the occupying Japanese (see Chapter 1), the Communist Chinese Forces (CCF) were very experienced in combat. They were excellent tacticians—well-versed in employing forces in combat—with strong roots in guerrilla warfare, an irregular form of combat that often involves small groups of warriors who use ambushes and surprise attacks to harass or even destroy much larger armies.

The CCF was organized quite differently than the U.S. or even the Soviet and North Korean armies. The Chinese soldiers all wore the same uniform: in winter, a mustard brown quilted cotton garment with rubber-soled shoes and a cotton cap with ear flaps. The Chinese did not use a ranking system like the American military hierarchy, although there were certainly officers and troops. The organization was created to be egalitarian, with each person in it given more or less equal powers. This was evident to Americans when they captured Chinese prisoners: the privates knew the most intricate details

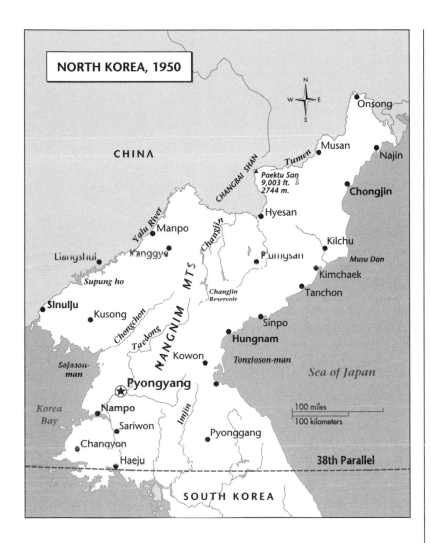

NORTH KOREA, 1950

CHINA

Onsong

Musan

Najin

Tumen

Paektu San
9,003 ft.
2744 m.

Chongjin

Hyesan

Kilchu

Manpo

Pumgsan

Musu Dan

Liangshui

Kanggye

Kimchaek

Supung ho

Tanchon

Changjin
Reservoir

Sinuiju

Kusong

Sinpo

Hungnam

Kowon

Tongioson-man

Sea of Japan

Sojoson-
man

Pyongyang

Nampo

Korea
Bay

Sariwon

Pyonggang

100 miles

100 kilometers

Changyon

Haeju

38th Parallel

SOUTH KOREA

of the Chinese strategy. At first the Americans dismissed what the prisoners of war (POWs) told them, but later they understood that the Chinese army sponsored discussion groups in which strategy and planning were discussed by all.

The People's Liberation Army

When the Korean War started, the Communist Party had only been in power in China for a year and a half. The Chinese were facing tremendous economic crises. They had little technology, and their military equipment was almost nonexistent. The famous Chinese attack signal—the sounding of eerie bugles along with drums, cymbals, and other loud

McCarthyism and Diplomacy

In February 1950, Joseph McCarthy (1908–1957), a little-known U.S. senator from Wisconsin, stood up at a conference in Wheeling, West Virginia, and announced that there were communists working in the U.S. State Department. In his ensuing speech McCarthy stated that the State Department was "thoroughly infested with communists," making his famous claim: "I have in my hand 57 cases of individuals who would appear to be either card-carrying members or certainly loyal to the Communist Party, but who nevertheless are still helping to shape our foreign policy." McCarthy never produced any evidence to back his allegations, but this speech and others he made on radio and television stirred up a political tempest in the new cold war era. A five-year witch-hunt for communists in the government ruined many careers and forced policymakers to go to extreme lengths to avoid being labeled communist sympathizers. It was not until 1954, after he had made serious allegations against the army, that McCarthy was himself investigated. At that time he was exposed as a dishonest opportunist who had taken advantage of public fears to boost his own career.

In McCarthy's early speech, he focused on one State Department diplomat in particular, John Service. Service was an accomplished expert on China who had

noises—was, in fact, a primitive way of communication necessitated by a lack of radios and telephones. The Chinese army used humans and animals to transport their supplies because they had few vehicles. Even their railroad system had fallen into disrepair. They had very little air or naval support. And they had never fought in a battle with the kind of weapons the United Nations (UN) forces were using.

But the Chinese had several things their enemy did not have. First, the Chinese army made sure that each soldier in battle was passionately committed to the war. The Chinese believed that if China lost the war, the United States would enter their country as an occupying force. To lose the war meant the loss of independence and freedom in China. The Chinese stressed this in the "political training" of a soldier, which was, to them, as important as tactical training. Second, the Chinese had the advantage of manpower. They had many

Joseph McCarthy. *Reproduced by permission of AP/Wide World Photos.*

kept up communications with Mao Zedong and the Communist Party during the 1940s. He had urged the U.S. government to not dismiss the importance of the Communists, for he believed they were likely to take power. Service had been arrested on suspicion of being a communist and was forced to resign from his work for the State Department in China. All charges were quickly dropped, and he was reinstated in the State Department but was not returned to China. Service, and other diplomats like him, were never to have the opportunity to share their knowledge about China with the U.S. government during the Korean War, when their help was desperately needed.

troops in Korea, always with more on the way. As Edwin Hoyt pointed out in his book *The Day the Chinese Attacked Korea, 1950:* "Mao Tse-tung chose to put force against force; his force of human hordes against the American force of modern weapons and technology." This meant that when a Chinese soldier went down in battle, another stepped in and quickly took his place. The gruesome fact was that UN forces could fire continuously on an attacking unit of Chinese soldiers; although many soldiers were killed, the group would keep coming on at full strength.

The Chinese, unlike the Americans, also had the advantage of knowing what they were up against. South Korean general Paik Sun Yup (1920–) noted this in his memoirs *From Pusan to Panmunjom:* "The Chinese understood combat tactics thoroughly, and unlike the UN Command, the Chinese Army knew its enemy well." Paik then quoted a bulletin that

Corsairs returning from a combat mission over North Korea circle the U.S.S. *Boxer* as they wait for planes in the next strike to be launched from her flight deck, September 1951. The U.S. military's air-to-ground attack capability was one of its stronger aspects during the Korean War. *Reproduced by permission of Double Delta Industries, Inc.*

was published by the Chinese military on November 20, 1950, on the results of the battle at Unsan. Written by Chinese deputy commander Teng Hua, the pamphlet provided a solid description of its enemy:

> The U.S. Army relies for its main power in combat on the shock effect of coordinated armor and artillery . . . and their air-to-ground attack capability is exceptional. But their infantry is weak. Their men are afraid to die, and will neither press home a bold attack nor defend to the death. . . . Their habit is to be active only during the daylight hours. They are very weak at attacking or approaching an enemy at night. . . . If their source of supply is cut, their fighting spirit suffers, and if you interdict their rear, they withdraw on their own.

China is snubbed by the UN

It is clear that China wished to avoid this war. Having just come out of a civil war, the Communist government needed time to establish economic and political stability and also wanted to continue its efforts in claiming Taiwan (formerly Formosa; where the Chinese Nationalists had settled) and Tibet, which had resisted China's claim to it as a "special territory" of China. China was willing to go through the channels of diplomacy in order to come to a resolution in Korea but was impeded in this because of its exclusion from the United Nations. (Since 1949, when the Communists defeated the U.S.-backed Nationalists in the Chinese Civil War, the United States and the UN did not recognize Communist China.) At the same time that Chinese troops were moving to Manchuria, an area in northern China just north of the Korean border, in August 1950, the People's Republic of China was trying to gain admittance to the United Nations.

On August 1, the Soviet delegate to the United Nations Security Council, Jacob A. Malik (1906–1980), returned. He had been boycotting (refusing to take part in) the proceedings during the prior resolutions on Korea in a show of Soviet displeasure at the UN's refusing to recognize the People's Republic of China as the legitimate Chinese nation. The Soviet delegate introduced a resolution to invite representatives of the People's Republic of China and both Koreas to the Security Council to discuss the war. A second part of his proposal was to stop hostilities and withdraw all foreign troops from Korea. For over a month the proposal was debated, with American representatives pushing instead for a commitment to eliminate the North Koreans and unify the country. The Soviet resolution was defeated in the Security Council on September 6 and September 11: there would be no representation of Korea or China in discussions about the war, and there would be no cease-fire.

On October 2, 1950, after China's foreign minister Zhou Enlai (Chou En-lai; 1898–1976) sent a message through the Indian ambassador that China would intervene in the war if the Americans crossed the 38th parallel, the Soviet foreign minister tried again, proposing to the UN General Assembly an immediate cease-fire in Korea and the withdrawal of all foreign troops, to be followed by all-Korean elections. But this was not to be. On October 7, the United Nations passed the vaguely worded, U.S.-created resolution that authorized UN troops to take "appropriate steps . . . to ensure conditions of stability throughout Korea," as quoted in Bevin Alexander's *Korea: The First War We Lost,* and to pave the way for a unified Korean government elected under United Nations supervision.

The UN resolution meant that the North Koreans, to whom Chinese loyalty was strong, would certainly be destroyed if they did not receive help. It also meant that the United States would have its forces at the Chinese borders for a long time to come, if not permanently. The United States had been tied to Chiang Kai-shek and the Nationalists for many years and already had a naval fleet poised between Taiwan and mainland China. The Communist Chinese foresaw the United States constantly trying to reinstate the Nationalists, as MacArthur, commander of the UN forces, had so pointedly said he wanted to do. One other factor must have stirred China toward an unwanted war. The resolution and the public statements of American and European statesmen had demonstrated a general lack of respect for the Chinese, who took pride in being one of the largest and oldest countries of the world.

The Chinese prepare

UN forces began to cross the 38th parallel soon after the UN resolution of October 7. With that provocation, Mao Zedong met with the top generals of his army to discuss intervening in the Korean War. Many Chinese commanders strongly urged against entering the war, believing the army too weak to take on the technologically superior Americans. They were also concerned about the air strength of the UN forces and the potential use of the atomic bomb on China, which had been dropped on Hiroshima and Nagasaki, Japan, effectively ending World War II in 1945. On October 8, Mao selected Peng Dehuai (P'eng Teh-huai; 1898–1974), a general who had been with Mao and the Communists for decades, to be commander of the forces in Korea.

The troops targeted for Korea were to be called the Chinese People's Volunteers (CPV), although they were all part of the regular army. (By calling the troops in Korea volunteers, the Chinese may have been leaving the door open to denying they had formally entered into the war.) The CPV troops had been accumulating and organizing around the Manchurian towns of Andong and Shenyang throughout the summer and the fall of 1950. From October 14 to October 18, Peng oversaw the movement of 180,000 troops from Manchuria into North Korea.

The Chinese troops wore North Korean uniforms as they silently traveled by night through the mountainous terrain to take up defensive positions. They carried American-made mortars (muzzle-loading cannons) and machine guns captured from the Nationalists in the Chinese Civil War, as well as rifles seized from the surrendering Japanese in Manchuria at the end of World War II. Preparing to meet the enemy, many formed the *Haichi Shiki,* a Chinese battle formation in which the soldiers fan out to form a huge V shape. Once advancing enemy soldiers marched into the open end of the V, the soldiers at the mouth of the formation close in, effectively cutting off the escape route, isolating and enveloping a small unit for battle. Because they were precise in their defense formations, the Chinese, silent and camouflaged (disguised to look like the surrounding plants and environment), allowed unsuspecting UN troops to march right past them before launching their first offensive.

The first United Nations troops to cross the 38th parallel pose with a sign to show their crossing, 1950. *Reproduced by permission of Archive Photos, Inc.*

Excerpt from Peng Dehuai's Memoirs

Peng Dehuai, a field commander in the army and one of Chinese leader's Mao Zedong's longtime associates, was summoned to attend an October 4, 1951, meeting with Mao and the Chinese Communist Party Central Committee at Zhongmanhai, part of the Imperial Palace. He was to report on the army's readiness for war. He arrived the night before the meeting and spent a sleepless night worrying about what lay ahead for China, as he wrote in his memoirs, quoted in Edwin Hoyt's *The Day the Chinese Attacked Korea, 1950:*

> I could not fall asleep that night. I thought it might be because I could not enjoy the soft, cozy, spring bed, so I lay down on the carpeted floor. But sleep still did not come, and a train of thoughts flashed across my mind. The U.S. occupation of Korea, separated from China only by a river, would threaten northeast China. Its control of Taiwan posed a threat to Shanghai and east China. The United States could find a pretext at any time to launch a war of aggression against China. The tiger wanted to eat human beings; when it would do so would depend on its appetite. No concession could stop it. If the United States wanted to invade China, we had to resist its aggressions. Without going into a test with U.S. imperialism to see who was stronger, it would be difficult for us to build socialism. If the United States was bent on warring against China, it would want a war of quick decision. While we would wage a protracted war, it would fight regular warfare and we would employ the kind of warfare we had used against the Japanese invaders. As we had a national government and Soviet assistance, our situation was much better than it had been during the War of Resistance to Japanese Aggression. We should dispatch troops to Korea to safeguard our national construction.

Source: Edwin P. Hoyt. The Day the Chinese Attacked Korea, 1950: The Story of the Failure of America's China Policy. New York: McGraw-Hill, 1990.

The first Chinese offensive

While the U.S. troops were advancing toward the Yalu River after successfully taking the North Korean capital of Pyongyang on October 20, the South Korean (ROK) forces met with an unexpected blow as they hurried to the border in the east. On October 25, a regiment of the ROK First Division advancing past the town of Unsan was suddenly attacked by a unit of Chinese troops. On capturing an enemy soldier, the ROK were told that there were two groups of ten thousand Chinese soldiers facing them and another ten thousand facing the ROK Sixth Division. By the afternoon of October 26, the entire ROK First Division was surrounded by Chinese troops.

On October 26, as the ROK Sixth Division's Seventh Regiment neared the shores of the Yalu River at Onjong, it was attacked by what the regiment assumed were North Korean soldiers. The attack, in fact, came from a roadblock of Chinese soldiers. Fierce fighting continued through the next day, when the entire regiment scattered in defeat.

On October 28, two more ROK regiments went to Onjong to try to retrieve some of the weapons and vehicles that had been left behind during the battle. These regiments were shattered by the Chinese as well. On that same day the ROK Seventh Regiment came upon a Chinese roadblock at Kojang. After brutal fighting that day, the Seventh Regiment was ambushed. As many as twenty-seven hundred men were lost. The ROK II Corps was shattered.

Americans in denial

The Chinese attacks at Onjong and Unsan were initially casually dismissed by MacArthur. It was not until Octo-

Young workers in a Chinese textiles factory sign a document, pledging that they will increase production in support of China's recent entry into the Korean War.
Reproduced by permission of the Corbis Corporation.

ber 31, with great loss of lives and ground near the border, that MacArthur's chief intelligence officer conceded that the reports of the Chinese invasion were turning out to be all too true. By that time General Walton H. "Johnnie" Walker (1889–1950) had sent in the First Cavalry to support the surviving South Korean troops. He found that the entire ROK II Corps had disintegrated and was retreating south. Still, the Americans thought the end of the war was just around the corner and that the Chinese soldiers were not a real threat.

General Paik Sun Yup, commander of the ROK First Division, knew better. In his book *From Pusan to Panmunjom* he said:

> Although we were now capturing a succession of Chinese prisoners who unequivocally [without doubt] identified their units as part of the conventional Chinese Army, the Americans continued to fool themselves because the Chinese had yet to challenge a U.S. Army division directly, and because to the American eye, the Koreans and Chinese looked and sounded very much alike. To us, of course, the differences were vast. The Americans clung to the view that at worst we were facing small numbers of Chinese volunteers who had joined defeated NKPA [North Korean People's Army] units.

China's first offensive

On November 1, many observers reported huge columns of Chinese soldiers marching toward the town of Unsan. The Chinese were hidden by smoke they had produced by burning the forests in the area so air support could not locate them. During the night the Chinese surrounded the Eighth Cavalry Regiment at Unsan as well as the ROK Fifteenth Regiment. After destroying most of the Fifteenth, the Chinese trapped and attacked the Third Battalion of the Eighth Cavalry. Attempts were made to rescue the Third Battalion without success, and it became painfully clear that nothing more could be done. After three days of being trapped and in close combat with the Chinese, more than one-half the battalion's survivors were seriously wounded. The two hundred remaining able-bodied men decided to try to escape, leaving behind the battalion's chaplain and surgeon with the two hundred fifty wounded. In all, six hundred died or were missing in action.

Sharp, short attacks began to hit many units of the Eighth Army, mainly at night and always entailing heavy casualties. Although the Americans were seasoned by combat, the power of this new enemy seemed over-whelming. "The attackers came in the hours before the dawn, making enormous noise with drums, whistles, and off-key bugles," Hoyt described in *The Day the Chinese Attacked Korea, 1950.* "Their attacks were ushered in by machine gun fire and mortar fire, but no artillery. The use of grenades was extensive. The attackers would come out of the night, rush a position, kill and wound men, and then withdraw." Facing this new and unknown enemy, Walker could see that the Eighth Army was vulnerable. He ordered a withdrawal to Kunu-ri, at the Chongchon River line.

Then a very unusual turn of events occurred. Starting November 6, the Chinese units—even as they were defeating the enemy—began, one by one, to pull out of combat and march away. By November 7, the Chinese had withdrawn into the mountains. In many instances the Chinese, before they withdrew, placed American and ROK wounded on stretchers and carried them up to the road, leaving them to be rescued by their comrades. Before freeing them, the Chinese told the wounded to tell their friends about China's compassionate treatment of them. The Chinese People's Volunteers did not strike again for three weeks, leaving enough time for the UN and U.S. policymakers to reconsider.

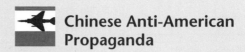

Chinese Anti-American Propaganda

Chinese troops were expected to firmly believe in their cause. Political leaders within the Chinese military attempted to ensure that the soldiers were passionate in their hatred of the enemy, as can be seen in this piece of Chinese military propaganda:

> The United States is the paradise of gangsters, swindlers, rascals, special agents, fascist germs, speculators, debauchers, and all the dregs of mankind. This is the world's manufactory [maker] and source of such crimes as reaction, darkness, cruelty, decadence, corruption, debauchery, oppression of man by man, and cannibalism. This is the exhibition ground of all the crimes which can possibly be committed by mankind. This is a living hell, ten times, one hundred times, one thousand times worse than can be possibly depicted by the most sanguinary [bloodthirsty] of writers. Here the criminal phenomena that issue forth defy the imagination of human brains. Conscientious persons can only wonder how the spiritual civilization of mankind can be depraved to such an extent.

Source: Reprinted in Patrick C. Roe. The Dragon Strikes, China and the Korean War: June-December 1950. *Novato, CA: Presidio, 2000.*

The pause in battle: November 7–24, 1950

The Americans were puzzled by the Chinese withdrawal-in-victory. Unfortunately, there was little expertise available. The Chinese tactic of withdrawing to lure the enemy deeper into their trap had been written about extensively by

Mao Zedong in his book on warfare. But Mao's books had not even been published in the United States and no copies were available. On November 3, the Joint Chiefs of Staff (the advisors to the president and the secretary of defense on matters of war) asked MacArthur for a report on the situation. He replied that he could not at that time foresee whether the Chinese would actually execute a large invasion. MacArthur then sent a message to the United Nations, reporting that UN forces were meeting hostile Chinese troops in battle. The UN Security Council met but did not make any decisions about what to do.

Despite the lack of urgency in his November 3 message to the Joint Chiefs, on November 5 MacArthur ordered the Far East Air Force to prepare a large-scale bombing offensive, in which the Korean sides of all the bridges crossing the Yalu River into Manchuria, as well as all North Korean cities and towns, factories, and lines of communication, were to be destroyed. In order to prevent any more Chinese troops from entering Korea, he ordered the air force bombers to work around the clock, if necessary, to accomplish the bombings within a two-week period. When the Joint Chiefs got word of MacArthur's order—he had not bothered to inform them of his intent—they ordered him to stop this attack. MacArthur responded with a cable on November 7, 1950, quoted by Bevin Alexander in *Korea: The First War We Lost:*

> Men and material are pouring across all bridges over the Yalu from Manchuria. This movement not only jeopardizes but threatens the ultimate destruction of the forces under my command. The actual movement across the river can be accomplished under cover of darkness and the distance of the river and our lines is so short that the forces can be deployed against our troops without being seriously subjected to air interdiction. The only way to stop this reinforcement of the enemy is the destruction of these bridges and the subjection of all installations in the north area supporting the enemy advance to the maximum of our air destruction. Every hour this is postponed will be paid for dearly in American and other United Nations blood.

Bombings at the Yalu River

On November 7, MacArthur reported that some enemy aircraft had been striking UN aircraft and then flying back across the border into China. MacArthur wanted permission to bomb aircraft in the skies above Manchuria. UN forces had no authority to cross the Yalu, and widespread international concern over the extent of American aggression in Korea ruled this out. But the U.S. Joint Chiefs of Staff and then the National Security Council met and eventually decided that MacArthur should be allowed to continue his operations as he wished, with the Joint Chiefs continuing to closely monitor the situation.

It was agreed that nonmilitary negotiations with the Chinese would be conducted in the meantime. The Chinese were invited to attend a United Nations meeting to discuss MacArthur's November 6 report. The Chinese foreign ministers agreed to come to the UN to discuss American aggression in Taiwan, not MacArthur's report. They were to arrive at the UN's headquarters in New York on November 19, but they intentionally delayed, not arriving until November 27, after their second offensive in Korea had started. MacArthur's bombings in North Korea and at the Yalu had begun on November 8 and continued until December 5.

Britain proposed that the United Nations forces fall back to provide China a buffer zone on the Korean side of the Yalu River. U.S. Secretary of State Dean Acheson (1893–1971) liked this idea. At a November 21 meeting of the heads of the military services and the State Department, China's entry into the war and dissatisfaction with the UN's position were on everyone's minds. The demilitarized zone south of the Yalu was discussed, as were the grave concerns shared by all about the split in command between the X Corps, led by Major General Edward M. Almond (1892–1979), and the Eighth Army, led by Walker. But no firm decisions were reached at the meeting. Acheson wrote later in his memoirs *Present at the Creation:*

> We were all deeply apprehensive. We were frank with one another, but not quite frank enough. I was unwilling to urge on the President a military course that his military advisors would not propose. They would not propose it because it ran counter to American military tradition of the proper powers of the theater commander. . . . If General [George C.] Marshall and the Chiefs had proposed withdrawal to the Pyongyang-Wonsan line and a continuous defensive position under united command across it—and if the President had backed them, as he undoubtedly would have—disaster would probably have been averted. But it would have meant a fight with MacArthur, charges by him that they had denied him victory—and his relief under arguable circumstances. So they hesitated, wavered, and the chance was lost. While everyone acted correctly, no one, I suspect, was ever quite satisfied with himself afterward.

The split in the ground command

On November 24, the day MacArthur set aside for the start of the UN's "final drive," the Far East Command estimated that there were anywhere from 40,000 to 70,935 Chinese troops in Korea and about 82,800 North Korean troops. In fact, by that time there were about 380,000 Chinese troops in North Korea. Once his bombing campaign was underway, MacArthur began movement of all UN forces to the northern border of Korea. The Eighth Army was to advance in the west and X Corps was heading for the Chosin (Changjin) Reservoir from the east.

Not everyone was as enthusiastic about this advance as MacArthur. As the November 24 offensive began, it was clear to many military planners that the UN forces were too spread out and lacked proper communication, and that Almond's X Corps should have been in a position to support the Eighth Army if it were in trouble. General Walker, commander of the Eighth Army, and General Oliver Smith, commander of the First Marine Division (in X Corps, under General Almond), were very concerned about their assignments to advance without coverage at their flanks (sides).

There were ill feelings between the generals of the Eighth Army and the X Corps, Walker and Almond. Almond made it clear he did not want to report to Walker, who was his superior. General Walker wanted both armies to advance slowly together, in the east and the west. Almond wanted to head north as quickly as possible, in line with MacArthur's plans, leaving the Eighth Army to its caution.

Where to Learn More

Acheson, Dean. *Present at the Creation: My Years in the State Department.* New York: W. W. Norton, 1969.

Alexander, Bevin. *Korea: The First War We Lost.* New York: Hippocrene Books, 1986, revised edition, 2000.

Hoyt, Edwin P. *The Day the Chinese Attacked Korea, 1950: The Story of the Failure of America's China Policy.* New York: McGraw-Hill, 1990.

Paik Sun Yup. *From Pusan to Panmunjom: Wartime Memoirs of the Republic of Korea's First Four-Star General.* Dulles, VA: Brassey's, 1992.

Roe, Patrick C. *The Dragon Strikes, China and the Korean War: June-December 1950.* Novato, CA: Presidio, 2000.

Whiting, Allen S. *China Crosses the Yalu: The Decision to Enter the Korean War.* Stanford, CA: Stanford University Press, 1960.

Web sites

"Joseph Raymond McCarthy." CNN Interactive. [Online] http://www.cnn.com/SPECIALS/cold.war/kbank/profiles/mccarthy (accessed on August 14, 2001).

"Senator Joseph McCarthy, Speech at Wheeling, West Virginia, February 9, 1950." [Online] http://138.110.28.9/~kemarsh/mccarthy/speech.html (accessed on August 14, 2001).

The Second Retreat of the United Nations Command

In mid-November 1950, winter set in quickly in North Korea—almost overnight, according to some of the soldiers. The weather dropped as low as twenty degrees below zero, bringing new chaos to the units. Rifles would not fire, vehicles would not start, and many men were taken out of commission by frostbite. Morale dropped steadily with the temperature. Walton H. "Johnnie" Walker (1889–1950), commander of the Eighth Army, was having trouble getting supplies for his troops, and there was already a shortage of winter equipment, significantly delaying northward advances of the Eighth Army from the Chongchon River front.

The plan for the Eighth Army to advance to the northern Korean border on the western frontier, devised by American general Douglas MacArthur (1880–1964), commander in chief of the United Nations (UN) Forces in Korea, was at last put into action. This was the beginning of the optimistically named "Home by Christmas" offensive. At 8:00 A.M. on November 24, 1950, the entire Eighth Army began its northward advance—now including the I Corps, which included the Twenty-fourth Division, the South Korean (ROK) Army First Division, and the Twenty-

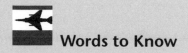

Words to Know

annihilate: to destroy or kill.

automatic weapon: a weapon that fires repeatedly without needing reloading or other extra actions by the person shooting it.

battalion: a military unit usually made up of about three to five companies. Generally one of the companies is the headquarters unit, another the service unit, and the rest are line units. Although the numbers differ greatly, a battalion might consist of about 35 officers and about 750 soldiers.

casualties: those who are killed, wounded, missing, or taken prisoner in combat.

division (or infantry division): a self-sufficient unit, usually about 15,000 to 16,000 strong, under the command of a major general. Communist Chinese army divisions were closer to 10,000 soldiers strong.

gauntlet: a terrible ordeal; a ritual in which an individual is forced to run through a formation of two facing rows of people armed with clubs or other weapons who are striking him or her from both sides.

grenades: a small explosive weapon that can be thrown, usually with a pin that is pulled to activate them and a spring-loaded safety lever that is held down until the user wants to throw the grenade; once the safety lever is released, the grenade will explode in seconds.

infiltrate: to enter into enemy lines by passing through gaps in its defense.

mortar: a muzzle-loading cannon that shoots high in the air.

napalm: a jellylike material that turns to flame as it is shot from bombs and flame throwers; napalm is known for sticking to its targets as it burns them.

POW: prisoner of war.

refugee: someone who is fleeing to a different country to escape danger in his or her own nation.

regiment: a military unit composed of three battalions.

---

seventh British Commonwealth Brigade, and the IX Corps, which included the Twenty-fifth and Second Divisions and the Turkish Brigade (which had just arrived in Korea). On the right of the line was the repaired ROK II Corps, which included the recently battered ROK Sixth, Seventh, and Eighth Divisions.

The Communist Chinese Forces (CCF) hit the Eighth Army on November 25. Knowing that the ROK units were

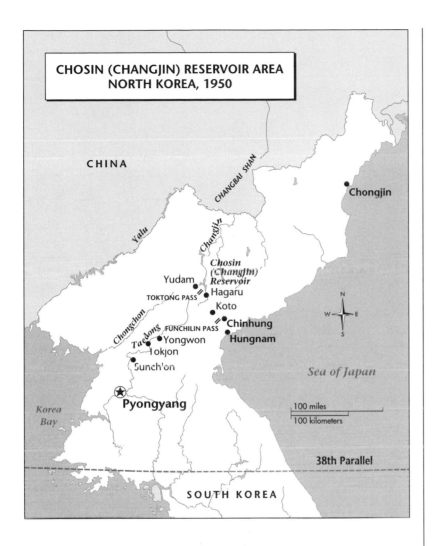

**CHOSIN (CHANGJIN) RESERVOIR AREA
NORTH KOREA, 1950**

CHINA

Chongjin

CHANGBAI SHAN

Yalu

Changjin

Chosin (Changjin) Reservoir

Yudam

TOKTONG PASS

Hagaru

Koto

Chongchon

FUNCHILIN PASS

Chinhung

Taedong

Yongwon

Hungnam

Tokjon

Sunch'on

Sea of Japan

N

W—E

S

Korea Bay

Pyongyang

100 miles

100 kilometers

38th Parallel

SOUTH KOREA

poorly armed and often weaker than the other UN forces, they concentrated their efforts at strategic points where the ROK Seventh held Tokjon and the ROK Eighth held Yongwon. The Chinese decisively shattered both divisions that day. Using the holes in the Eighth Army line left by the ROK divisions, the CCF forces then surrounded unit after unit of the IX Corps, inflicting terrible damage to the Second Division in particular. The exposed areas of the Eighth Army left it vulnerable to the infiltrating Chinese troops. Outnumbered and without sufficient protection on its flanks (sides), the Eighth Army faced certain disaster. Walker had no choice but to request a withdrawal order for the entire army. He received the authority to

Turkish soldiers search Chinese prisoners for weapons shortly after capture, December 1950.
Reproduced by permission of the Corbis Corporation.

withdraw on November 28. The Eighth Army units withdrew under cover of the Second and Twenty-fifth Divisions, which held the high ground on either side of the route of withdrawal as the main column passed.

The gauntlet

The Second Division held the roads open for the Eighth Army withdrawal as long as it could, with Chinese forces bearing down from three sides. When the time came for the Second Division to join in the general withdrawal to Sunch'on on November 30, most of the exit routes were impassable. The Second Division chose a route that seemed the least blocked. They did not know the Chinese had set up a deadly roadblock there, later called "the gauntlet" or the "fire wall." At this roadblock, the mountains surrounding the roads provided cover for at least two full regiments of Chinese soldiers. They perched—poised to fire—along a line that stretched down the road for six or seven miles. As the withdrawing troops of the Second Division entered the gauntlet they would remain the target of continuous shooting for miles. If one vehicle on the road stopped, everyone was stuck in the line of fire. Unable to communicate with the units behind them, the best anyone could do was to try to get themselves out of the gauntlet as quickly as possible. The Second Division had three thousand casualties that morning alone, bringing their casualties during the second Chinese offensive to a total of five thousand. No longer combat effective, the remainder of the division was sent to the South Korean capital of Seoul to rebuild.

On December 3, MacArthur ordered a retreat of all UN forces to the 38th parallel, the dividing line between North and South Korea. As the Eighth Army quickly withdrew, thousands of North Korean refugees followed in the bitter cold. General Paik Sun Yup (1920–) of the South Korean (ROK) Army remembers that day sadly in his memoirs *From Pusan to Panmunjom:* "For us in the ROK Army, December 3, 1950, lives as the day when our dream of national unification by force was dashed forever. MacArthur's Christmas Offensive had run full tilt into Peng's Second Offensive and collapsed completely." Peng Dehuai (P'eng Teh-huai; 1898–1974) was commander of the Chinese troops in Korea.

The X Corps heads north

On the other side of the mountains, the X Corps (the First Marine Division, the Third and Seventh Infantry divisions, and ROK I Corps), under the command of Major General Edward M. Almond (1892–1979), had begun the advance up to the Yalu River in October. By mid-November, MacArthur's headquarters directed the X Corps to advance

A seemingly endless file of Korean refugees slogs southward through the snow outside of Kangnung, January 1951. *Reproduced by permission of Double Delta Industries, Inc.*

north to the Chosin (Changjin) Reservoir, a huge man-made lake surrounded by four-thousand-feet plateaus at the northern border of Korea. From there, they were to head west to link up with the Eighth Army. MacArthur issued a statement to be read to all the troops saying that if this operation were successful, the war would doubtless be over.

By the end of November, the U.S. Marines and parts of the Seventh Division had formed a base in the town of Haguru. There, a new airstrip was built, with engineers working on it around-the-clock. The airstrip would serve to bring in supplies and to evacuate the wounded, and a hospital unit was built there as well. The Seventh and Fifth Regiments of the First Marines had gone on to the village of Yudam on November 26. Other X Corps units were stationed at Koto and Chinhung. Since it had been generally agreed that there was only a minor Chinese presence in Korea, no one was prepared for the massive attack of the Chinese on the night of November 27.

The attack at Chosin

Twelve CCF divisions were sent into Chosin. Spotting the weakness in the UN plan that had drawn fire from within its ranks—the division of the two armies—they had marched down the gap between the X Corps and the Eighth Army in the mountains. The Chinese struck the night of November 27 at seven different fronts: three places in the village of Yudam, held by the marines, and at Hagaru, Koto, Neidongjik, and Sinhung. They struck the hardest at Yudam, with orders to "annihilate" the marines there. Having learned that the marines were the most powerful fighting force of the United States, the Chinese wished to destroy them at the outset.

During the first night's attack, the Chinese set up roadblocks that separated Yudam, Hagaru, and Koto from each other, dangerously isolating some of the units. Hagaru was only lightly defended. In order to keep the airstrip work going night and day and to protect the base, troops were sent from Koto to Hagaru. Task Force Drysdale was hastily put together and pre-

U.S. Marines sit covered with ice and snow at the Chosin Reservoir in North Korea, December 1950. *Reproduced by permission of AP/Wide World Photos.*

While the troops were fighting in the Chosin Reservoir during the frigid winter of 1950–51, their food, equipment, and supplies were dropped to them by parachute. Among the rations they received was a tremendous supply of Tootsie Rolls candies. While the candies were a welcome treat to the exhausted troops, they froze in the bitter temperatures so thoroughly it took more than twenty minutes to thaw them so they could be eaten.

Some clever soldier in Chosin saw an opportunity in this and soon new Tootsie Roll procedures were known to all the troops. When the Chinese bullets made holes in the gas tanks, fuel drums, and radiators of military vehicles at the battlefront, the men would call "Tootsie to the rear!" Soldiers chewing the candies would then make their way to the vehicle. They stuck the chewed up candy into the bullet hole, and it immediately froze so solid it sealed the hole like a true metal welding job had been done. Many of the survivors of Chosin campaign have a special fondness for Tootsie Rolls to this day.

pared to move up the road with arms and troops to strengthen the base. The task force faced well-prepared Chinese forces and roadblocks and was hit hard on its trip. Out of 922 men who made the journey, 321 were killed or wounded. But the majority of the Royal Marine Commando and Company G of the First Marine Division made it to Hagaru and secured the village for the rest of the UN effort in Chosin.

Three surrounded battalions

The Thirth-second Regiment of the Seventh Division was northeast of Hagaru near the village of Sinhung when it was attacked by the Chinese around midnight on November 28. True to form, the Chinese surrounded three battalions in a double-envelopment and then infiltrated, coming in wherever there was an opening for close combat. For several days, the Chinese continued to infiltrate, causing heavy casualties and loss of ground during the night. By day the American soldiers made progress against them. Eventually the three battalions managed to come together through the roadblocks and the Chinese forces, but they were still surrounded. The continuous bloody combat and the freezing weather threatened them with utter destruction.

By December 1, it was clear that no help was coming. The survivors of the three battalions decided to attempt to make it to Hagaru. Loading the severely wounded into trucks and forcing the less wounded to walk, they set off. At once, they were attacked by the Chinese. U.S. planes came in to help, but in trying to hit the Chinese they misfired, dropping napalm right onto the American troops, killing several and severely wounding others. Things broke down further as the troops came upon a blown-up bridge and were once again ambushed by the Chinese. On December 2, the survivors of the three battalions limped into Hagaru. There had been 2,500 men in the battalions; 1,050 survived, but more than 600 of them were severely wounded or frostbitten.

The marines at Yudam

During the first year of the Korean War (1950), observers noted frequently that the U.S. Army was not ready for combat. The U.S. Marines were understrength as well. Unlike the other military services, however, the marines were not drafted (required to participate in compulsory military service), but volunteered to be soldiers. They were trained to be tough, enduring, disciplined, and combat-ready at all times. The marines had their own air support and coordinated it well with ground activities. Professional soldiers, they had shown great skill and courage in the war so far. The Chinese, appreciating the skill of this enemy, sent massive numbers of their own well-trained troops to annihilate the First Marine Division troops at Yudam. The marines put up a mighty fight.

On the night of November 27, as the marines of the Fifth and Seventh Regiments set up positions in the hills, three Chinese divisions attacked: two at Yudam and the third to the south of them through the mountains, to block the road between Hagaru and Yudam. The marines were outnumbered by more than three to one.

The Chinese struck at 10:00 P.M. that night, pouring through any holes available between companies and surrounding small units so they could then attack them at close

Telegram from Mao Zedong to His Military Leaders in Korea, November 12, 1950

It is said that the American Marine First Division has the highest combat effectiveness in the American armed forces. It seems not enough for our four divisions to surround and annihilate its two regiments. [You] should have one to two more divisions as a reserve force. The 26th Army of the 9th Army Corps should be stationed close to the front. Combat must be fully prepared for, and the campaign commands must be carefully organized. Please continuously instruct Song [Shilun] and Tao [Yong] to accomplish their task.

Source: "Mao's Telegrams During the Korean War, October-December 1950." Cold War International History Project at the Woodrow Wilson International Center for Scholars. [Online] http://cwihp.si.edu/ (accessed on August 14, 2001).

range. Because the Chinese succeeded in isolating units from each other, each company fought its own small war. The American casualties were tremendous.

That night, General Oliver Smith, commander of the First Marines, anxiously listened by radio to the reports of what was happening to his marines in Chosin. He knew that the mission to meet up with the Eighth Army in the west was impossible due to the Eighth Army's defeat; his men were being slaughtered for a doomed mission. He desperately tried to reach General Almond to get new orders. He did not hear back from Almond for nearly two days. Unable to order a retreat without permission, Smith ordered the Fifth and Seventh Marines to forget their offensive but to continue to defend their positions around Yudam.

On the morning of November 28, Almond had flown into Hagaru and other points on the front. According to Patrick C. Roe in *The Dragon Strikes, China and the Korean War,* Almond's parting words as he left the front were a characteristically gross (and racist) underestimation of the Chinese: "The enemy who is delaying you for the moment is nothing more than remnants of a Chinese division fleeing north. . . . We're still attacking and we're going all the way to the Yalu. Don't let a bunch of Chinese laundrymen stop you."

"When you break out, you attack"

In the late hours of November 28, General Smith finally received orders to retreat. He was instructed to bring his troops into the secure village of Hagaru. From there they were to make their way to Hungnam. The marines had no history of retreating and this turn of events shocked everyone. When war correspondents questioned Smith about it, he snapped, "Retreat, hell, we are simply attacking in another direction." The quote became famous. In *The Korean War: Pusan to Chosin: An Oral History,* Donald Knox provided Smith's explanation from a later interview: "You can't retreat or withdraw when you are surrounded. The only thing you can do is break out. When you break out, you attack. That's what we were doing." In fact, the retreat to Hagaru from November 28 through December 5 presented some of the most brutal fighting in the Korean War.

One of the Heroes at Chosin

One private in the Fox Company, twenty-one-year-old rifleman Hector A. Cafferata, stood firm as the Chinese tried to push through and separate the Second and Third Platoons at Toktong Pass on the night of November 27, 1950. He was awarded a Congressional Medal of Honor for his actions that night. According to the U.S. Army:

> When all the other members of his fire team became casualties, creating a gap in the lines . . . Pvt. Cafferata waged a lone battle with grenades and rifle fire as the attack gained momentum and the enemy threatened penetration through the gap and endangered the integrity of the entire defensive perimeter. Making a target of himself under the devastating fire from automatic weapons, rifles, grenades, and mortars, he maneuvered up and down the line and delivered accurate and effective fire against the onrushing force, killing 15, wounding many more, and forcing the others to withdraw so that reinforcements could move up and consolidate the position. Again fighting desperately against a renewed onslaught later that same morning when a hostile grenade landed in a shallow entrenchment occupied by wounded marines, Pvt. Cafferata rushed into the gully under heavy fire, seized the deadly missile in his right hand and hurled it free of his comrades before it detonated, severing part of 1 finger and seriously wounding him in the right hand and arm. Courageously ignoring the intense pain, he staunchly fought on until he was struck by a sniper's bullet and forced to submit to evacuation for medical treatment.

Source: United States Army. "Korean War Medal of Honor Recipients." United States Army. [Online] http://www.army.mil/cmh-pg/mohkor2.htm (accessed on August 14, 2001).

Fox Company's ordeal

Every Fifth and Seventh Marine company in the vicinity of Yudam at the end of November 1950 had its own battles with the Chinese troops in some of the most horrible conditions imaginable. One frequently told tale is the ordeal of the Fox Company of the Second Battalion of the Seventh Regiment. When the withdrawal order came through for X Corps, Fox Company received the assignment to hold open the Toktong Pass (later named Fox Hill), which was on the withdrawing troops' route to Hagaru. It was far too big to be defended by one company, but the survival of the entire division depended on the route being open. Fox Company was ordered not to withdraw under any circumstances.

Freezing

The bitter cold in North Korea took a great toll on the soldiers—both communist and of the United Nations. The experiences of being out in twenty below temperatures for weeks at a time are tales of unimaginable misery. Soldiers taking off their socks would accidentally pull the skin off the bottom of their feet, which had frozen to their socks. Food was frozen and nearly impossible to thaw, and eating frozen food caused terrible digestive problems. Most soldiers were sick to their stomachs and limping from painful frostbite. Sentries (guards) could not hear the invading Chinese because they had on heavy hats, but without the hats, their ears quickly froze. The cold also numbed the mind. Orders given were often immediately forgotten. Responses to danger that are normally automatic came slowly, if at all.

So many wounded were coming into the medical stations at Hagaru and Yudam, there were not enough tents for all of them. Many had to be placed on top of straw on the frozen ground and covered with a tarpaulin (a canvas or plastic sheet). These soldiers were so frozen by the time they got medical attention that doctors and nurses could only tell if they were alive by checking their eyes for movement.

An infantryman uses his poncho as protection against the bitter cold, January 1951.
Reproduced by permission of Double Delta Industries, Inc.

Blood for transfusion froze and could not be used. It was difficult or impossible for doctors to work on patients. Without gloves, their hands were too frozen to work. It was also nearly impossible to cut a patient out of his uniform to work on a wound without the patient freezing to death. In some cases the freezing temperatures actually stopped the flow of blood from the wounds—the one positive aspect of the terrible winter conditions.

The men in Fox Company were already at their position on Fox Hill when the withdrawal order was issued. Going to sleep the night of November 27, most of the men were concerned with trying not to freeze in the well below zero weather. It was nearly impossible to dig in for the night because the ground was so frozen. All around them, the marines heard the sound of firefights and knew their turn was coming. The Chinese struck at 2:00 A.M. Although the Chinese killed twenty men and injured many more, the Fox Company rallied and threw back the CCF.

The fighting continued each night, and the few survivors on Fox Hill held on, managing to inflict heavy casualties on their Chinese attackers. On November 29, General Smith ordered a rescue party to Fox Hill from Yudam, but it could not get through the Chinese resistance. A new cross-country rescue force was assembled and set out on the night of December 1, taking with them only what they could carry on their backs. The crew hiked all night through the frozen mountain terrain, in and out of firefights with the Chinese, and moved beyond the limits of exhaustion in order not to freeze to death. They got through to the Fox Company on its sixth day on the hill. The rescuers were able to carry the ninety wounded down to trucks waiting in the roads below. The rest of Fox Company chose to stay with the cross-country force to hold the Toktong Pass open for the withdrawing troops to pass through. Both the captain of Fox Company and the lieutenant colonel leading the rescue expedition received Medals of Honor for their bravery and sacrifice.

Leaving the Chosin Reservoir

The marines withdrew down the main supply route from Yudam to Hagaru, fighting the Chinese and smashing through their frequent roadblocks with the ever-present aid of their air support. On December 3, they broke through the strong Chinese barrier at Toktong Pass after incurring many casualties. The bloodiest combat was over, but there were many more firefights before the four-day retreat was completed on December 4 at 2:00 P.M. in Hagaru. Having just completed one of the most fierce ordeals in marine history, the marines came in exhausted, cold, wounded, hungry, sick, dirty, and frostbitten. They had not been able to carry out their mission, but they had defied the Chinese efforts to annihilate them. The Chinese had sent twelve CCF divisions to face three American and two ROK divisions, and they had focused most of their manpower on the First Marine Division. By managing to survive at such odds, the First Marines had a true victory.

Some of the nearly one-hundred-thousand civilian refugees evacuated from the Hungnam beachhead, December 1950. *Reproduced by permission of the Corbis Corporation.*

In five days, from December 2 to December 6, air force and marine planes evacuated forty-five hundred wounded from Hagaru. On December 6, X Corps was on the move again: ten thousand men were on the road to Koto and then on to the coastal city of Hungnam, where they could be transported out by sea.

The Chinese had not attacked at Hagaru, but had used the time to fortify blocking positions on the road south. The marines had to fight their way out. Assault teams launched out ahead of the troops, securing the hills by the road before the main column got to it. The casualties on both sides were often very heavy and it was slow moving. But it was clear by this time that the Chinese troops were exhausted, frozen, and starving. At one battle site, the X Corps found foxholes with what turned out to be fifty Chinese soldiers in them. In *Korea: The Untold Story of the War,* author Joseph Goulden quoted Major W. D. Sawyer, who was there at the time: "They [the Chinese soldiers] were so badly frozen that our men simply lifted them from the holes and sat them on the road."

The troops marched on to Chinhung, and then on to Hungnam. There, a huge fleet was prepared to evacuate the soldiers and the fleeing Korean civilians who had been following them on their miserable retreat. Over the course of two weeks beginning December 11, 105,000 troops and nearly 100,000 Korean civilians were evacuated from Hungnam. The X Corps burned and bombed the city mercilessly as they left. The longest retreat in U.S. history was over. There were approximately 25,000 troops from the allied nations in the Chosin campaign and there were 6,000 casualties. One in every four men had been killed, wounded, or was missing in action.

Where to Learn More

Alexander, Bevin. *Korea: The First War We Lost.* New York: Hippocrene Books, 1986, revised edition, 2000.

Goulden, Joseph C. *Korea: The Untold Story of the War.* New York: Times Books, 1982.

Hoyt, Edwin P. *The Day the Chinese Attacked Korea, 1950: The Story of the Failure of America's China Policy.* New York: McGraw-Hill, 1990.

Knox, Donald. *The Korean War: Pusan to Chosin: An Oral History.* San Diego: Harcourt Brace Jovanovich, 1988.

Roe, Patrick C. *The Dragon Strikes, China and the Korean War: June-December 1950.* Novato, CA: Presidio, 2000.

Web sites

United States Army, "Korean War Medal of Honor Recipients." United States Army. [Online] http://www.army.mil/cmh-pg/mohkor2.htm (accessed on August 14, 2001).

"Mao's Telegrams During the Korean War, October-December 1950." Cold War International History Project at the Woodrow Wilson International Center for Scholars. [Online] http://cwihp.si.edu/ (accessed on August 14, 2001).

Negotiations at the 38th Parallel

On December 23, 1950, Eighth Army commander Lieutenant General Walton H. "Johnnie" Walker (1889–1950) was speeding down a Korean road north of the South Korean capital city of Seoul when his jeep collided with a truck. He died almost immediately. Walker had commanded the Eighth Army through the worst of times with a steady hand. He was not liked by all, least of all by his superior, commander of the United Nations (UN) Forces General Douglas MacArthur (1880–1964). But many close observers believed that Walton's leadership had made the saving difference in the breakout at the Pusan Perimeter (see Chapter 6), and that his quick perception of the Chinese strength and his order for rapid withdrawal from North Korea in November had avoided the massacre of his troops.

Lieutenant General Matthew B. Ridgway (1895–1993) was appointed to replace Walker as the commander of the Eighth Army. A hero in World War II (1939–45), Ridgway was serving as deputy to the army chief of staff at the time of Walker's death. Ridgway lost no time in getting to the front to assess the condition of the troops, arriving on December 26.

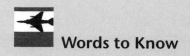

Words to Know

atomic bomb: a powerful bomb created by splitting the nuclei of a heavy chemical, such as plutonium or uranium, in a rapid chain reaction, resulting in a violent and destructive shock wave as well as radiation.

bunker: a reinforced underground room dug into a battle area for protection against enemy gunfire and bombs.

grenade: a small explosive weapon that can be thrown, usually with a pin that is pulled to activate it and a spring-loaded safety lever that is held down until the user wants to throw the grenade; once the safety lever is released, the grenade will explode in seconds.

hawkish: advocating for all-out war or military action.

intelligence (military): information about the enemy.

isolationism: the view that a country should take care of its problems at home and not interfere in conflicts in other countries.

Joint Chiefs of Staff: an agency within the Department of Defense serving to advise the president and the secretary of defense on matters of war. The Joint Chiefs of Staff consists of a chairman, a vice chairman, the chief of staff of the army, the chief of naval operations, the chief of staff of the air force, and the commandant of the marine corps.

limited warfare: warfare with an objective other than the enemy's complete destruction, as in holding a defensive line during negotiations.

stalemate: deadlock; the state in which the efforts of each party in a conflict cancels out the efforts of the other party so that no one makes any headway.

38th parallel: the 38th degree of north latitude as it bisects the Korean Peninsula, chosen by Americans as the dividing line between what was to be Soviet-occupied North Korea and U.S.-occupied South Korea in 1945.

unilaterally: one-sided; acting only on one's own part, without reference to others.

warmongering: pushing for war.

He was disturbed by what he found, as he recorded in his memoirs, *The Korean War:* "After meeting all ranks of officers and men, it was my impression that they were deficient in vigor, bravery, and fighting spirit." Ridgway placed a grenade in the flap of his vest as a sign that he meant to fight. The grenade can be seen in almost every photograph of the general during the war.

The Communist Chinese Forces (CCF), siding with the communist North Koreans, launched their third offensive on New Year's Day, 1951, shortly after Ridgway arrived. In an all-out effort, the Chinese successfully defeated the Eighth Army, pushing it south some fifty miles below the 38th parallel, the dividing line between North and South Korea. On January 4, South Korean president Syngman Rhee (1875–1965) and his government were evacuated from Seoul for the second time with the Eighth Army behind them. The capital city was once again in the communists' hands. Behind the retreating Eighth Army was a stream of Korean refugees.

This was the third of four times that Seoul changed hands. First the incoming communists persecuted those suspected of participating in or helping the Rhee regime, and then, during the recapture, the South Koreans arrested and often killed suspected communists. Anyone involved in either side's politics or military by this time had either fled or been arrested and often executed. The capital city was burnt and bombed. It was a terrifying time to be living in Korea, and the lines of fleeing refugees on the icy Korean roads grew longer and longer.

By Ridgway's orders, the Eighth Army's retreat went farther south than may have been necessary in order to give the troops a chance to recover. In mid-January, the Eighth Army formed a defense line across the 37th parallel. In the meantime, most of the X Corps (the First Marine Division, the Third and Seventh Infantry divisions, and ROK I Corps, under the command of Major General Edward M. Almond [1892–1979]), was in the southern part of the peninsula, waging attacks on guerrillas. (Guerrillas are soldiers who fight an irregular form of combat; in small groups, the warriors use ambushes and surprise attacks to harass or even destroy much larger armies.) General Ridgway was ready for a counteroffensive.

Worldwide fears

During the UN forces' long retreat from North Korea, panic set in around the world. The chances for a third world war—complete with U.S. and Soviet atomic bombs—seemed high. General MacArthur was making the leaders of many nations nervous. He wanted authority to bomb the Chinese bases in Manchuria, an area in northern China just north of

A Soviet 7.63-millimeter .42 Federou rifle resting on a North Korean flag that would be taken at Heartbreak Ridge, Korea, in November 1952. With the Soviets supplying the North Koreans with war materiel, it was feared that the Korean War would lead to a third world war—complete with nuclear weapons. *Reproduced by permission of Archive Photos, Inc.*

the Korean border. He wanted to use troops offered by Chinese Nationalist leader Chiang Kai-shek (1887–1975) in Korea. MacArthur was unwilling to go along with any aspect of fighting a limited war, one in which the military held a defense line in Korea while the politicians negotiated the terms of ending the war. And he was making his views known.

The Joint Chiefs of Staff and the State Department became increasingly concerned about MacArthur's contradictory statements and his failure to communicate his intentions to them. (The Joint Chiefs of Staff is an agency within the Department of Defense serving to advise the president and the secretary of defense on matters of war.) Some blamed MacArthur for failing to alert the UN forces to the presence of the Chinese armies. Many felt that he had been wrong in separating the command of the Eighth Army and the X Corps and rushing into an unknown situation (see Chapter 7). In UN countries, fear of MacArthur's warmongering was rising. On December 6, 1950, President Harry S. Truman (1884–1972) had issued a directive requiring all public officials to clear in advance with the State Department and Department of Defense any statements they made concerning foreign or military policy. This was intended for MacArthur.

On November 30, 1950, the president himself had created more worldwide panic. When asked by a reporter whether the atomic bomb was being considered as a weapon for the Korean War, Truman, as quoted in Joseph C. Goulden's *Korea: The Untold Story of Korea,* answered that "there has always been active consideration of its use." He went on to imply that it would be up to MacArthur to decide if a situation necessitated the use of the atom bomb. This was not true; only the president had the power to make such a decision. Since Truman was very clear about what he said to the reporter, many historians believe he made the incorrect statement deliberately to frighten the Chinese out of the war. The Chinese did not take the bait, but many UN allies became very disturbed.

British Prime Minister Clement Attlee (1883–1967) responded to the other nations' concerns by quickly heading for Washington, D.C., to meet with Truman. Soon after their four-day conference, U.S. Secretary of State Dean Acheson (1893–1971) introduced to the Joint Chiefs of Staff the idea of a cease-fire in Korea with the UN forces holding the 38th parallel, so that Korea would be as it was before the war. No one liked giving up the prospect of unification, but most agreed that a cease-fire made sense. The proposal was made to China through the United Nations. China rejected the proposal. On December 23, Communist Chinese Premier and Foreign Minister Zhou Enlai (Chou En-lai; 1898–1976) announced that China would not negotiate a cease-fire unless: (1) all foreign troops were withdrawn from Korea, (2) U.S. troops were withdrawn from Taiwan (formerly Formosa), and (3) Communist China received representation in the United Nations.

Ridgway takes over

By the time General Ridgway arrived to take General Walker's place, the X Corps had finally come under the command of the Eighth Army. MacArthur had given Ridgway the authority to make his own decisions about attacking, without referring back to headquarters. Ridgway surveyed a truly international army, with troops from sixteen nations

The Twenty-fourth RCT, an African American Unit

While the Twenty-fourth Division was fighting at Taejon, the First Cavalry Division and the Twenty-fifth Division arrived in Korea. Among the incoming troops was the Twenty-fourth Regimental Combat Team (RCT), an all-black unit of the Twenty-fifth Division. Up to that time, the American military had been segregated, with African Americans separated from whites. Although President Harry S. Truman had signed Executive Order 9981 in 1948, which provided for "equality of treatment and opportunity for all persons in the Armed Forces," only the air force had actually integrated its troops, having African Americans and other groups living and working in the same facilities. The army, showing considerable racism, had dragged its feet on the issue. The Twenty-fourth RCT was the only all-black regiment in the army.

On July 21, the Twenty-fourth RCT led a very successful attack on the town of Yechon, defeating a large unit of North Koreans. But soon afterwards, the army began to discredit the feat, saying it had not really happened. The victory was the last one for the Twenty-fourth. According to army history, in several battles in the next few weeks the Twenty-fourth RCT panicked and ran away (bugged-out). Many army officers made much out of this, saying they could not rely on the team. But members of the Twenty-fourth RCT disputed the way they were represented. According to them, they were forced to retreat as all other units had been; that they "bugged-out" seemed to be no different than what other troops in Korea were doing daily. The dispute about the Twenty-fourth RCT was great enough that the army began to integrate. The Twenty-fourth RCT was dissolved and its men were absorbed into other units and there were no more segregated units.

amounting to nearly 365,000 men. After witnessing the January 1 Chinese offensive and the retreat of his command to the 37th parallel, Ridgway quickly instilled a sense of purpose and professionalism to his huge army and then planned a strategy for attack.

By this time, the Chinese practice of attacking full force and then withdrawing to resupply, replace casualties, and rest was well known. While the system had worked well in the northern parts of the Korean peninsula where the Chinese

Soldiers of the Twenty-fourth Infantry Regiment move up to the front in Korea. *Reproduced by permission of Double Delta Industries, Inc.*

were not far from their supply bases, it was a rough system for soldiers so far from home. The Chinese soldiers were generally given food for four days of attack. After that they were on their own. Many of the Chinese captured in battle were starving and exhausted.

After the January 1 offensive was over, there was little sign of the Chinese. Dissatisfied with the intelligence he was receiving, Ridgway began sending out patrols to find out where the enemy troops were. From January 15 to February 11, 1951, the patrols, working slowly and with a united front, made their way north, encountering only light enemy resistance. Although Seoul was heavily defended, the UN forces moved up to a new defensive line that closed in around the capital city.

On February 11, the Chinese launched a massive counterattack. The main thrust of the offensive took place at Chipyong-ni on February 14 and 15. The UN forces were hit very hard and they requested permission to withdraw fifteen miles to avoid being surrounded. But General Ridgway would not allow retreat. Somehow, the UN forces held and soundly defeated the Chinese. When the Chinese withdrew from the battle at Chipyong-ni, they left behind more than five thousand of their dead.

Ridgway began to regularly gather his own intelligence on the location of the communist armies. Knowing that the Chinese troops were in desperate straits from exhaustion, cold, and hunger, he made it his business to find out when they were going to withdraw to resupply. His new method of attacking was to put units right on the trail of the withdrawing enemy so that they could not rest or get new supplies. The advances were slow and at times strong resistance from the communist armies pushed back the UN forces, but continuous progress was made.

On March 14 and 15, the communist forces withdrew from Seoul in order to avoid being surrounded by UN forces. Seoul, although nearly a ghost town by this time, was back in UN control after changing hands four times, and the Eighth Army was again approaching the 38th parallel. In April, they had advanced farther, to a line north of the 38th parallel called the Kansas line.

MacArthur goes too far

On March 20, the Truman administration put together a plan for a cease-fire. Since the Eight Army was approaching the 38th parallel, Truman and the Joint Chiefs of Staff felt they could come to terms with the communists from a position of strength and try to put an end to the killing. Their proposal left the key issues open for future discussion; instead of rejecting the idea of withdrawing U.S. troops from Korea, for example, they proposed that discussions on the issue begin with the cease-fire. While they were drafting the plan, the Joint Chiefs sent a letter to MacArthur telling him to postpone any advances through the 38th parallel until after the president presented his cease-fire proposal.

The State Department went to work on a draft of a proposal to China, but before they got a chance to broadcast it to China, MacArthur issued a statement of his own to the enemy. MacArthur's March 24 statement, quoted here from Bevin Alexander's *Korea: The First War We Lost,* read like an ultimatum (an "or else" kind of threat):

> The enemy therefore must now be painfully aware that a decision of the United Nations to depart from its tolerant effort to contain the war to the area of Korea through expansion of our military operations to his coastal areas and interior bases would doom Red China to the risk of imminent military collapse . . . Within my area of authority as military commander, however, it should be needless to say I stand ready at any time to confer in the field with the commander in chief of the enemy forces in an earnest effort to find any military means whereby the realization of the political objectives of the United Nations in Korea, to which no nation may justly take exception, might be accomplished without further bloodshed.

In other words, MacArthur was telling the Chinese that they had their choice between all-out war in their own land or to accept the peace that the United Nations dictated. This directly contradicted the intentions of Truman's peace initiative. The proposal for peace had to be temporarily dropped, since it reflected such a wide split within the U.S. government.

Truman, a Democrat, was constantly attacked by Republicans in the U.S. Congress who criticized his Korean War policies, whether from the standpoint of isolationism (the view that the United States should take care of its problems at home and not fight in other countries) or the hawkish (war-

Matthew B. Ridgway, Major General Doyle Hickey, and Douglas MacArthur at a command post in Yang Yang, fifteen miles north of the 38th parallel, Korea, April 3, 1951. *Reproduced by permission of Double Delta Industries, Inc.*

ready) attitude of MacArthur. The Republican leaders in the U.S. House of Representatives had picked up on MacArthur's disagreements with the Truman administration and wrote to MacArthur asking why Chinese Nationalist troops were not being used in the war. MacArthur responded, and on April 5 the representatives read to the House MacArthur's letter, which both insulted the Truman administration's policy and supported a policy that the administration was against. This was, of course, very politically damaging to the president.

The sacking of a hero

Truman realized that he could not have a commander in Korea on whom he could not rely. There was general agreement among his top advisers and the Joint Chiefs that MacArthur must be relieved of his command, and the decision was made. MacArthur was informed on April 11, 1951. General Matthew B. Ridgway would take MacArthur's place as commander of the UN forces and General James A. Van Fleet (1892–1992), a corps commander during World War II, would succeed Ridgway as commander of the Eighth Army. MacArthur came back to the United States less than a week later. Although he was relieved of his command, he was met with a tremendous hero's welcome, with huge crowds turning out for his every public appearance. President Truman was attacked harshly throughout the country.

MacArthur would later present his side of things in hearings arranged by Congress to investigate the way the Truman administration had handled the Korean War. In the end, even many of MacArthur's supporters understood that a commander of armies who sidesteps the democratic process in order to carry out his own agenda is a true danger to his country. In the words of Korean War historian Bevin Alexander in his book *Korea: The First War We Lost*: "Whether MacArthur had been right or wrong made little difference; by taking it upon himself to make policy unilaterally, he was operating outside the American political system."

The Iron Triangle

The communist armies had been preparing for a spring offensive for months, gathering troops at a place north of the 38th parallel known as the Iron Triangle, the area set within a triangle defined by the North Korean cities of Chorwon, Kumwha, and Pyongyang. On April 21, the UN forces, now at about half a million strong, struck near Chorwon and Kumwha. The next day, the Chinese and North Korean armies counterattacked in force. They struck particularly hard on the British Twenty-ninth Brigade, which battled the enemy for two difficult and bloody days and nights. The Chinese, it is estimated, lost about ten thousand men in that battle, while the Twenty-ninth Brigade had about one thousand casualties. The Chinese continued to send more troops into battle and in mid-May the communist forces formed another offensive. Although they inflicted many casualties and scattered two South Korean divisions, when the attack was over a day later, the communists had suffered worse casualties than they had inflicted.

Defeating the enemy

Although the Chinese were suffering badly from exhaustion, severe casualties, and a lack of ammunition and supplies, they continued to strike at the UN line during the

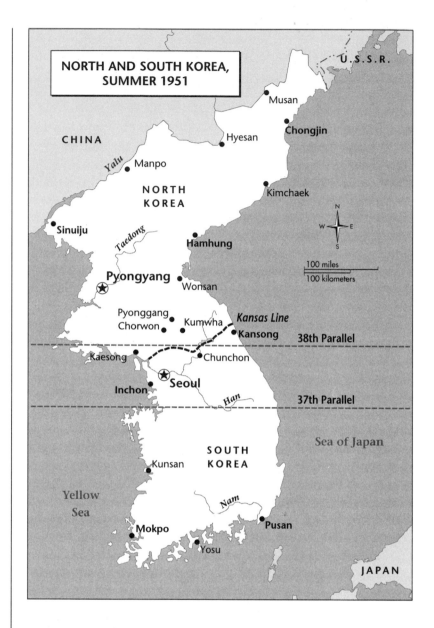

NORTH AND SOUTH KOREA, SUMMER 1951

month of May. Without food and ammunition they could never sustain an attack. By the end of the month, the Chinese were at such a severe disadvantage that they began to surrender in large numbers. An offensive at the Iron Triangle and points north was launched by the UN forces at this time, with the U.S. Marines attacking a volcanic crater called the Punchbowl. When it was over, the UN held the lower lip of the Punchbowl and had moved north on the east coast above Kansong. The Chinese casualties were terrible, in the range of twenty-seven thousand. In his book *In Mortal Combat: Korea, 1950–1953,* John Toland quoted a platoon sergeant, who wrote his reaction to the slaughter in a letter to his wife:

> We crossed the parallel again yesterday and we have the Chinks on a wild retreat. . . . There's a hell of an air strike going on about 3 miles up the road . . . the Air Force and Artillery are giving us fits with their noise. And this place we are in now is a horrifying sight. We caught a bunch of Chinese in the open here (we are in a long valley along a river bed) and it certainly is a mess. Over a hundred vehicles, plenty of cannons, uncounted dead horses and of course, Chinese. We caught them about day before yesterday and it really was a slaughter. The days are warm now and the sun is getting to them and the stink is terrible. No exaggeration this we can't turn around without sighting dead men or horses. . . . We use bulldozers for the horses and mules, but naturally we have to pick the Chinese men up and place them in graves. A lot of people figure the more you bury the less you have to fight (I do too) but boy! When it comes to planting them I wish the Air Force and Artillery and our marksmanship weren't so thorough and precise. Boy! I wish I could see a little peace for a while. I'm sick of the stench of the dead and dying and seeing torn bodies scattered like waste paper on a windy day.

In early June, the Chinese were no longer capable of attack, but they were prepared to defend their position, whatever it took. During the spring, they had built bunkers—reinforced underground rooms—that were nearly impossible to penetrate. The Chinese had set up a defense line that they could hold, across the Punchbowl from the UN forces. In this stalemate, the time had come to negotiate a peace for Korea.

Where to Learn More

Alexander, Bevin. *Korea: The First War We Lost.* New York: Hippocrene Books, 1986, revised edition, 2000.

Blair, Clay. *The Forgotten War: America in Korea, 1950–1953.* New York, Times Books, 1987.

Goulden, Joseph C. *Korea: The Untold Story of the War.* New York: Times Books, 1982.

Ridgway, Matthew B. *The Korean War.* Garden City, NY: Doubleday, 1967.

Shinn, Bill. *The Forgotten War Remembered: Korea, 1950–1953; A War Correspondent's Notebook and Today's Danger in Korea.* Elizabeth, NJ: Hollym International, 1996.

Toland, John. *In Mortal Combat: Korea, 1950–1953.* New York: William Morrow, 1991.

War and Peace Talks

In the spring of 1951, the Communist Chinese Forces (CCF) and the United Nations (UN) forces had "dug in" to defensive positions just north of the 38th parallel, the dividing line between North and South Korea. Like the trench warfare of World War I (1914–18), both sides were fairly secure in their positions. The war stopped moving. The most the combatants could really hope for in battle was to kill a lot of enemy soldiers, and that is what both sides did. Small gains were made by the UN in moving their line of defense north, but at a very high cost of lives.

By that time, international opinion had swung to the side of peace, even if it meant giving up the idea of a unified Korea. Without U.S. General Douglas MacArthur in command (he had been asked to step down as commander of the UN forces in April), the only strong voice in favor of a war to the finish was South Korean (ROK) President Syngman Rhee (1875–1965). General Matthew B. Ridgway (1895–1993), MacArthur's successor, was not ready to concede very much to the communists, but he did not heed Rhee's push for all-out war either. In the limited warfare he was waging, his job depended

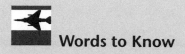

Words to Know

agenda: a list or outline of things to be discussed, planned, or undertaken.

armistice: talks between opposing forces in which they agree to a truce or suspension of hostilities.

artillery: large weapons, such as howitzers, rockets, and 155-millimeter guns, that shoot missiles, and generally take a crew to operate.

bug-out: to panic and run away from a battle in confusion; a disorderly retreat without permission.

bunker: a reinforced underground room dug into a battle area for protection against enemy gunfire and bombs.

China Lobby: a group of Americans during the late 1940s and early 1950s who fervently supported Chinese Nationalist leader Chiang Kai-shek in his struggles against the Communist Chinese, and who held a romanticized and sometime patronizing view of the Chinese people and their relations with Americans.

concessions: things that are given up and granted to the other side in an argument or conflict.

demilitarized zone (DMZ): an area in which military presence and activity are forbidden.

disarmament: taking away a group's weapons and other military equipment in order to render it unable or less able to make war.

impasse: the position of being faced with a problem for which there seems no solution; a stalemate.

limited warfare: warfare with an objective other than the enemy's complete destruction, as in holding a defensive line during negotiations.

ROK: an acronym standing for Republic of Korea; "ROK" was frequently used to refer specifically to South Korean soldiers.

trench warfare: combat in which enemies dig into ditches facing each other across the battlefield; the ditches then serve as defensive positions. Trench warfare is usually associated with World War I (1914–18).

ultimatum: a demand made of an opponent, in which he or she must accept a condition or request or face consequences.

war correspondent: someone who provides news stories to a newspaper or television or radio news program from the battlefront or on location in a war.

on some kind of negotiations. The U.S. State Department began to search for contacts on the communist side to begin negotiations for an armistice (a truce or suspension of hostilities).

Finding the right party with whom to enter into peace discussions proved to be difficult. Officially, the enemy was North Korea, but the U.S. negotiators believed the threat—and the power to negotiate—came from elsewhere. Approaching Communist China was problematic on several fronts. The United Nations did not recognize Communist China as a nation, so it was difficult to communicate as one government to another. (Ever since 1949, when the Communists defeated the U.S.-backed Nationalists in the Chinese Civil War, the United States and the UN did not recognize Communist China.) Furthermore, the American diplomats who had understood China had long ago lost their jobs and returned to the United States, having been accused themselves of being communists or communist sympathizers (see Chapter 8). On top of this, the United States was still deluded in its belief that the Soviet Union was in charge of all communist nations. (The Soviet Union was the first communist country and was made up of fifteen republics, including Russia. It existed as a unified country from 1922 to 1991. Communism is a set of political beliefs that advocates the elimination of private property. It is a system in which goods are owned by the community as a whole rather than by specific individuals and are available to all as needed.)

The Soviet Union urges peace

Eventually a former U.S. diplomat contacted Soviet UN ambassador Jacob A. Malik (1906–1980). These two discussed the possibility of a cease-fire in Korea. On June 23, shortly after their second meeting, Malik surprised the State Department by broadcasting a message on UN radio. He stated that the "Soviet people" believed that a cease-fire and an armistice could be arranged between the hostile nations. The Soviet Union insisted that it did not know China's intentions regarding a cease-fire and that the discussions would have to be between the United States and China. In a different conversation, Soviet deputy foreign minister Andrei A. Gromyko (1909–1989) suggested that terms could be reached if the parties focused on ending the battles and getting their armies out of Korea and left the future Korean government for later discussions.

On June 30, 1951, the Joint Chiefs of Staff drafted a message for General Ridgway to broadcast by radio to the

A machine gun crew dug in for the night in Korea. In the spring of 1951, the war stopped moving.
Reproduced by permission of Double Delta Industries, Inc.

enemy. (Created in 1949, the Joint Chiefs of Staff is an agency within the Department of Defense serving to advise the president and the secretary of defense on matters of war.) Ridgway told the communist leaders that if they were interested in holding a meeting to discuss a cease-fire, then he would send representatives at such a time as they determined. He suggested meeting in a Danish hospital ship in Wonsan Harbor. On July 2, Peking Radio (from Beijing [Peking], China) broadcast a response signed by North Korean Premier Kim Il Sung (1912–1994) and General Peng Dehaui (P'eng Teh-huai; 1898–1974), the commander of the Chinese troops in Korea, that said: "We are authorized to tell you that we agree to suspend military activities and to hold peace negotiations, and that our delegates will meet with yours. We suggest, in regard to the place for holding talks, that such talks be held at Kaesong, on the 38th parallel. If you agree with this, our delegates will be prepared to meet your delegates between July 10 and 15, 1951."

In this message, the communist forces publicly agreed to stop fighting immediately. This would leave the troops on each side holding the positions they were in at that time, which was what the Americans wanted. This could have been the end of combat in the Korean War, but Ridgway did not trust his opponents. Ridgway believed that the Chinese and North Koreans would use a cease-fire to build up their strength and attack the UN forces unexpectedly and forcefully. After receiving Joint Chiefs and State Department approval, Ridgway wrote back to the communist leaders agreeing to meet, but saying that military activities would continue during the talks. In fact, the Joint Chiefs urged that military efforts be stepped up during the talks. Two more years of vicious fighting and hundreds of thousands of deaths resulted.

The talks begin

The talks began at Kaesong, a town at the 38th parallel in the hands of the communists at that time, with a preparatory meeting on July 8, at which the agenda and practical matters for further meetings were discussed. Disagreement and disagreeableness marked this meeting, as it would future ones. On July 10, at a once elegant but recently bombed teahouse in Kaesong, the chosen delegates of the opposing forces met. On the UN side, Vice Admiral Charles Turner Joy (1895–1956), commander of the Far East Naval Forces, was the senior delegate. Three other Americans—the Eighth Army chief of staff, the vice commander of the Far East Air Forces, and the deputy chief of staff of the Naval Forces—and one South Korean, ROK General Paik Sun Yup (1920–), also attended. On the communist side, the chief delegate was Lieutenant General Nam Il, the chief of staff of the North Korean People's Army. Nam Il had lived much of his life in the Soviet Union and had fought with the Russians in World War II (1939–45), coming back to Korea after the war. Two other North Korean officials attended. The Chinese army delegates were Teng Hua, deputy commander of the Chinese army, and Chieh Fang, chief of staff and political commissar of the Chinese army.

No pleasant exchanges occurred at this or in any of the meetings. The mood was cold and formal to begin with and heated up only with insults and arguments. At first there were showdowns over little things, such as whose chair was taller, whose flag was exhibited more prominently on the table, or who faced south. As the meetings continued, more important practical matters arose. On the first day of talks, fully armed communist troops came through the area, pointing guns in a manner that felt threatening to the UN delegates. Another matter that arose in the early meetings was that communist journalists were at hand, but no other war correspondents. These issues were quickly resolved. A five-mile circle around Kaesong was proclaimed a neutral area. The armed North Korean troops were banished from the neutral zone where talks were held, and foreign journalists were permitted in.

These concessions did not help the discussions. The negotiators spent the next ten sessions arguing about the items to be included on an agenda for the talks, in effect, arguing about what they were going to argue about. On July 26, the negotiators compromised on the agenda. The five points listed for discussions were:

1. adoption of the agenda;

2. the location of the military demarcation line and the demilitarized zone;

3. arrangements for a cease-fire and armistice, including a supervisory organization to oversee it;

4. arrangements for exchanging prisoners of war;

5. recommendations for governments on either side.

This agenda omitted the areas of contention. It did not mention the UN demand that the International Red Cross, an international relief organization, be allowed to inspect prison camps, or the Chinese demands that all foreign troops withdraw from Korea and that the demarcation line be set at the 38th parallel. Although these points were left out of the agenda, they were still very much at issue. In the first meeting after the agenda was adopted, the delegates were immediately at an impasse. The communists wanted the demarcation line at the 38th parallel. The United States wanted it at the existing battlefront, slightly north of the 38th parallel. No one would budge. In his book *In Mortal Combat: Korea, 1950–1953*, John Toland provided a sample of how this argument—with no one giving any ground at all—played out in the negotiations:

General Nam Il: It has been proved that your proposal is untenable and that our proposal is based on reason. Therefore, whatever novel and ridiculous arguments you fabricate, they would never bolster your proposal. I can tell you frankly that as long as you do not abandon your unreasonable proposal, it will not be possible for our conference to make any progress. As for our proposal, its reasons are irrefutable: therefore, it is unshakable. We insist on our proposal of making the 38th parallel the military demarcation line.

Vice Admiral Joy: Yesterday you used the word "arrogant" in connection with a proposal the United Nations Command delegation now has before this conference. The United Nations Command delegation has been in search of an expression which conveys the haughty stubbornness of your attitude. "Arrogance" is indeed the word for it. By your obdurate and unreasonable refusal to negotiate you have brought these meetings to a standstill. You have slammed every door leading to possible progress.

Stymied

Toward the end of August 1951, the communists called off the talks because, they claimed, UN aircraft had bombed the neutral zone at Kaesong. The United States denied any bombing and claimed that the communists were trying to discredit the United Nations. On September 10, another bombing occurred in Kaesong. The United States again denied responsibility but soon learned that one of their bombers had, in fact, accidentally bombed Kaesong. General Ridgway apologized to the communist delegates, who rejected his apology. Ridgway was growing increasingly hostile to the communist negotiators. He found them rude and insulting to his delegates, and he felt it to be beneath American dignity to give any ground to them. He threatened to stop the meetings entirely if the communists would not agree to hold them at a different location than Kaesong. The Joint Chiefs of Staff and President Harry S. Truman all urged him not to offer ultimatums to the Chinese. Worldwide opinion would not support the United States if it walked out of the peace talks. In the end, the Chinese compromised without being forced. In October, the meetings resumed at Punmanjom, a small village six miles east of Kaesong.

Back at the front

Although the terms were very different after the truce talks began, combat raged on as violently as ever. In the sum-

A Soldier Remembers Trench Warfare

Beverly Scott was a communications officer with the Twenty-fourth Regiment, Twenty-fifth Infantry Division during the summer of 1951. When his all-black regiment was deactivated, he became a platoon leader with the Fourteenth Regiment. In the fall of 1951, his regiment experienced trench warfare. Scott described it later to oral historian Rudy Tomedi:

It was now the fall of 1951. We'd just moved to the Iron Triangle area. Three towns arranged in a triangle around a long valley, the valley surrounded by steep hills.

That valley had been one of the main invasion corridors to the south, but the truce talks had started, and now they were digging in. Every morning we'd see fresh piles of dirt on the ridges. You never saw the Chinese, but you saw the dirt. They were always digging, and they churned out that dirt like worms.

We were digging in too, until what you had were two armies facing each other from opposing trenchlines. Between the two trenchlines there was maybe five hundred or six hundred yards of no man's land. And what the war came down to for us was patrolling that no man's land.

It was a miserable time. Just a miserable, miserable time. We lost men almost every day, killed or wounded, and it was hard to see the point. The lines stayed exactly where they were.

Source: Rudy Tomedi. No Bugles, No Drums: An Oral History of the Korean War. *New York: Wiley, 1993.*

mer of 1951, a new form of battle became established. It was no longer a war of large movements of advance and retreat. Slight gains were made by either side in getting control of a ridge or a hill, which was then often lost again. Gaining a hill in this warfare could cost more lives than gaining a city had in the first stages of the war. The most famous of the battles— Bloody Ridge and Heartbreak Ridge—came early in the truce period and set the model for the many battles to come.

Bloody Ridge and Heartbreak Ridge

The Battle of Bloody Ridge started with a U.S. plan to straighten out the defensive line. This involved taking the northern ridge of the Punchbowl, a large crater surrounded by hills that lay in the midst of the battlefront that was the scene of many battles during the last two years of the Korean War. The

With mortar and napalm
and brutal fighting, the U.S.
troops secured Bloody
Ridge, September 13, 1951.
*Reproduced by permission of
the Corbis Corporation.*

attack began in the summer with a daylong barrage of artillery fire, completely wiping out all plant life in the area. However, artillery fire was not enough to destroy the underground bunkers (protected underground rooms) protecting the communist troops. The bunkers were strongly fortified with heavy timber and rock and were nearly impossible to penetrate with standard army weapons. When the South Korean (ROK) Army units approached the scorched land, the enemy fired on them

Down off Heartbreak Ridge after two weeks of bloody battle, soldiers of the Second Division carry their buddies through the rain to an aid station just behind the front lines, October 1951. *Reproduced by permission of AP/Wide World Photos.*

from their bunkers with machine guns and grenades, sending the ROK troops back time after time. After several attempts, some of the ROK forces broke and ran. In early September, the Eighth Army sent in the marines and the Second Division as well as two more ROK divisions. Three weeks of brutal fighting ensued, and the North Koreans finally withdrew from Bloody Ridge. There had been twenty-seven hundred Eighth Army casualties and fifteen thousand communist casualties.

From September 13 to September 26, a similar battle was fought at Heartbreak Ridge, another ridge in the Punchbowl. With many casualties, the assault had to be called off: the North Koreans were too firmly entrenched to be forced to move. Then in early October, the Eighth Army attacked at Mundung-ni, a spot near Heartbreak Ridge, sparking another drawn-out assault. Heartbreak Ridge was gained after thirty days of battle, but the Second Division alone had suffered 3,700 casualties. The communist casualties were estimated at 25,000. The benefits of these offensives were minimal, and attacks like them were occurring throughout the front. From July to November 1951, the casualty rate soared: some estimate that there were up to 60,000 UN casualties and 234,000 communist casualties.

Syngman Rhee

As the Americans, North Koreans, and Chinese delegates fiercely argued about the fate of Korea, Syngman Rhee made it known that he would accept nothing less than what the United Nations had resolved: the unification of Korea and the withdrawal of foreign troops. According to Joseph Goulden in *Korea: The Untold Story of the War,* Rhee made his own agenda for a truce, which he sent to the U.S. State Department:

1. complete withdrawal of Chinese forces from Korea;

2. disarmament of North Korea;

3. UN commitment to prevent any third-party support of the North Koreans;

4. South Korean participation in any UN consideration in "any aspect of the Korean problem";

5. preservation of the sovereignty and territorial integrity of Korea.

In a July 16 letter to General Ridgway, signed by Rhee and six other Republic of Korea government officials, he expressed his determination: "The substance of the position of my government is that we cannot maintain our nation in half our country. A divided Korea is a ruined Korea, unstable economically, politically, and militarily. . . . In every Korean heart and in every Korean mind the fact is clear that our nation

South Korean leader
Syngman Rhee reviewing
the troops. *Reproduced
by permission of Archive
Photos, Inc.*

would be plunged into irrevocable disaster by any acceptance of a continued dividing line."

South Korean general Paik attended the early truce meetings knowing Rhee's opposition to the truce. He also realized that the UN delegates did not accept Rhee's position and were not taking it into account in their dealings with the communists. Paik was frustrated and did not speak at the meetings. The anticommunist South Koreans were losing patience with the UN and greatly feared the compromises they might make. But their only option was to fight the North Korean and Chinese armies alone, and they did not have the strength.

Van Fleet restructures the ROKs

Throughout the war the American military and the American press had been scornful of the ROK Army. Although the South Koreans had lost many times the number of soldiers that the UN forces had lost, they had frequently broken ranks

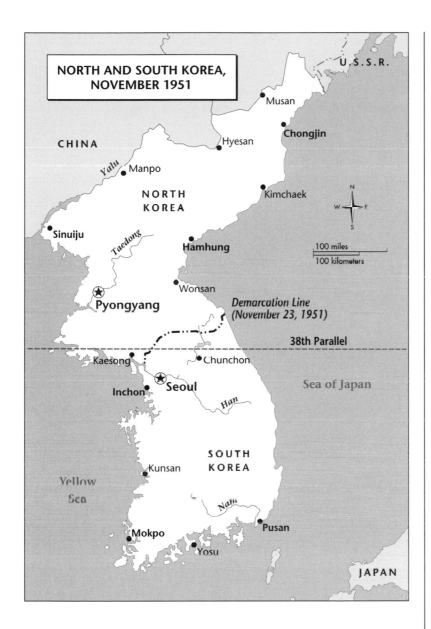

NORTH AND SOUTH KOREA, NOVEMBER 1951

U.S.S.R.

Musan

Chongjin

CHINA

Hyesan

Yalu Manpo

NORTH KOREA

Kimchaek

Sinuiju

Taedong

Hamhung

Wonsan

Demarcation Line (November 23, 1951)

Pyongyang

38th Parallel

Kaesong Chunchon

Sea of Japan

Inchon Seoul

Han

SOUTH KOREA

Kunsan

Yellow Sea

Nam

Mokpo Pusan

Yosu

JAPAN

and scattered when the enemy was fierce. The Chinese knew to hit the defense lines of the Eighth Army at the ROK positions, where there was often weakness. The ROKs never had sufficient equipment or arms and ammunition, and they had little training when the war began. The leadership was also inconsistent. Despite all this, they had proven repeatedly to be dedicated fighters.

After the truce talks began, General James A. Van Fleet (1892–1992), commander of the Eighth Army, decided to take all the ROK divisions out of the line and retrain them. His training program was intensive, and after training the South Koreans were finally provided with a more reasonable supply of arms and ammunition. When they went back to the line, the South Korean army was strong and skilled and had no more "bug-outs," or disorganized retreats. By December 1952, three out of four Eighth Army soldiers at the battlefront were ROKs.

The demarcation line

When the truce talks continued, the next item for consideration was the demarcation line and demilitarized zone (DMZ) that would separate the north from the south. The communists quit insisting that the line be at the 38th parallel, but at that point General Ridgway began to insist that the town of Kaesong—once a capital city of Korea—should be in the hands of the southerners. The communists would agree to a line at the existing front, but not to giving up Kaesong. Ridgway initially insisted on Kaesong but was overruled by the Joint Chiefs of Staff. On November 23, 1951, a new demarcation line was established at the front, with a DMZ that stretched out two kilometers on each side of the line.

Proceeding on to the third agenda item, the negotiators spent several weeks disputing the arrangements for a cease-fire and a supervisory organization to oversee it. Ridgway was particularly interested in having free inspections on both sides of the demarcation line, and the Chinese wanted to be able to rebuild the roads, airports, and buildings in North Korea without hindrance. After a good deal of compromising on both sides, all the terms were arranged but one, whether and when airfields could be rebuilt. It was agreed to go on to the next agenda item and come back to this issue.

The next item on the agenda was the exchange of prisoners of war (POWs). Truce talks had already been going on for five months. No one imagined that the fourth item on the agenda would take more than a year to negotiate.

Where to Learn More

Alexander, Bevin. *Korea: The First War We Lost*. New York: Hippocrene Books, 1986, revised edition, 2000.

Blair, Clay. *The Forgotten War: America in Korea, 1950–1953*. New York, Times Books, 1987.

Goulden, Joseph C. *Korea: The Untold Story of the War*. New York: Times Books, 1982.

Toland, John. *In Mortal Combat: Korea, 1950–1953*. New York: William Morrow, 1991.

Tomedi, Rudy. *No Bugles, No Drums: An Oral History of the Korean War*. New York: Wiley, 1993.

Varhola, Michael J. *Fire and Ice: The Korean War, 1950–1953*. Mason City, IA: Savas Publishing, 2000.

Prisoners of War and the Peace Negotiations

12

ost of the prisoners of war (POWs) of the Korean War were taken during the first year of fighting, from mid-1950 to mid-1951. The United Nations (UN) forces, fighting for the South Koreans, had taken only about one thousand prisoners in the first two months of the war, while they were being pushed south by the North Korean People's Army (NKPA). After the successful landing at Inchon (see Chapter 7) and the advance into North Korea, however, tens of thousands of prisoners were taken. By December 1950, the UN forces had taken more than 130,000 prisoners of war. Most of them were held in camps at Inchon and in the south at Pusan. When the Communist Chinese Forces (CCF) entered the war on the side of the North Koreans and began pushing the UN troops south again, the problem of what to do with prisoners became urgent. Depending on how far the enemy forced the UN to retreat, the camps might become difficult to maintain.

In February 1951, preparations for a prison camp began on an island off the coast of Korea, called Koje-do ("do" means island). The island, not very suitable for a prison camp,

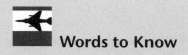

Words to Know

beriberi: a disease caused by inadequate nutrition that attacks the digestive system as well as the heart and nervous system.

biological warfare: the act of spreading disease germs or other living organisms through enemy territory, using the germs as a weapon with which to kill or disable the enemy.

brainwashing: the use of carefully planned psychological techniques to try to change the way someone thinks and believes, often against the will of, or even without the knowledge of, the person.

classified: kept away from public view; being placed in a category (as a document) in which only select people have access to it.

commandant: commanding officer.

compound: a walled-in area within which there are buildings, usually places of residence.

dysentary: a disease caused by infection resulting in severe diarrhea.

Geneva Convention: a series of agreements about the treatment of prisoners of war and the sick, wounded, and dead in battle, signed by many nations.

humanitarian: promoting the good of humanity.

impressed: forced to enlist as a soldier.

indoctrination: to thoroughly teach or train someone with a particular, and one-sided, set of beliefs, practices, or principles.

malnourished: having a poor diet lacking in proper nutrients, resulting in ill health.

parasite: an insect or animal that lives off another animal, usually hurting the host animal; a person who lives off someone else.

paratroopers: soldiers who are trained to jump from airplanes with parachutes.

repatriation: the act of sending someone (often prisoners of war) back to his or her own country.

reprisal: violence or other use of force by one side in a conflict in retaliation for something bad that was done by the other side; a system of getting even for harm done.

was rocky and hilly, inhabited by about 200,000 natives on about 150 square miles. The UN put up four barbed-wire enclosures on a large site on the island. Each of these was then separated into eight compounds. By April, 130,000 Korean and 20,000 Chinese prisoners were packed into Koje-do. This was more than five times as many people as the camp had room to hold.

At the prison camp at Koje-do, there was an unusually divided group of prisoners. Among both the North Koreans and the Chinese, there was a significant proportion of inmates who had defected to the UN side, creating a big split between communists and anti-communists. The North Korean Army sent agents—soldiers who allowed themselves to be captured—into the camp to organize the inmates and to make sure that principles of communism and anti-United States propaganda were promoted within the prisons. Governing bodies formed among the communist prisoners. In some cases, they held trials and the anticommunists were executed by the communists. Throughout the war, the Communist Chinese and the North Koreans kept open communication with their agents in the Koje prison camp.

A North Korean prisoner of war awaits his fate, September 25, 1950.
Reproduced by permission of Archive Photos, Inc.

The communists take prisoners

For the UN troops captured in battle, the prospects were very grim. Those captured in the first six months of the war had it the worst. The North Koreans forced them to march under very harsh conditions to the prison camps. POWs who could not make the long marches were generally shot as they dropped out of the line. There was little food, and the POWs were not provided clothing for the trip.

After the spring of 1951, China ran most of the prison camps in North Korea, which were situated along the Yalu River near the Korean border with China. The Chinese had more humanitarian ideas about prison camps and conditions improved, but the captured POWs' accounts of life in the Chinese prison camps are still nightmarish. Some of the prison cells were so crowded that if one soldier moved, everyone else was forced to move as well. There were no facilities for washing. Body lice and other parasites abounded. The communists were

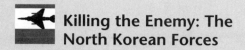

Killing the Enemy: The North Korean Forces

U.S. Marine private Ernest Gonzalez described an unofficial practice at the frozen Chosin Reservoir in the battles of November 1950:

> Word was passed to kill all enemy wounded. I found one Chinese curled up, lying facedown. He had a head wound shaped like a perfect pie-cut that exposed his brain. I fired into his midriff. He turned slowly and looked at me as if saying, "Why must you make me suffer more?" Although it remained a common practice on both sides, I never again killed another wounded Chinese soldier.

Source: Donald Knox. The Korean War: Pusan to Chosin, An Oral History. San Diego: Harcourt Brace Jovanovich, 1988.

so low on supplies and medicines that their own soldiers and civilians were dying in great numbers. Food for the prisoners was often a small handful of ground meal that was mixed with water or snow to make a mash; once in a while the prisoners got a ball of rice. Many of the men developed dysentery, often caused by an infection that causes severe diarrhea, and could no longer force themselves to eat. Even those who were able to keep eating the meager fare in order to survive were severely malnourished. The disease beriberi, caused by a lack of nutrients and resulting in diarrhea and fever, was widespread in the camps. There was little or no medical care available to the prisoners in many camps, and death from sickness and hunger was commonplace.

In the communist camps, prisoners were subjected to intense indoctrination programs, lectures, discussion groups, and interrogations directed at converting the soldiers to communism and anti-Americanism. There were many attempts to get American soldiers to sign statements about American wrongdoing in the war, some of which were successful. Although the Chinese prided themselves on not using violence on the inmates, there were many cases in which their tactics were cruel and painful. POWs later described the process they were put through as "brainwashing": the enemy used carefully planned psychological techniques to try to change the way the prisoners thought.

Missing in action

Army intelligence investigations revealed that some American POWs were being taken to China. A classified army report (only select people could see it) dated December 15, 1951, only recently declassified in 1996, concluded that there were about twenty-five hundred American POWs in

Killing the Enemy: The United Nations Forces

In late October 1950, as the Eighth Army advanced into North Korea, a paratroop drop was organized to look for a group of American prisoners of war (POWs) being transported by the enemy to prison camps in the north. The following excerpt describes what was found of the United Nations' POWs:

> The assistant commander of the First Cavalry Division, Brigadier General Frank A. Allen, Jr., and his party discovered a sad and sickening sight: around a railroad tunnel near Myongucham, about five miles northwest of Sunch'on, were the bodies of sixty-six American POWs who had been murdered and seven more American POWs who had either starved to death or died of disease. In addition, General Allen and his party found twenty-three Americans who had escaped from their North Korean captors, some of them critically wounded (two died during the first night).
>
> The survivors told the story: two trains, each carrying about 150 American POWs, left Pyongyang on October 17, crawling slowly and repairing the heavily broken tracks as they went. These were survivors of a group of 370 Americans the North Koreans had marched north from Seoul shortly after the Inchon landing. Each day five or six Americans died of dysentery, starvation, or exposure. Their bodies were removed from the train. A few Americans escaped along the way. On October 20, while the paratroop drop [to save these

A North Korean soldier guards an unidentified POW. *Reproduced by permission of AP/Wide World Photos.*

> prisoners] was in progress, the second of the two trains remained in the Myongucham tunnel. It still had about 100 Americans, crowded into open coal gondolas and boxcars. That evening, the North Korean guards took the Americans in three groups to get their evening meal. The North Koreans shot them down as they waited for it. Most of the Americans who survived did so by feigning [pretending] death. The guards and the train left that night.

Source: Bevin Alexander. Korea: The First War We Lost. New York: Hippocrene Books, 1986, revised edition, 2000.

Manchuria, an area in northern China just north of the Korean border, and about fifteen hundred in other parts of China. "Specially selected groups are sent to China in relatively small numbers to undergo political indoctrination," the report,

U.S. and South Korean
prisoners of war paraded
through the streets of
Pyongyang, October 3,
1950. *Reproduced by
permission of Archive
Photos, Inc.*

which was quoted in the *Detroit News* on February 16, 1998,
stated. "Of those POWs processed in Manchuria, the ones not
going to China are apparently being sent to mines and labor
camps in Manchuria itself. Because of obvious diplomatic com-
plications, it follows that the communists would neither wish
to return these men to U.S. control nor admit to their existence
at this time." There were about eighty-one hundred American
soldiers not accounted for at the end of the war, and it is possible that POWs in China make up some part of those missing.

Another much smaller group of the missing may have been taken to various places in the Soviet Union, never to return. (The Soviet Union was the first communist country and was made up of fifteen republics, including Russia. It existed as a unified country from 1922 to 1991.) During the war, some U.S. military aircraft were shot down by the Russians. There is evidence that the Soviets captured some of the pilots. Since the fall of communism in the Soviet Union in 1989, more and more Russian people are speaking up about encounters they had at that time with American soldiers in Russia. The Russians have worked with the United States to try to find out what happened to these soldiers, but so far there have been no solid results.

The truce talks focus on POWs

On December 11, 1951, the delegates at Panmunjom began to discuss the repatriation (sending home) of prisoners. The communists were not initially willing to provide a list of the UN prisoners they held, but the United States stood firm, and eventually the lists were exchanged. The UN list accounted for about 133,000 POWs: 95,531 North Korean, 20,700 Chinese, and 16,243 South Koreans who had been impressed (forced to enlist) into the North Korean Army. Another 44,000 South Koreans had been earlier reported as prisoners of war but were then reclassified (as South Koreans and not enemy troops) and released. The communists noted the discrepancy and claimed that the UN was withholding the 44,000 soldiers. The communist list, on the other hand, reported only 11,559 POWs: 3,198 American, 7,142 ROKs, and the rest other UN soldiers. The UN claimed that there were 88,000 ROKs and 11,500 U.S. troops missing in action. The communists explained the huge difference as the consequence of prisoner deaths by disease and by prison camps being bombed by UN aircraft (which was a frequent occurrence). They also claimed to have released many POWs.

The repatriation issue

By January 1952, the two sides agreed to exchange prisoners, but an unexpected problem arose almost immediately. The United States realized it was holding prisoners who did not want to be sent back to the communist countries.

Claims of U.S. Use of Biological Warfare

In the spring of 1951, Brigadier General Crawford Sams, the public health and welfare chief of the United Nations (UN) Command in Tokyo, Japan, launched a highly secret mission in an epidemic-control ship equipped with medical laboratory facilities. Landing at Wonsan, he and his crew made a trip through the enemy territory. On his return, he announced that the army had received intelligence that there had been an outbreak of the bubonic plague on the east coast of North Korea, and he had gone to examine whether this was true. In April 1951, *Newsweek* magazine reported that "landing parties have been grabbing off numbers of Chinese Reds from the tiny islands of the harbor and taking them back to the ship, where they are tested for symptoms of the dread bubonic plague."

In February and March 1952, the communists accused the United States of engaging in biological warfare. They held that Sams had gone into North Korea to test out biological weapons on prisoners taken there. Among the weapons the Chinese and North Koreans accused the United States of using were a variety of germ-carrying insects and infected feathers, which were dropped from aircraft over North Korea and Manchuria, China. The United States flatly denied these claims.

Twenty-five U.S. soldiers being held as prisoners of war confessed to the

There were soldiers in the UN prison camps who were Nationalist Chinese who had been impressed into the communist forces. Many had surrendered to the Americans rather than fight for the communists. Another group of prisoners were South Koreans impressed into the North Korean Army when North Korea occupied the south. Americans argued that these groups risked severe reprisals (punishment) upon repatriation.

The communists were outraged at the suggestion. They felt that the Americans were trying to discredit them by saying that the POWs did not want to return. And not sending the POWs back conflicted strongly with the Geneva Convention of 1949, which stated that POWs were to be "repatriated without delay after cessation of hostilities." (The Geneva Convention was a series of agreements about the treatment of prisoners of war and the sick, wounded, and dead in battle, signed communists that they had been involved with the germ warfare. After they were released, none of these prisoners ever went on to claim that their confessions were true. Many, but not all, retracted their confessions after their release, saying they had been coerced by the communists into making the confessions.

The Chinese and North Koreans raised a tremendous outcry about American inhumanity, both in the prison camps and with the use of germ warfare. It was certainly an advantageous time for them to rally worldwide opinion against the United States. However, the International Scientific Commission for the Facts Concerning Bacterial Warfare in China and Korea created by the World Peace Council conducted a two-month investigation that corroborated the communists' allegations. Since that time, some very distinguished scientists and historians have concluded that the United States *was* guilty of biological warfare, especially when it came to light that the Japanese had shared their data on the subject with the United States. Other experts have concluded that there was no biological warfare in Korea. There is some evidence, but no solid proof, that the United States dropped fleas and spiders infested with deadly epidemic germs over enemy lands. This issue remains controversial.

by many nations.) Most of the U.S. State Department officials and Joint Chiefs of Staff (an agency within the Department of Defense serving to advise the president and the secretary of defense on matters of war) agreed that the idea of separating out the prisoners who did not want repatriation would be against the Geneva Convention and very difficult as well. But on this issue President Harry S. Truman stood firm: the United States would not force anyone to go back to a communist country who did not want to go. The communists stood just as firm on the principle of an all-for-all exchange of prisoners.

Unrest at Koje-do prison camp

In February 1952, U.S. troops at Koje-do began to screen the POWs to determine which prisoners would go along with repatriation. When the troops went into the compound that housed the core of the communist governing group, more than one thousand inmates attacked with homemade but deadly weapons. The troops began firing. In this incident, fifty-five Korean prisoners were killed, twenty-two died later, and one hundred forty were wounded. One American was killed and thirty-eight were wounded. At the tables in Panmunjom, the communist delegates loudly protested the "massacre" at Koje. In March, there was another incident at Koje, in which North Korean prisoners threw stones at Korean prisoners who were anticommunist. The Korean guards began shooting at the North Koreans, killing ten and wounding twenty-six, of whom two died later. Again the North Korean and Chinese delegates at Panmunjom raised an outcry.

The screening of POWs turned up many more prisoners who did not want to return to communist countries than expected, with 40,000 out of 132,000 opting not to go home. On April 28, the UN delegates presented a compromise package to the communists, offering to release the prisoners who were willing to be repatriated and, as a compromise, giving up any more demands about how the North Koreans rebuilt their airfields, a stumbling block in earlier negotiations. The communists, horrified at the huge number of prisoners the UN claimed to be unwilling to go home, rejected the package and the truce meetings were once again brought to a halt.

The kidnapping of the commander

Meanwhile, the ruling prisoner groups at Koje-do had been working out a plan. On May 7, 1952, the prison camp commander, Brigadier General Francis T. Dodd, went to see some inmates who claimed they had been beaten in one of the compounds. In a planned attack, the inmates kidnapped Dodd. The U.S. Army's response was to try to calm the prisoners; no one wanted a large revolt at this time. Dodd understood this from his cell and agreed to act as a go-between for the prisoners, helping them to present their demands to the United Nations. They treated Dodd well. In turn, they got telephone systems throughout the camp and a few vehicles. In the meantime, Eighth Army Commander General James A. Van Fleet (1892–1992) ordered a battalion of tanks to Koje-do. Brigadier General Charles Colson assumed command of the prison.

On May 9, the prisoners staged a trial for Dodd, in which he was charged with nineteen counts of death or injury to inmates. The next morning, as the trial continued, Colson prepared for a massive attack on the compound. But before it was launched, the prisoners sent out this crudely written list of demands, as quoted in Bevin Alexander's history *Korea: The First War We Lost:*

- Immediate ceasing the barbarous behavior, insults, torture, forcible protest with blood writing, threatening, confinement, mass murdering, gun and machine gun shooting, using poison gas, germ weapons, experiment object of A-bomb, by your command.

- Immediate stopping the so-called illegal and unreasonable repatriation of North Korean People's Army and Chinese People's Voluntary Army.

- Immediate ceasing the forcible [screening] which thousands of POWs of NKPA and CPVA be armed and falled in slavery.

U.S paratroopers clash with prisoners during a stretch of bloody fighting at the Koje-do prison camp following the kidnapping of the commander, June 1952. *Reproduced by permission of the Corbis Corporation.*

- Immediate recognition of the P.W. Representative Group (Commission) consisted of NPKA and CPVA PW's and close cooperation to it by your command. This Representative Group will turn in Brig. Gen. Dodd, USA, on your hand after we receive satisfactory declaration to resolve the above items by your command. We will await your warm and sincere answer.

General Colson responded to these demands by delaying the attack and writing a letter back to them in which he denied that Americans had committed all the offenses listed in the prisoners' list of demands. He agreed to halt the repatriation screenings and asked that Dodd be freed by noon. Then he heard from Dodd himself, who argued that Americans *had* been responsible for POW deaths, and offered to write in the changes to Colson's letter that were demanded by the prisoners. Colson agreed. As it stood in the end, the letter stated that there had been many deaths at the hands of the UN personnel in the prison. It also promised that the inmates at Koje-do could expect "humane treatment." General Matthew B. Ridgway (1895–1993), commander of the UN Forces, tried to stop the signing of this letter, but it was too late. Victory was all on the side of the prisoners. The army tried to repudiate Colson's statement, and General Dodd was immediately relieved of command.

General Mark W. Clark (1896–1984), who had recently assumed command of the Far East Forces, was furious. He had both Colson and Dodd reduced to the rank of colonel and put a tough new commander in charge of Koje. The prisoners were placed in smaller compounds so there was less possibility of revolt. When the prisoners resisted being placed in smaller groups, armed troops forced them. In the violent uprising that followed, thirty-one prisoners were killed and many more were wounded; there was little resistance afterward. The troops who went into the prisoner's former quarters found the bodies of murdered inmates and thousands of weapons.

Where to Learn More

Alexander, Bevin. *Korea: The First War We Lost.* New York: Hippocrene Books, 1986, revised edition, 2000.

Blair, Clay. *The Forgotten War: America in Korea, 1950–1953.* New York, Times Books, 1987.

Deane, Hugh. *The Korean War, 1945–1953.* San Francisco: China Books, 1999.

Goulden, Joseph C. *Korea: The Untold Story of the War.* New York: Times Books, 1982.

Knox, Donald. *The Korean War: Pusan to Chosin: An Oral History.* San Diego: Harcourt Brace Jovanovich, 1988.

Toland, John. *In Mortal Combat: Korea, 1950–1953.* New York: William Morrow, 1991.

Web sites

Burns, Robert. "China Held U.S. POWs During Korean War, Army Reports Reveal." *Detroit News.* [Online] http://detnews.com/1998/nation/9802/16/02160106.htm (accessed on August 14, 2001).

United States Army. "African Americans in the Korean War." Fiftieth Anniversary of the Korean War Commemoration Site. [Online] http://korea50.army.mil/history/factsheets/afroamer.html (accessed on August 14, 2001).

An End to the Fighting

The year 1952 was an election year in the United States. President Harry S. Truman (1884–1972) had decided not to run for another term. The Democrats nominated the governor of Illinois, Adlai Stevenson (1900–1965), to run for president. The Republicans nominated Dwight D. Eisenhower (1890–1969), supreme commander of the NATO forces in Europe. (NATO stands for North Atlantic Treaty Organization, an alliance of nations in Europe and North America formed in 1949 primarily to counter the threat of Soviet and communist expansion.) Eisenhower returned home from Europe to campaign in June 1952, leaving his NATO command position open.

When Eisenhower won the Republican nomination, General Matthew B. Ridgway (1895–1993)—still fighting the Korean War in battle and at the negotiating tables as the commander of the Far East Forces and the United Nations (UN) Command—was given the NATO command. He immediately left Korea for Europe. Mark W. Clark (1896–1984), a four-star general and commander of U.S. forces in Italy during World War II (1939–45), replaced him just as the Koje-do prison takeover erupted (see Chapter 12).

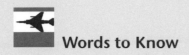

Words to Know

atomic bomb: a powerful bomb created by splitting the nuclei of a heavy chemical, such as plutonium or uranium, in a rapid chain reaction, resulting in a violent and destructive shock wave as well as radiation.

casualties: those who are killed, wounded, missing, or taken prisoner in combat.

civilian: someone who is not in the military or any other security forces.

collaborator: someone who cooperates with, or helps out, enemies to his or her own nation.

coup d'etat: the overthrow of an existing government through force or violence.

gross national product (GNP): a measurement of the output of goods and services of a nation.

impasse: the position of being faced with a problem for which there seems no solution; a stalemate.

limited warfare: warfare with an objective other than the enemy's complete destruction, as in holding a defensive line during negotiations.

nationalize: to place ownership, usually of a factory or a business, in the hands of the government.

Pentagon: the headquarters of the Department of Defense and therefore of all U.S. military activity.

repatriation: the act of sending someone (often a prisoner of war) back to his or her own country.

unification: the process of bringing together the separate parts of something to form a single unit; in Korea, the hoped-for act of bringing North and South Korea together under a single government.

unlimited war: a military conflict in which a combatant nation uses every means within its power to pursue the goal of completely defeating the enemy.

"I shall go to Korea"

In his campaign for the presidency, Eisenhower promised to try to end the Korean War quickly and fairly. A month before the elections, he won great public favor by saying simply "I shall go to Korea." He easily beat Adlai Stevenson in the elections and in early December made his promised trip to Korea. There, General Clark and Eighth Army commander James A. Van Fleet (1892–1992) presented Eisenhower with plans for an all-out war on the communists, including the use of atomic bombs and Chiang Kai-shek's (1887–1975) Chinese Nationalist troops. (Chiang Kai-shek and the Chinese Nationalists were driven to the island of Taiwan [formerly Formosa] after being defeated by Mao Zedong [Mao Tse-tung; 1893–1976] and the Communists in 1949 following the Chinese Civil War.) Eisenhower, who had certainly considered using atomic bombs to end the war, did not appear interested. He was an advocate of a limited war, preferring, if possible, to end the war in Korea with negotiation rather than resorting to extreme military means that could lead to world war. However, early in his administration, Eisenhower let it be known among the communist leaders that nuclear weapons would be considered if the peace talks were not resumed. In this "get-tough" position, Eisenhower also removed an order issued by Truman in 1950 prohibiting Nationalist China (whom the United States was supporting) from taking military action in mainland Communist China. Other than these gestures, the new president followed fairly closely in Truman's footsteps regarding Korea.

More changes in command

On March 5, 1953, Soviet Premier Joseph Stalin (1879–1953) died. Replacing him as the head of the Soviet Union was Georgy M. Malenkov (1902–1988), who, promptly after taking over, broadcast a speech expressing the Soviet Union's desire for peace in Asia. Eisenhower responded favorably to Malenkov's speech. Earlier, the International League of Red Cross Societies had arrived at a resolution that both sides in Korea should repatriate (send home) the sick and wounded prisoners of war (POWs). The United States approved of this resolution. Perhaps as a result of the change in Soviet leadership or due to international pressure, the North Koreans and Communist China announced their wish to exchange sick and wounded POWs with the UN Command. Almost immediately after this announcement, they expressed a desire to exchange all POWs, agreeing to allow a neutral nation to interview those communist POWs who did not wish to return to their home countries. These statements did not take place in the truce talks, which had not resumed, but the communists were publicly agreeing to the compromises proposed in earlier truce talk meetings.

Limited War versus Unlimited War

In 1945, near the end of World War II, the United States dropped an atomic bomb on Hiroshima, Japan. Nearly 130,000 people were killed or injured and 90 percent of the city was leveled. Two days later in Nagasaki, Japan, 75,000 were killed or injured and about 35 percent of the city was destroyed when the United States dropped a second bomb. The bombs quickly brought an already weakened Japan to surrender, but the use of this destructive new weapon horrified people throughout the world.

The United States tested the first atomic bomb in 1945. The Soviet Union tested its first atomic bomb in 1949. Atomic bombs have a powerful explosive force that can destroy large areas and cause tremendous death and pain. They also create powerful radiation that damages living tissue. Unlimited nuclear warfare could destroy great portions of the planet, perhaps even making it uninhabitable for human and other life. After the two world powers had this tremendous capacity to destroy, the nature of warfare and the concept of war itself began to change. In wars prior to the atomic bomb, the use of

all possible force to defeat an enemy was standard. After 1945, some limits would always be necessary.

Throughout the Korean War, the U.S. president, the State Department, and the Joint Chiefs of Staff all considered using the atomic bomb as a military solution. After consideration, they consistently returned to the idea of a "limited war," one in which the enemy was not thoroughly destroyed. Unfortunately, in Korea this limited war stretched on and on, leaving thousands dead and showing no sign of ending. Several of the military commanders in Korea, notably commanders of the United Nations (UN) forces Douglas MacArthur and Mark W. Clark, were advocates of an "unlimited war" in which the United States would use everything in its power, including atomic bombs, to defeat the enemy. They wished to fight China, who supported the communist North Koreans, on the Chinese mainland and to use the remaining Chinese Nationalist troops, who were exiled on Taiwan since the Chinese Civil War. Advocates of an unlimited war were generally called "hawks."

"Little Switch": A step forward

On April 20, 1953, the first exchanges of Korean War POWs began with a transfer of the sick and wounded. The operation was called "Little Switch." By May 3, the United

A survivor of the Hiroshima bombing.
Reproduced by permission of the Corbis Corporation.

With the brutality of the atomic bombs dropped in Hiroshima and Nagasaki and World War II within such recent memory, there was a great deal of international resistance to the idea of unlimited war in Korea. In the United States, no one seemed greatly concerned, and few were even aware, that the air attacks on North Korea had virtually wiped out whole cities and villages and killed hundreds of thousands of civilians. But President Dwight D. Eisenhower wrestled with the consequences of unlimited versus limited warfare, according to his biographer Stephen E. Ambrose, as quoted by Hugh Deane in *The Korean War: 1945–1953:* "The truth was that Eisenhower realized that unlimited war in the nuclear age was unimaginable, and limited war unwinnable." Privately horrified by the idea of nuclear war, Eisenhower was able to speak calmly about it with his staff and the press and did not hesitate to scare the enemy with the prospect. After his visit to Korea in December 1952, Eisenhower wrote in his memoirs, as quoted by Ambrose: "My conclusion as I left Korea was that we could not stand forever on a static front and continue to accept casualties without any visible results. Small attacks on small hills would not end this war." Although he saw the need for a quick end to the killing, he still sought peace without all-out destruction. In a speech in the spring of 1953 called "The Chance for Peace," Eisenhower pushed for "the conclusion of an honorable peace in Korea."

Nations had returned 5,194 North Korean and 1,034 Chinese POWs and 446 civilians. The communists returned 684 prisoners: 471 South Korean, 149 American, 32 British, 15 Turkish, and 17 other UN POWs. There were no difficulties in the exchange.

Refugees from Pyongyang and nearby areas crawl perilously over the shattered girders of the city's bridge across the Taedong River, December 4, 1950. By the end of the war, the city—and much of North Korea—was destroyed. *Reproduced by permission of AP/Wide World Photos.*

Bombing the North Korean food supply

The war had continued throughout the talks and cessations of talks, at times very violently and with many casualties on both sides. Truce talks resumed on April 26, as the sick and wounded POWs found their way home. The talks focused on forming a commission of neutral nations to oversee the armistice and repatriation of POWs. There was little agreement across the tables about which nations were neutral. In May

1953, the truce talks once again threatened to stall. General Clark wanted to launch another massive bombing of North Korea to push the communists to negotiate.

The Joint Chiefs of Staff—the president's and the secretary of defense's advisors on matters of war—agreed to another bombing of North Korea, but the plan was held up because, at this point in the war, North Korea had almost no buildings left standing to bomb. The North Korean capital of Pyongyang was leveled, as were the villages and cities in the north as well as the factories, plants, and industrial complexes. After consideration, the U.S. strategists decided to bomb the North Korean dams along the Yalu River, near the border with China. By destroying the dams, they hoped to flood the rice crops that would feed the nation through the year. Their intention was to starve the civilian population of North Korea in order to force the communist delegates to come to terms. The air force went to work, bombing the area for two weeks, successfully ruining the all-important rice crops. It is not known exactly how much starvation this caused, but there is no doubt that it caused much suffering in the year to come. Whether it had any effect on the communist delegates at Panmunjom is not determined, but the Chinese forces on the front followed the bombings with a fierce attack, gaining a few hills and killing many UN troops.

Syngman Rhee sabotages peace efforts

Although there were many details that provoked argument in the truce talks—particularly as to which nations were to be chosen as neutral—progress was being made. Both sides wanted to end the fighting. Unfortunately, South Korean President Syngman Rhee (1875–1965) did not. He had never been a willing participant in the armistice process. Rhee had proclaimed it unacceptable to create a peace that would leave the nation divided, with Chinese troops in the north to prevent the south from taking control of the whole country. He had done what he could to turn public opinion against the truce by staging mass rallies and making radio broadcasts and press releases.

In the spring 1953 negotiations, the UN made a concession to the communists, agreeing to send North Koreans who did not want to be repatriated to neutral nations (earlier they had said they would release them in South Korea). Rhee let it be known that he would not allow any Koreans to be released to a neutral nation, and that he did not believe India (the designated neutral nation) to be neutral. Further, he said he would not allow Indian troops into South Korea.

Despite the continuing and often vicious military conflicts at the battlefront, by June 1953 the armistice was nearing completion. Rhee stepped up his anti-armistice campaign in South Korea. He announced that South Korea would not go along with the terms of the truce and that he would remove the South Korean (ROK) Army from the UN forces and continue the war on his own. In his usual manner, he went after anyone in his own country who did not agree with him. Sydney Bailey described this in his book *The Korean Armistice:* "Opponents of the regime were being persecuted, alleged collaborators executed without trial, governmental 'goon squads' were at large, ministers with unsavory reputations had been appointed, corruption was rife, Rhee and his supporters were threatening to subvert the constitution, and the campaign against an armistice was gaining momentum." Rhee also threatened to shoot the Indian troops that were to come into South Korea to supervise the prisoner exchange.

Knowing that the UN armistice provided for North Korean prisoners who did not wish to be repatriated to be sent to neutral nations for interviewing and processing, on June 18 Rhee ordered the ROK officers at the prison camps to release these prisoners. He did this with the help of some high-ranking American officers. That night, prison guards sent about twenty-five thousand North Koreans out of the prison camps and into the population of South Korea. Then Rhee ordered all South Koreans, army and civilian, to cease working for the UN forces. He began to prepare his troops for fighting on their own.

The UN delegates and General Clark immediately gave the North Koreans and Chinese a written apology for Rhee's actions. Although the communists accepted the apology, they reasonably asked how the United Nations could comply with the terms of the peace in Korea if South Korea was not included in it. The truce was at a new impasse.

Eisenhower sent a team to try to reason with Rhee. On July 11, with promises of enormous economic aid and the continued presence of U.S. troops to provide security in South

Korea, Rhee agreed not to obstruct the armistice. Two days later the Chinese concluded a brutal assault directed almost entirely at the ROK troops at the battlefront. Whole ROK divisions were shattered and the casualties were in the tens of thousands by the time the fighting ceased. Rhee then publicly promised to cooperate with the terms of the armistice.

The armistice is signed

On July 27, 1953, at 10:00 A.M., the delegates to the peace talks at Panmunjom filed into the Peace Pagoda to sign the armistice agreement. No one spoke during this stiff and uncelebrated ending of the war. The delegates simply signed their names in eighteen different places. The armistice agreement then went to the supreme commanders of the armies for signing. At 10:00 P.M. that day the fighting stopped. (The delay was set to give the Chinese, who had poor communications systems, time to let all their troops know of the cease-fire.) There was celebration in North Korea when North Korean Premier Kim Il Sung (1912–1994) announced the end of the war. In South Korea, it was quiet. In the United States, too, there was little fanfare upon news of the end of the war. Although few wanted to put it into such terms, many felt that the United States had suffered a true defeat, its first lost war. Eisenhower was criticized by many for not using nuclear warfare to bring about a victory in Korea, but for the rest of his life Eisenhower remained proud of getting the United States out of a dangerous and miserable war, viewing it as one of his greatest accomplishments while in office.

Operation Big Switch

Operation Big Switch, the exchange of all prisoners of war between the opposing sides, took place from August 5 to September 6, 1953. The communists returned a total of 12,773 UN prisoners. Of these, 7,862 were South Koreans; 3,597 were Americans; nearly 1,000 were British; and the rest were from the other UN contributing nations. From this POW population, there were 359 prisoners who did not wish to be repatriated. Of these, 335 were South Korean, 23 were Americans, and 1 was British.

The UN Command released 75,823 POWs directly to the communists in the demilitarized zone in Korea. Of these, 70,183

An exchange of prisoners between the United Nations and the North Koreans and their allies at Panmunjom, North Korea, August 11, 1953. *Reproduced by permission of Archive Photos, Inc.*

were North Koreans and 5,460 were Chinese. They released to the Neutral Nations Repatriation Commission another 22,604 POWs who did not wish to be repatriated. Of these, 14,704 were Chinese and 7,900 were Koreans. (There had been 25,000 more North Koreans who refused repatriation that had escaped into South Korea due to Rhee's release order.) The repatriation committee, headed by Lieutenant General Timaya of the Indian army, heard the stories and decided the futures of the voluntary exiles and in many cases sent them to live in neutral nations like Argentina, Brazil, and India. The Chinese who refused repatriation, however, were most often sent directly by the UN to Taiwan.

Casualties

The tally of dead, missing, and wounded from the Korean War is still, more than half a century later, in question. The Pentagon (headquarters of the U.S. Department of Defense) estimate of casualties from the war was 996,937 UN casualties. Of these, 850,000 were ROK (South Korean) soldiers; 17,000 were non-American UN troops; and 157,530 were Americans. Of the American casualties, 33,629 were killed and 103,284 were wounded. There were another 20,617 deaths within the military during the years of the Korean War, but not necessarily in Korea. Although a figure of 54,000 deaths—which includes the deaths of people who did not die or necessarily serve in Korea—has been used for many years and is engraved on the Korean War Veterans Memorial in Washington, D.C., the Pentagon revised these numbers in 1994. The new estimate of battle deaths in Korea is 33,652, with "other deaths"—those occurring in Korea during the war due to illness, accidents, and other nonbattle causes—at 3,262. Thus, 36,914 American troops died in the Korean War. During the last two years of the war, while the delegates argued at the truce meetings, there were 62,000 American casualties, with 12,300 killed.

On the communist side, the Pentagon estimated 1,420,000 casualties. There were 520,000 North Korean casualties and 900,000 Chinese casualties. Some recent historians find these figures too high.

The worst of the casualties occurred among the civilians in North Korea and South Korea. Although the figures are not precise, there were probably significantly more than four million civilians killed during the Korean War. With the cities and towns of the nation flattened by bombing, millions of civilians also found themselves homeless and without means of survival; the suffering on both sides of the newly drawn demarcation line was vast and terrible.

After the armistice, North Korea and South Korea were still at war (and still were at the start of the twenty-first century). In 1954, the Geneva Conference raised the issue of unification of Korea. No progress was made in two months of discussion and none has been made since then. North Korea has remained staunchly communist and isolated from Western trade and culture. South Korea has modernized under a sometimes wildly successful capitalist economy. Both countries have experienced considerable turmoil.

South Korea after the armistice

Within six months of the armistice, most of the UN troops that were going home had flocked out of Korea. The

United States, however, was far from done with its role in Korea. Rhee had made sure of this before he accepted the terms of the truce. The United States had promised to leave significant numbers of U.S. troops and provide military aid indefinitely in South Korea; it also agreed to help expand the ROK Army to twenty divisions and to provide long-term economic aid, with an initial installment of $200 million and $9.5 million in food to the Korean people.

In his memoirs *From Pusan to Panmunjom*, ROK General Paik Sun Yup (1920–) said "Once the armistice was a fait accompli [a done deal], President Rhee accepted it almost casually." Rhee had other things to worry about. The end of his second term as president came in 1954. He amended the constitution, which allowed only two terms, to allow him to stay in office indefinitely. Rhee was facing a different kind of opposition than he had before. After the war, South Korea opened its schools and had its own independent education system for the first time. With more education, people were less inclined to accept his strong-arm tactics. By 1960, the public was in an uproar about the corruption and violence within Rhee's government. Civil disorder, particularly among students, raged out of control, and Rhee was forced to resign at the age of eighty-five. He and his wife moved to Hawaii.

Democracy did not come easily for the Republic of Korea (South Korea). A democratic government followed Rhee's, but within one year, in May 1961, the military staged a coup d'etat (pronounced coo-day-tah; the overthrow of an existing government through force or violence). A military government under Park Chung Hee (1917–1979) remained in power until 1979. During those years, healthy economic progress was made, with a rapid buildup of business and industry. But the booming economy was not stable. In 1979, as inflation raced out of control, students took to the streets in powerful demonstrations against the increasingly repressive government.

Park was assassinated by the Korean Central Intelligence Agency, and a short period of democracy followed. In 1980, however, another military coup placed the Republic of Korea in the hands of dictator Chun Doo Hwan (1931–). Under his ironfisted government, spectacular economic strides were made in Korea, but freedom and democracy were lacking. The

South Korean public rose up against the rigid dictatorship. The Korean people wanted democracy, and a new constitution was drawn up in 1987, calling for a popular election for the president and five-year term limits. Roh Tae Woo was elected in 1988, but it was not until 1998 that former dissident Kim Dae Jung (1924–), the first South Korean president ever to be elected from the political opposition, brought some much-desired freedom and democracy to the country.

North Korea after the armistice

In the meantime, Kim Il Sung remained premier of the Democratic People's Republic of Korea (North Korea) and leader of the Workers' Party until his death in 1994. The nation never veered from its communist economy. (Communism advocates the elimination of private property. It is a system in which goods are owned by the community as a whole rather than by specific individuals and are available to all as needed.)

Tied to a rope, students arrested at an anti-government demonstration are led away by Republic of Korea Army soldiers in the riot-torn city of Kwangju, May 1980. *Reproduced by permission of the Corbis Corporation.*

The government revolved strictly around one man, its leader. Kim instituted a "cult of personality" in which he, the "great and glorious leader," was the center of adoration for all his people. His picture and statue were visible all over North Korea for this purpose. Free speech, the right to practice religion, and freedom of movement were almost nonexistent in his country. Outside of North Korea, knowledge of Kim's rule and his nation remain sketchy. After the war, North Korea returned to its position from previous centuries as the "Hermit Kingdom" (see Chapter 1). It held out against Western intrusion long after the other former communist nations opened their countries to world trade or diplomacy.

North Korea was faced with a monumental task in rebuilding its cities, factories, and facilities, which were frequently described as "rubble," after the war. With the help of the Soviet Union and China, the country succeeded in rapid reconstruction in the first ten years after the armistice. Its nationalized (owned by the state) industry was held up as a model among communist nations. Until the mid-1970s, it is believed that North Korea's gross national product (GNP; a measurement of the output of goods and services) was similar to South Korea's.

In 1994, Kim Il Sung died and his son Kim Jong Il (1942–) took his place as premier of North Korea. It was a difficult time to step into power. In the early 1990s, the Soviet Union and China, which had assisted North Korea to that time, withdrew necessary support. The North Korean economy collapsed. Problems with floods and collective farming added to the growing crisis. There was a dire food shortage and the nation faced widespread famine. From 1994 to 1998, between two to three million people died from starvation or from diseases due to hunger—as many North Koreans as were killed in the war.

At the end of the twentieth century, the two leaders of the Koreas, Kim Jong Il and Kim Dae Jung, began a new era of communication between the two estranged nations. They held meetings to try to relax tensions and arranged for a few Koreans to travel across the border to meet with relatives they had not seen or heard from in fifty years. South Koreans were anxious to send aid to North Korea when they learned of the famine. Although it was clear that the Korean people on both

sides of the border wanted reunification, the divisions set in 1945—when the 38th parallel was arbitrarily (randomly) carved across the peninsula—were too deeply entrenched for any short-range resolution.

The demilitarized zone (DMZ) remained at the turn of the century where negotiations left it in 1953, partly at the 38th parallel and partly just north of it. The armies of the two nations, greatly strengthened after years of military buildup, continued to face each other across the DMZ. Included in South Korea's military were thirty-seven thousand U.S. troops, the legacy of a fifty-year-old promise to Syngman Rhee to coerce him to accept the armistice.

Facing each other, a South Korean soldier and a North Korea soldier guard the demilitarized zone, circa 1996. *Reproduced by permission of the Corbis Corporation.*

Where to Learn More

Alexander, Bevin. *Korea: The First War We Lost.* New York: Hippocrene Books, 1986, revised edition, 2000.

Blair, Clay. *The Forgotten War: America in Korea, 1950–1953.* New York: Times Books, 1987.

Bailey, Sydney D. *The Korean Armistice.* London: Macmillan, 1992.

Eisenhower, Dwight D. *The Eisenhower Diaries.* Edited by Robert H. Ferrell. New York: W. W. Norton, 1981.

Goulden, Joseph C. *Korea: The Untold Story of the War.* New York: Times Books, 1982.

Paik Sun Yup. *From Pusan to Panmunjom: Wartime Memoirs of the Republic of Korea's First Four-Star General.* Dulles, VA: Brassey's, 1992.

Shinn, Bill. *The Forgotten War Remembered: Korea, 1950–1953; A War Correspondent's Notebook and Today's Danger in Korea.* Elizabeth, NJ: Hollym International, 1996.

Toland, John. *In Mortal Combat: Korea, 1950–1953.* New York: William Morrow, 1991.

Web sites

Savada, Andrea Matles, ed. "North Korea: A Country Study." The Federal Research Division, Library of Congress. [Online] http://lcweb2.loc.gov/frd/cs/kptoc.html (accessed on August 14, 2001).

Savada, Andrea Matles, and William Shaw, eds. "South Korea: A Country Study." The Federal Research Division, Library of Congress. [Online] http://lcweb2.loc.gov/frd/cs/krtoc.html (accessed on August 14, 2001).

Primary Sources

Otto F. Apel Jr., M.D.

MASH: An Army Surgeon in Korea
Published in 1998

When the war broke out in Korea on June 25, 1950, there were only two hundred doctors in the entire Far East Command, or the U.S. military in Japan, Guam, the Philippines, and Korea. In order to boost necessary medical services in the combat area, the U.S. Congress quickly passed the Doctors Draft Act, requiring all medical doctors under the age of fifty-one to register for military service. Otto F. Apel Jr. was twenty-eight years old and recently out of medical school when he received his draft notice.

Apel was shipped to Korea in the summer of 1951. He was assigned to the 8076th Mobile Army Surgical Hospital (MASH), supporting the Second, Seventh, and Twenty-fourth U.S. Infantry divisions and the Second and Sixth Republic of Korea (ROK; South Korea) divisions, along with elements of other divisions near Chunchon, which is near the 38th parallel, the dividing line between North and South Korea and the scene of heavy fighting. What he found when he got there was beyond any of his worst expectations.

Personnel and equipment assembled at the headquarters of the 8225th Mobile Army Surgical Hospital in Korea in October 1951. *Reproduced by permission of Double Delta Industries, Inc.*

Things to remember while reading this excerpt from *MASH: An Army Surgeon in Korea:*

- The first MASH unit was created by the army in 1948 as a sixty-bed unit, fully equipped for surgery, that could be moved around with army units. Each unit was to have fourteen doctors, twelve nurses, two medical service corps officers, one warrant officer, and ninety-three enlisted personnel.

- There were no MASH units available in the Far East when the Korean War broke out. By the end of the war, there were six U.S., two South Korean, and one Norwegian MASH units in Korea.

- When a soldier was wounded at the battlefront, he was first attended on the spot by medics and doctors attached to his unit. If the wound was serious, he was evacuated (removed) to a MASH unit for surgery. After surgery and recovery, the soldier was evacuated to a larger hospital unit and if the wound was very serious, sent home from there.

- The use of emergency helicopter evacuation became an important part of the medical program in the Korean War for the first time.

- Casualties (the killed, wounded, missing, and captured) were so high in Korea that the MASH units, though understaffed, were made over from sixty-bed units to two-hundred-bed units within the first six months of the war.

Excerpt from MASH: An Army Surgeon in Korea

*I had never seen a MASH before. I thought I had an idea of what to expect, but even in the glaring midday sun I never would have recognized as a medical facility the **conglomeration** of dark brown tents, the sides down and tied, that appeared quickly in the field away from the dusty dirt road. I could hear in the distance an **artillery battery** limbering up. . . .*

[Although he had just traveled from Japan, Apel was shown directly into the surgical tent without a chance to see his quarters or wash up first.]

*The chief of surgery of the 8076th MASH was Maj. John Coleman, who had trained at the University of Louisville. He looked up from the operating table. Two nurses and another doctor surrounded a young American on a **litter**. They had attached an **intravenous** to his arm and covered him with a white sheet. One naked light bulb hung over the table. My first sensation upon entering the surgical tent was not the darkness or the smell of dirt and dust mixed with rubbing alcohol and soap. The sensation that crawled all over you was the stifling heat.*

"Scrub up," Major Coleman barked.

*He pointed with a **scalpel** toward the door, and I turned. A young African American private who served as an **orderly** took my coat and hat and said, "Follow me, Doctor."*

He took several steps to a five-gallon bucket that I had not seen when I entered. It was in a corner, and it was dark even in midday. No light entered the tent from the outside.

Conglomeration: A mix of very different things.

Artillery battery: A group of large, mounted firearms, such as rockets, guns, and howitzers, and the crews that fire them.

Litter: A stretcher or other device for carrying the sick and wounded.

Intravenous: A needle injected into a vein through which medicines or fluids can be delivered to a patient.

Scalpel: A thin-bladed knife used in surgery.

Orderly: An attendant in a hospital.

"Scrub up here. When you're ready to rinse, I'll pour the water through that bucket."

For the first time I noticed a second bucket hanging from a tent pole. It had holes punched in the bottom of it so that water could run through. I scrubbed, and the private poured the water, and I rinsed and put on a white surgical coat and hung the mask over my head.

The injured were brought in through one end of the surgery tent from a preparation area in the **pre-op** tent. They were brought on litters and placed on one of the three metal tube tables lined in the surgery tent. Each table had two doctors and two or three nurses clustered around it. Several enlisted personnel assisted the surgery by bringing supplies and necessities. Each of the wounded had been examined before he came in, and the nurse who brought him briefed us on the injuries.

The nurse knew her stuff. She wore olive drab army fatigue pants, boots bloused, and a white T-shirt. A surgical mask covered her face. She looked me over carefully.

"We're glad to have you aboard, Doctor," she said.

I nodded.

"We're way short of doctors."

A second nurse joined us, and we examined a young white soldier with a nasty sucking chest wound. My first thought was that he was younger than my younger brother. His close buzz cut made him look even younger. His eyes were closed and his face turned to the side as if he was peacefully asleep. His gasping chest heaved regularly, then sputtered. I probed momentarily and looked away to prepare for surgery.

"Get used to this," she said. "There's a lot more where he came from. . . ."

[Apel worked throughout the night and through the next morning, suffering badly from swollen ankles and feet, a sore back, and the stifling heat. Patient after patient was brought in.]

At noon the mess hall sent lunch to the five-gallon can. I do not remember what it was, but by that time it made no difference. We slugged it down and wished for more. None of us had showered, so we all smelled like billy goats. I could hardly keep my eyes open.

"Drink more coffee," Major Coleman said.

Pre-op: Short for preoperative, or before surgery.

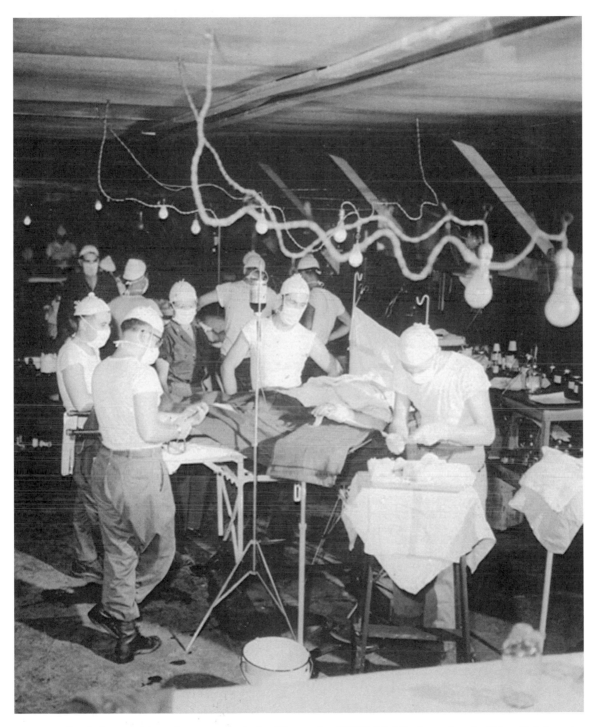

An operation being performed on a wounded soldier at the 8209th Mobile Army Surgical Hospital, twenty miles from the front lines in Korea, August 1952. *Reproduced by permission of Double Delta Industries, Inc.*

"When's our shift over?" I asked.

He smiled. "When the last litter comes through that tent flap back there."

I glanced at the tent flap that led to the pre-op tent.

He patted my shoulder. "That could be days from now."

"Are we it?"

"We're it," he said. "There are three surgeons here, and you see every one of them in this tent."

"We don't take a break?" I asked.

"If you need it," he said. "Sit down here by the five-gallon can. But remember, while you're napping there are men dying out there on litters waiting for you to get up from your nap.". . .

Eighty hours after my arrival at MASH 8076, Major Coleman came to my operating table. He was as worn as I was.

"That's it for now," he said. "Go get some sleep. Choi, the Korean boy, is outside, and he will take you to the officers' tent."

"What time is it?" I asked.

"I don't know," he said. "I don't wear a watch in surgery. The sweat ruins it."

"Is it day or night outside?"

"I don't know that either. It doesn't make any difference."

Both of us turned to go to the five-gallon can. As we stepped forward, we bumped into each other. Suddenly, we laughed.

"After you get some sleep, come to the headquarters tent. We have to get you in-processed."

The private took me by the arm and pulled me toward the five-gallon can. I could not have made it without him.

As I stepped through the tent flap, John Coleman said to me, "Welcome to the 8076th, Doctor." (Apel, pp. 21–23, 33, 42)

What happened next . . .

Apel served out his one-year term in the Korean War and returned home to his wife and three children. He was a surgeon in private practice for forty-four years.

By late 1951, the Korean War stopped moving: the battlefront remained at nearly the same spot until the war was over in the summer of 1953. There was no longer any need for the hospitals at the front to be mobile. The medical units were no longer technically "MASH" units, but everyone continued to use the term.

MASH units and the helicopter evacuations that had developed during the Korean War were to become a standard part of the medical operations in the war in Vietnam (1954–75).

At the turn of the twenty-first century, there was only one MASH unit left in the world, in Albania. The MASH unit that inspired the novel, movie, and TV show *M*A*S*H* was deactivated (shut down) in 2001. Replacing MASH units are smaller, more efficient medical units called "Forward Surgical Teams."

Did you know . . .

- The man who wrote the novel *MASH: A Novel about Three Doctors* under the pseudonym Richard Hooker was Captain H. Richard Hornberger, a doctor who served in the 8055th MASH. The novel was the basis of a later movie and the very popular TV show.

Where to Learn More

Apel, Otto F. Jr., M.D., and Pat Apel. *MASH: An Army Surgeon in Korea.* Lexington: The University Press of Kentucky, 1998.

Cowdrey, Albert E. *United States Army in the Korean War: Medic's War.* Washington, DC: United States Government Printing Office, September 1987.

Hooker, Richard. *MASH: A Novel about Three Army Doctors.* New York: William Morrow, 1968.

Keyes Beech

"Fire and Ice" from Tokyo and Points East
Published in 1954

Pulitzer prize-winning *Chicago Daily News* war correspondent Keyes Beech was an ever present figure during the Korean War (1950–53). His experience with Korea and the ways of war made him an outstanding observer of the battlefront and he had the nerve to be out there when it mattered. In his career as correspondent and as a veteran of World War II (1939–45), Beech had seen more than his share of shocking things; very little surprised him. But his description of the First Marine Division's conflict with the Chinese at the Chosin (Changjin) Reservoir in November and December 1950, one of the most ferocious battles of military history, shows that even a tough, battle-wise correspondent like him could be overwhelmed by the heroism and suffering that occurred there.

The worst Chosin fighting started in the village of Yudam on November 27, 1950. Beech arrived in Hagaru on December 4, where he met up with the Fifth Regiment of the First Marines and its commander, Lieutenant Colonel Raymond Murray, who had just come in from Yudam. Beech was stunned to learn that the marines, for the first time in history, were in retreat, and perhaps even more surprised when the

A bitter fight in the bitter cold: a U.S. Marine in Korea, December 1950. *Reproduced by permission of Double Delta Industries, Inc.*

commander admitted that, while fighting it out in Yudam, he had seriously doubted that he or his men would ever get out of there. At that time, although Murray tried repeatedly to relate the experience to Beech, he could not get any words out without choking on his tears. Beech recorded the story over the next couple of weeks from Murray and his men, parts of which comprise a chapter called "Fire and Ice" in his 1954 book *Tokyo and Points East.*

Things to remember while reading this excerpt from "Fire and Ice":

- Because the U.S. Marines were so highly esteemed, Chinese leader Mao Zedong (Mao Tse-tung; 1893–1976) sent massive forces to try to "annihilate" the First Marine Division at the beginning of the offensive. The Chinese were allied with the North Koreans.

- Although there had been a strong Chinese offensive only three weeks prior to the conflict at Chosin, United Nations forces commander General Douglas MacArthur (1880–1964) was issuing "end-of-the-war" statements about having the American troops "home-by-Christmas" as the marines moved into the Chosin Reservoir in November 1950.

Excerpt from "Fire and Ice," in Tokyo and Points East

[On November 27, Lieutenant Colonel Raymond Murray arrived at Yudam with the Fifth Regiment of the First marines Division; Colonel Litzenberg's Seventh Regiment was already there.]

Yudam lay in a valley about twenty-five hundred yards long. . . . As for Yudam, there wasn't much left of it. Most of the houses had been destroyed by artillery fire and only a few miserable Koreans remained. When the temperature dropped to 17 degrees below zero Marines learned to call Yudam the "Ice Bowl."

As night came snow began to fall. Packed into this picturesque little valley and ringing the silent mountains around it were ten thou-

2000: 8 P.M. military time.

Company: The basic army unit comprised of a headquarters and two or three platoons.

Infiltrated: Penetrated behind friendly lines.

mopped up: Cleared out of the area

Gooks: A degrading, offensive term used to mean people of Asian descent.

Casualties: Those killed, wounded, missing, or captured in battle.

Command post: The quarters where the commander of a unit exercised command.

Battalion: A battalion is usually made up of two or more companies led by a lieutenant colonel. Army and Marine Corps regiments during the Korean War followed the same system of designating their companies by a letter. In First Battalion, A, B, C were rifle companies, D was a weapons company. In Second Battalion, E, F, G were rifle companies, H was a weapons company, and so on. To avoid confusion, the letter designations became words: H Company was How Company, etc.

CP: Command post.

Hand grenades: Small explosive weapons that can be thrown.

sand Americans, a long way from home and, for Marines, a long way from salt water. What the Marines didn't know was that on the other side of the mountains lay thirty thousand Chinese.

For the moment, however, cold was a more deadly enemy than the Chinese. But at dusk a disquieting thing happened: one truck and two jeeps which had been ordered back to Hagaru were fired upon only a few hundred yards from Yudam. The two jeeps turned back, but the truck, too cumbersome to turn around in the narrow road, was abandoned.

The Chinese were closing their trap.

At **2000** Murray received word that Fox Company was under attack by an estimated **company** of Chinese. [Lieutenant Colonel] Hal Roise, a doggedly unspectacular man, told Murray the attack was nothing to be concerned about. A few Chinese had **infiltrated** Fox Company's position, but they were being **mopped up** and no assistance was required. One hour later Roise reported the attack ended and said Fox Company had "stacked up a lot of dead **gooks.**"

How [H] Company of the 7th, which was holding a hill that formed the north end of the valley, was hit next. How Company's **casualties** were so heavy that it was driven off the hill. Murray rang up Litzenberg, whose **command post** was four hundred yards away, and "Litz" said How Company was counterattacking to restore its position.

While the issue was in doubt as to who owned that hill, the 3rd **Battalion**, 5th, guarding the northeast rim of the valley, was struck with sudden and appalling ferocity. Literally pouring down the draws that led to the ridge line, the Chinese overran the 3rd Battalion command post. Lieutenant Colonel Robert D. Tapplitt's journal for that period read:

"Have lost ridge line north of my **CP**, George Company is attacking to regain ridge line. Item Company still in position. Have no wire communication. Switchboard knocked out.". . .

By now the whole valley was aflame. Having gained the ridge line, the Chinese were shooting directly down into the valley. In Taplitt's command post things were, to say the least, difficult. Taplitt stayed in his tent and ordered Major John J. Canney, his exec, to set up a defense line with command post personnel.

Four Chinese **hand grenades** ripped Taplitt's tent to shreds. Canney was killed instantly forty minutes after the fire fight began. Three

Chinese **burp guns** swept the command post area from the high ground above. When the fight ended two hours later there were six dead Chinese only twenty feet from where Taplitt stood and fifty more scattered around the CP perimeter. And George Company was sweeping back up to its lost ridge line killing Chinese right and left.

Captain Sam Jaskilka, **CO** of Easy Company, had thoughtfully set up a machine gun section at the bottom of a draw. The Chinese were only twenty yards away when the Marines spotted their white uniforms.

"Jesus Christ, they're coming down in droves," yelled Sam. "For Chrissakes somebody do something."

Evidently somebody "did" something. When daylight came there were three hundred Chinese dead lying in front of Easy and Fox Companies.

"Most of us were fighting without our shoes on," said Pfc. Philip A. Calvert. "We took 'em off when we got into our sleeping bags and they hit us so fast we didn't have time to put them back on."

"The Chinese were yelling . . . I don't know what the hell they were saying. Anyway we started yelling back. We yelled 'Gung ho! Long live the Marine Corps!' and kept on shooting. One kid was kind of surprised when a **Chink** hit him with his fist and broke his glasses. He hit the Chink back.

"They set up a heavy machine gun about twenty yards in front of us, but they never got a chance to fire it. We knocked it out with grenades. My **squad** leader got three of them before they got him, in the chest, and that's how I became squad leader.". . .

The order for the following day, November 28, was to continue the attack to the west. The order was not carried out. It had now become plain to the marine commanders that, far from carrying on their attack, they would do well to fight their way out. They didn't know that Radio Peking was itching to announce the destruction of the 1st Marine Division. But they did know they had been caught in a cleverly laid trap. . . .

For the next two days the Marines stayed where they were. Back at Hagaru, Lieutenant General Oliver P. Smith, the 1st Division's bony, white-haired commander, sat in a rocking chair in a bullet-riddled Korean hut and decided to disobey orders. His orders from General Almond, X Corps commander, were to continue the advance. But Smith didn't need to be hit on the head by the whole Chinese Army

Burp guns: Small submachines guns.

CO: Commanding officer.

Chink: A degrading, offensive term meaning Chinese.

Squad: A unit consisting of about twelve riflemen.

Frostbitten soldiers of the First Marine Division and the Seventh Infantry Division during the Korean War, 1952. *Reproduced by permission of Archive Photos, Inc.*

to know that the farther his men advanced the less their chance of returning. . . .

On November 30, the Litzenberg–Murray joint command got orders from division headquarters to begin the withdrawal to Hagaru eighteen miles away. . . .

As the Marines pulled out of Yudam, the Chinese came swarming into it. Many of them were without weapons. The Marines shot at them but the Chinese didn't return fire. They were more interested in scrounging for food and clothing. It was not until several days later that the Marines had the satisfaction of knowing the enemy was in worse shape than they were. . . .

In the meantime it had grown colder. It was so cold that men's feet froze to the bottom of their boots and the skin peeled off when the socks were removed; so cold that men had the feeling their faces would pop; so cold that men who might have died from loss of blood didn't die because the blood congealed and bleeding stopped.

"It was very strange to see blood freeze before it could **coagulate**," said Lieutenant Commander Chester M. Lessenden, regimental surgeon. "Coagulated blood is dark brown but this stuff was pinkish.". . .

The Marines left Yudam with six hundred casualties. En route to Hagaru, they acquired two or three hundred more. Transportation was dreadfully short and all the wounded who could walk walked. That, however, is a slight exaggeration, for some walked who could not. . . .

Seldom has the human frame been so savagely punished and continued to function. Many men discovered reserves of strength they never knew they possessed. . . .

> [After a desperate march out of Yudam, fighting the Chinese, the freezing temperatures, and a difficult terrain, the First Marines made their way to Hagaru, which had been secured by United Nations forces.]

To the men from Yudam, Hagaru had been a dim and distant goal which promised some **respite** from the unending Chinese attacks and the ever present cold that froze everything it touched, including their bodies, the bolts on their rifles, and their **rations**. To some of them Hagaru meant shoes, for many of them had been shoeless when attacked, warming their feet in their sleeping bags. . . .

For years to come, wherever marines gather, . . . the battle of Yudam and the breakthrough to the sea will be fought and refought. And any man who wasn't there will always be an outsider in the presence of those who were. I served at Tarawa and Iwo Jima, two of the fiercest battles of the **Pacific war,** but at neither of these places did I see such mass suffering as I witnessed and, to a small degree, shared in the snow-covered mountains of North Korea.

The **redoubtable** [commander of the First Regiment Colonel Lewis B.] "Chesty" Puller **admonished** me: "Remember, this was no retreat. We just found more Chinks behind us than in front of us, so we attacked in the opposite direction."

Whatever it was, retreat, defeat, or withdrawal, one thing can be said with certainty: in American military history there has never been anything to compare with it. (Beech, pp. 191–201)

Coagulate: To thicken into a mass or a clot.

Respite: Rest.

Rations: Food provision.

Pacific war: The part of World War II that was fought against Japanese forces in the Pacific Ocean area.

Redoubtable: Awe inspiring, or worthy of great respect.

Admonished: Reprimanded; scolded.

What happened next . . .

On December 11, 1950, a huge fleet of ships started a two-week evacuation of 105,000 troops from the port of Hungnam. Another 98,000 Korean civilians were also evacuated. North Korea was fully in the hands of the North Korean communists and remained so into the twenty-first century.

Did you know . . .

- Being at the front is a dangerous business. Fifteen war correspondents were killed in the Korean War, more than were killed in World War II. Many others were wounded and taken captive by the enemy.

Where to Learn More

Alexander, Bevin. *Korea: The First War We Lost.* New York: Hippocrene Books, 1986, revised edition, 2000.

Beech, Keyes. *Tokyo and Points East.* Garden City, NY: Doubleday, 1954.

Michener, James A. "Introduction," to *Tokyo and Points East,* by Keyes Beech. Garden City, NY: Doubleday, 1954.

Marguerite Higgins

"The Great Gamble at Inchon" from War in Korea:
The Report of a Woman Combat Correspondent
Published in 1951

Except for military nurses, there were few women from the United Nations countries in war-time Korea. Marguerite "Maggie" Higgins (1920–1965), the only female American war correspondent to cover the conflict, was probably the best-known exception. Higgins, an established journalist who had gained recognition covering the opening of the German death camps at the end of World War II (1939–45), had been assigned the post of Far East Bureau Chief for the *New York Herald Tribune* in Tokyo, Japan, in May 1950. When the war erupted in Korea, she was there to cover it within two days, and quickly became a familiar figure at the battlefront.

Higgins was not readily accepted in Korea. Within the first months of the war, General Walton H. "Johnnie" Walker (1899–1950), commander of the U.S. Eighth Army, issued orders for her to go home because he felt that Korea was no place for a woman. Later, General Douglas MacArthur (1880–1964), commander of the United Nations forces in Korea and Walker's superior, overruled him. But other military officials and even some of her colleagues were hostile to her. But Higgins was competitive and tough. She stood up to the

Marguerite Higgins interviews Douglas MacArthur in South Korea, June 1950. *Reproduced by permission of AP/Wide World Photos.*

dangers at the front and the extreme conditions that accompanied them as well or better than the other (male) correspondents. She worked hard to get her stories out and to be accepted as a journalist on equal terms with her colleagues. **Keyes Beech** (see entry), a correspondent for the *Chicago Daily News* who worked closely with Higgins, observed that, although she might never win a popularity contest, Higgins never stooped to giving the "woman's angle" that was expected of her. "In her quest for fame Higgins was appallingly single-minded, almost frightening in her determination to overcome all obstacles," he stated in his book *Tokyo and Points East.* "But so far as her trade was concerned she had more guts, more staying power, and more resourcefulness than 90 percent of her detractors. She was a good newspaperman."

In September 1950, learning that MacArthur was planning an amphibious assault (with coordinated air, land, and sea forces) behind enemy lines, Higgins quickly made arrangements to be on board a ship so she could cover the landing at the port city of Inchon. She met strong resistance from the naval officers, but managed to arrive on the beaches of Inchon along with the first waves of U.S. Marines. Braving the front as courageously as a seasoned soldier, Higgins may have found enemy fire a small obstacle compared to the restrictions placed upon her by the men on her own side.

Things to remember while reading this excerpt from *"The Great Gamble at Inchon"*:

- In the assault on Inchon on September 15, 1950, the United Nations forces were in their element, with naval and air power that far outstripped that of the North Koreans. Hundreds of ships and aircraft were deployed, engaging not only the skill of the U.S. Navy and air forces, but also those of Britain, Australia, New Zealand, Canada, and the Netherlands.

Excerpt from "The Great Gamble at Inchon," in War in Korea: The Report of a Woman Combat Correspondent

My request to go aboard an assault transport was greeted with about the same degree of horror as might have met a leper's request to share a bunk with the admiral. Navy tradition, I was told, was strictly anti-female, and of course there were no "facilities." (I later noted with some glee that the **flagship** *McKinley was fully equipped with a special ladies' room.)*

I gave Captain Duffy all my usual arguments: that women war correspondents were here to stay and the Navy might as well get used to them; that there were far more "facilities" on a ship than in the foxholes I'd been occupying; that it was not fair to deprive the New York Herald Tribune of coverage because I was a female. I might as well have been talking to myself. I was relegated to a hospital ship and told that I might not even be allowed to get off once the hospital ship reached the assault area. The prospect of wasting seven days on a ship and then not being certain of getting a story was discouraging to say the least.

But when I went to pick up my orders, Captain Duffy, apparently in a fit of absent-mindedness, handed me four neatly mimeographed sheets which announced that Miss Higgins could board "any navy ship." By the time I had grasped this wonderful switch, Captain Duffy was unavailable. . . .

[Higgins managed to get on a transport ship and had an uneventful four-day trip up to Inchon. On September 15, 1950, she and a couple of other correspondents were given instructions for landing with the soldiers on the as-yet-unsecured beaches in enemy territory.]

I was to go in the fifth wave to hit Red Beach. In our craft would be a mortar outfit, some riflemen, a photographer, John Davies of the Newark *Daily News, and Lionel Crane of the London* Daily Express. . . .

Flagship: The ship carrying the commander of the fleet; in this case General Douglas MacArthur's ship.

*Finally we [the fifth wave] pulled out of the circle and started toward the assault control ship, nine miles down the channel. It was an ear-shattering experience. We had to thread our way past the **carriers** and **cruisers** that were booming away at the beach, giving it a final deadly pounding. The quake and roar of the rocket ships was almost unendurable.*

After twenty minutes we rounded Wolmi Island—it looked as if a giant forest fire had just swept over it. Beyond was Red Beach. As we strained to see it more clearly, a rocket hit a round oil tower and big, ugly smoke rings billowed up. The dockside buildings were brilliant with flames. Through the haze it looked as though the whole city was burning.

Red Beach stretched out flatly directly behind the sea wall. Then after several hundred yards it rose sharply to form a cliff on the left side of the beach. Behind the cliff was a cemetery, one of our principal objectives.

*At the control ship we circled again, waiting for H hour. Suddenly the great naval barrage lifted and there was gigantic silence. Then the sky began to roar and the planes zoomed in, bombing and **strafing** the sea wall. It didn't seem possible that anything could survive the terrific hail of explosives.*

Silence again. Then H hour. The first wave pulled out of the circle and headed for the beach. There were only a few more minutes to wait. We all stared fixedly at the shore—about two thousand yards away—and tried to guess, from the expressions on the faces of the seamen returning from the beach in their empty boats, what it had been like.

The control ship signaled that it was our turn.

"Here we go—keep your heads down," shouted Lieutenant Shening.

*As we rushed toward the sea wall an amber-colored star shell burst above the beach. It meant that our first objective, the cemetery, had been taken. But before we could even begin to relax, brightly colored **tracer bullets** cut across our bow and across the open top of our boat. I heard the authoritative rattle of machine guns. Somehow the enemy had survived the terrible pounding they'd been getting. No matter what had happened to the first four waves, the Reds had sighted us and their aim was excellent. We all hunched deep into the boat. . . .*

Carriers: Aircraft carriers—huge ships that served as mobile bases for fighter planes.

Cruisers: General utility ships used as scouting vessels, leaders of groups of destroyers, and as guards for aircraft carriers.

Strafing: Machine-gun fire from low-flying planes.

Tracer bullets: Ammunition that leaves a trail of smoke or fire behind it.

Then our boat smashed hard into a dip in the sea wall. With the deadly crisscross of bullets whining above them, the marines involuntarily continued to crouch low in the boat.

"Come on, you big, brave marines—let's get the hell out of here," yelled Lieutenant Shening, emphasizing his words with good, hard shoves.

The first marines were now clambering out of the bow of the boat. The photographer announced that he had had enough and was going straight back to the transport with the boat. For a second I was tempted to go with him. Then a new burst of fire made me decide to get out of the boat fast. I maneuvered my typewriter into a position where I could reach it once I had dropped over the side. I got a footing on the steel ledge on the side of the boat and pushed myself over. I landed in about three feet of water in the dip of the sea wall.

A warning burst, probably a **grenade**, forced us all down, and we snaked along on our stomachs over the boulders to a sort of curve below the top of the dip. It gave us a cover of sorts from the tracer bullets, and we three newsmen and more of the marines flattened out and waited there. As we waited, wave after wave of marines hit the beach, and soon there must have been sixty or more of us lying on our bellies in the small dip.

One marine ventured over the ridge, but he jumped back so hurriedly that he stamped one foot hard onto my bottom. This fortunately had considerable padding, but it did hurt, and I'm afraid I said somewhat snappishly, "Hey, it isn't as frantic as all that." He removed his foot hastily and apologized in a tone that indicated his amazement that he had been walking on a woman. I think he was the only marine who recognized me as a woman—my helmet and overcoat were good camouflage.

The sun began to set as we lay there. The yellow glow that it cast over the green-clad marines produced a technicolor splendor that Hollywood could not have matched. In fact, the strange sunset, combined with the crimson haze of the flaming docks, was so spectacular that a movie audience would have considered it overdone.

Suddenly there was a great surge of water. A huge **LST** was bearing down on us, its plank door halfway down. A few more feet and we would be smashed. Everyone started shouting and, tracer bullets or no, we got out of there. Two marines in the back were caught and their feet badly crushed before they could be yanked to safety.

Grenade: A small explosive weapon that can be thrown, usually with a pin that was pulled to activate it and a spring-loaded safety lever that was held down until the user wanted to throw the it; once the safety lever is released, a grenade will explode in seconds.

LST: Tank Landing Ship: a huge craft with a large hold called a "tank deck" that opened out with a ramp to the beach, used for landing troops, vehicles, and other cargo onto enemy shores.

Troops of the Thirty-first Infantry Regiment land at Inchon Harbor, South Korea, aboard LSTs, tank landing ships, September 18, 1950. *Reproduced by permission of Double Delta Industries, Inc.*

Davies, Crane, and I vaulted the trenches on the other side of the sea wall and ran some twenty yards across the beach. There we found a mound, only about fifteen feet high, but it gave us some protection from the bullets. In the half-dark, marines started zigzagging toward the cliff on our left, and we had an anguished view of a half dozen of them hurled to the ground by tracer bullets.

There was another terrible moment when one of the LSTs mistook some men on the top of the cliff for the enemy and began banging rockets at them. They were marines who had seized the objective only minutes before. Frantic shouts and waves from the beach finally put a stop to it, but not before a number of our men had been hit.

Six LSTs were now at the beach with their planks down. Despite the **intermittent** *fire, they had to be unloaded. A marine colonel spotted our little group by the mound and yelled, "Hey, you big, brave marines by that mound—get the hell over here and start unloading." When we hesitated he rushed over, grabbed me by my coat lapels, and started pushing me toward the LST. I said that I'd be very glad to help if he wanted me to. When he heard my voice he dropped me hastily and very pleasantly allowed that it would undoubtedly be better if Davies, Crane, and I tended to our regular duties. I greatly admired the will and courage with which this particular marine colonel rallied his men to unload the ships in spite of severe fire. . . .*

> *[That night, as always, Higgins was attempting to find a way to write and then send out her story on the Inchon landing. She and the other correspondents boarded an LST, but found that its radio communications had broken down, so they flagged down a boat headed for the flagship McKinley, where they were promptly told they were not wanted. They boarded anyway. While the male journalists were made comfortable, Higgins was put through hours of questioning by an angry captain. They allowed her one night on the ship and she got the story out.]*

After that night Admiral Doyle decreed that ladies would be allowed on board the McKinley *only between 9 A.M. and 9 P.M. . . . As usual, my protests did no good.*

From then on I slept on the docks or at the front with the troops. This was no better or no worse than what I'd grown used to in the summer war, and I didn't complain. Still, when Keyes and the rest would leave me on the docks to go out to their warm showers and real scrambled eggs, I won't pretend that I blessed the Navy. (Higgins, pp. 136–37, 141–46, 149–50)

Intermittent: Coming and going; coming at intervals.

What happened next . . .

Marguerite Higgins won the Pulitzer Prize in 1951 for her coverage of the Korean War, and several other prestigious awards as well. Her book *War in Korea: The Report of a Woman Combat Correspondent* became a best-seller.

Inchon marked a major turning point in the war. After securing Inchon, the X Corps went on to recapture Seoul, the capital city of South Korea. The Eighth Army broke out of the Pusan Perimeter in the south of the peninsula and the combined UN forces overpowered the North Koreans and crossed the 38th parallel, the border between North and South Korea.

Did you know . . .

- During World War II (1939–1945), there were 127 female war correspondents accredited by the army. During the U.S. involvement in the war in Vietnam (1965–73), 467 women correspondents, including 267 Americans, covered the front.

- Marguerite Higgins was the only female war correspondent to cover the front in the Korean War.

Where to Learn More

Beech, Keyes. *Tokyo and Points East.* Garden City, NY: Doubleday, 1954.

Higgins, Marguerite. *War in Korea: The Report of a Woman Combat Correspondent.* Garden City, NY: Doubleday, 1951, pp. 135–50.

Toland, John. *In Mortal Combat: Korea, 1950–1953.* New York: William Morrow, 1991.

Kim Il Sung

"What Should We Do and How Should We Work This Year?"
Speech delivered on January 12, 1948; published in 1980

Kim Il Sung (1912–1994) became involved in the anti-Japanese struggle in Korea when he was still a boy. In 1910, two years before Kim's birth, Japan had annexed Korea. They had incorporated the country into Japan with the help of a very weak Korean monarch whom they had helped to the throne, and ruled it with an iron fist for the next four decades. Kim was an important member of the small Korean movement that helped the Chinese Communists fight the Japanese when they likewise occupied Manchuria, in northeast China, in the 1930s. In 1941, when the Japanese defeated the guerrilla movement or warriors who fought the Japanese with surprise attacks, Kim escaped to the Soviet Union, where he joined the Soviet Army. When the Soviets briefly occupied northern Korea in 1945 as part of the peace treaty ending World War II (the Americans occupied southern Korea), Kim Il Sung returned to his native land and immediately joined in the new governing People's Committees.

Kim Il Sung became the premier of the new People's Democratic Republic of Korea (North Korea) in 1948, not long after he delivered his "What Should We Do?" speech. In his first days as leader in the newly divided Korea, he was success-

A cartoon, circa 1904, of Japan marching across the back of Korea en route to Russia. Korean liberation from Japan in 1945, however, was followed by war. *Reproduced by permission of the Corbis Corporation.*

ful in building up the newly nationalized (government-owned) northern Korean industry. He relied strongly on aid from the Soviets and was very careful in his relations with China as well, but from the start he strove to maintain a separate Korean identity and government.

Things to remember while reading this excerpt from "What Should We Do and How Should We Work This Year?":

- Kim developed his own theory of communism called *juche,* a word meaning self-determination or self-reliance. Juche is Kim's attempt to adapt the communist principles of German philosopher Karl Marx (1818–1883) and Russian Communist leader Vladimir Lenin (1870–1924) to Korean society. It stresses developing a state-run economy with little help from outside nations. It also stresses the uniqueness of Korea's culture and history.

- Kim created a "cult of personality" in Korea, in which the one leader, himself, was revered almost as a god. Throughout his forty-six-year dictatorship, Kim was called "Great Leader" and his image was posted everywhere in North Korea. In order to maintain a strong position, he had to be a master of charisma (an almost magical power of appealing to people) and propaganda (information and ideas that are spread to further a cause, regardless of the truth).

Excerpt from "What Should We Do and How Should We Work This Year?"

*As you know well, what a cruel rule the Japanese **imperialists** bore over Korea! They oppressed the Korean people at will and robbed them of everything as they pleased, tried to **obliterate** the history of our country and **exterminate** our culture and our language and, to top it all, went so far as to force the Korean people to change their surnames, **desecrating** our ancestors. And they deprived the Koreans of the opportunities for education and prevented them from learning science and technology. An ordinary nation would probably have perished forever in the face of such persecution and oppression.*

*The Korean people, however, did not give in, they carefully preserved the history of their country and their national **sagacity**, loved their culture and did not abandon their language. The Koreans . . . fought through all difficulties for the day of our national **regeneration**. That is why our people set about building a genuinely independent and democratic state in north Korea without the slightest confusion from the first days of liberation. . . .*

*As they were driven out of Korea, the Japanese imperialists declared cynically that without them Korea's industry and transport would all be paralyzed. But we soon started operating factories and set trains running. . . . Big factories and enterprises such as the Hungnam Fertilizer Factory, Nampo Smeltery, Hwanghae Iron Works, Songjin Steel Plant and Supung Hydroelectric Power Station have been **rehabilitated** and are in normal operation, and all of them fulfilled their plans brilliantly last year. . . .*

Imperialists: Those who govern by forcibly imposing their rule over another country or territory.

Obliterate: Remove from existence; get rid of.

Exterminate: Kill off, or get rid of completely.

Desecrate: To treat disrespectfully or to violate the sanctity of.

Sagacity: Wisdom.

Regeneration: Renewal; the restoration of Korean independence.

Rehabilitated: Restored to the way they once were.

*The **reactionaries** mocked at our plan as an idle dream which would never be realized, and among us, too, there were some who were distrustful of the plan. But our people, displaying a high degree of patriotic zeal and creative activity, have creditably accomplished the things they once chose to. This is the strongest answer and counterblow to the US imperialists including **Hoover** and their **lackeys** who prattled that the Korean people should be placed under an **international trusteeship** for 25 years because they were incapable of self-government. This has convinced us more deeply, and **imbued** us with boundless national pride, that the Korean nation is a nation of superb ability, that no aggressor can ever conquer our nation again and our nation is able not only to attain independence but also to build a rich and strong, advanced democratic Korea. . . .*

*In a little more than two years following liberation . . . the Korean people were awakened and **tempered**, their strength grew incomparably and our national sense of dignity and power rose higher than ever before. The pride and self-respect of our nation which had been repressed and trampled down under the long Japanese imperialist colonial rule, began to revive and unfurled their wings and soared higher with each passing day in the struggle to create a new life after liberation. This is the most precious thing, which cannot be got for money nor can it be exchanged for any other things. This is a sure guarantee for our nation to grow stronger and our country to prosper and develop further in the future. . . .*

*Our nation can never again be reduced to a humiliating status as before. Our nation has already got out of that status completely and is waging an **indomitable** struggle for the independence, **sovereignty** and prosperity of the country. . . .*

*But the situation in south Korea is totally different. The rulers of dependencies who even fail to act as masters of their own countries but work for foreigners have been brought into south Korea by the US imperialists, and are now clamouring that they are going to make our Korea "independent." They are none other than the so-called "**UN** Temporary Commission on Korea." What on earth are they going to do in Korea, those fellows who are unable to run the affairs of their own countries properly and held in bondage to others, while driving their own peoples into a wretched plight?*

Today the Korean question can be solved only by the Koreans, and no one but the Korean people has the competence and right to solve it. It is much less possible for such a gang as the "UN Temporary Commission on Korea" to solve the Korean question. It is neither

the United States nor India nor Syria, but only the Korean people themselves that can solve the Korean question. . . .

Today the liberated people of north Korea are enjoying a happy and worthy life, and our livelihood is becoming more affluent every day. But we cannot forget even for a moment the cruel reality that half of our land of 3,000 **ri** is seized by the US imperialists and that our fellow countrymen and brothers, who are of the same ancestral blood as we are, groan under oppression and suffer from hunger. Under these circumstances it is natural that the north Korean people should feel deep sympathy for the bloody struggle of their south Korean brothers and extend them most enthusiastic encouragement. (Kim, pp.129–33, 135)

The verdant Korean countryside during rice-planting season, 1947. For decades following the Korean War, North Korea enjoyed greater prosperity than South Korea.
Reproduced by permission of AP/Wide World Photos.

Ri: Villages.

What happened next . . .

In 1948, when the United Nations Temporary Commission on Korea (UNTCOK) arrived in Korea to set up elections, after which Korea was to be an independent nation, Kim Il Sung and Soviet officials refused to let them enter northern Korea, claiming that the United Nations, of which Korea was not a member, had no authority to set up Korean elections. In southern Korea, too, there were great objections to the elections; many South Koreans of all political parties who were not directly tied to the now powerful leader Syngman Rhee (1875–1965) planned to boycott (refusal to participate in). In April 1948, a seven-day conference was held in Pyongyang in northern Korea with delegates from fifty-six northern and southern Korean political organizations and parties, including some of the most prominent southern Korean leaders. All parties quickly agreed to oppose the UNTCOK elections and the resulting creation of a separate South Korea. When elections proceeded and Rhee and his allies had won, several top South Korean leaders migrated to North Korea in disgust.

A second Pyongyang conference was held at the end of June, in which elections for a Korean government were set up—since they did not recognize the UN elections or the government they created in South Korea—to be held August 25 in the north, with underground votes for people in the south. In this election, the People's Democratic Republic of Korea (North Korea) was established with Kim Il Sung as the premier. Both governments claimed rule over all of Korea, and Korea was effectively divided into two nations. Rhee's rule in South Korea would last until 1960. Kim Il Sung remained the leader of North Korea until his death in 1994.

Did you know . . .

- At the turn of the twenty-first century, North Korea was one of the most hard-line Stalinist (following the authoritarian communism of Soviet Premier Joseph Stalin [1879–1953]) systems remaining in the communist world. The government remained committed to state control of the economy, and continued to launch great propaganda campaigns and to harshly suppress opposition. A major human rights report in 1989 documented the existence of thousands of political prisoners in North Korea.

Where to Learn More

Deane, Hugh. *The Korea War: 1945–1953*. San Francisco: China Books, 1999.

Kim Il Sung. *On Juche in Our Revolution*. Pyongyang, North Korea: Foreign Languages Publishing House, 1980.

Web sites

"Profile: Kim Il Sung." CNN Cold War. [Online] http://clinton. cnn.com/ SPECIALS/cold.war/kbank/profiles/kim/ (accessed on August 14, 2001).

Douglas MacArthur

"Address to Congress"
Delivered April 19, 1951

In the last weeks of March 1951, the Truman administration developed plans to negotiate with the Chinese and North Koreans to bring an end to the Korean War (1950–53). To their dismay, before they could draft their offer to the communists, Douglas MacArthur (1880–1964), commander of the U.S. forces in the Far East—who knew of the president's plans—foiled the negotiations with a public statement threatening the communists with all-out war on their own land. MacArthur wanted a complete victory in Korea and did not seem able to cooperate with the administration's effort at limited warfare accompanied by negotiation. Because this was not the only instance of MacArthur's failure to play by the rules, most of President Harry S. Truman's (1884–1972) advisers believed he could not be relied on to carry out the administration's orders. Truman decided that the seventy-plus year-old general must be relieved of command. MacArthur was informed of this on April 11, 1951.

To many, MacArthur was a hero of almost godlike proportions. When he left his headquaters in Tokyo, Japan, to return to the United States after being fired, there were crowds of Japanese people lining the roads to say goodbye. When he

Douglas MacArthur delivers his farewell address to a joint session of Congress, April 19, 1951. *Reproduced by permission of the National Archives and Records Administration.*

reached Hawaii, a huge, forty-mile parade was organized in his honor. Thousands of adoring fans met him when he arrived in San Francisco, California. Many newspapers attacked Truman and his administration for firing MacArthur. Immediately after the general's return, some of Truman's Republican opponents in the U.S. Congress began to talk about the possibility of impeaching the president (reprimanding him, and possibly removing him from office). After some debate, Congress invited MacArthur to speak about the Truman administration's Far East policy. He was received in Washington, D.C., on April 19, 1951, with full military honors (per Truman's instructions), and there he presented a televised speech to Congress outlining his views on the Korean War, part of which follows.

Things to remember while reading this excerpt from MacArthur's Address to Congress:

- More than five hundred thousand people showed up to greet MacArthur in Washington, D.C. His speech was interrupted more than fifty times with applause and cheering from the public galleries.

- The actual Senate hearings in which MacArthur was given a forum to contest the Truman administration's Far East policies did not occur until May 1951.

- Douglas MacArthur made two unsuccessful attempts at the Republican nomination for U.S. president, in 1948 and 1952.

- Communism is a set of political beliefs that advocates the elimination of private property. It is a system in which goods are owned by the community as a whole rather than by specific individuals and are available to all as needed. It is fundamentally at odds with the American economic system of capitalism, in which individuals rather than the state own the property and businesses.

Excerpt from MacArthur's Address to Congress, April 19, 1951

*While I was not consulted prior to the President's decision to intervene in support of the **Republic of Korea**, that decision from a military standpoint, proved a sound one. As I said, it proved to be a sound one, as we hurled back the invader and **decimated** his forces. Our victory was complete, and our objectives within reach, when **Red China** intervened with numerically superior ground forces.*

*This created a new war and an entirely new situation, a situation not contemplated when our forces were committed against the North Korean invaders; a situation which called for new decisions in the **diplomatic sphere** to permit the realistic adjustment of military strategy. Such decisions have not been forthcoming.*

While no man in his right mind would advocate sending our ground forces into continental China, and such was never given a thought, the new situation did urgently demand a drastic revision of strategic planning if our political aim was to defeat this new enemy as we had defeated the old one.

Republic of Korea: South Korea, with whom the United States was allied against North Korea and China.

Decimate: To destroy a large part of; annihilate.

Red China: Communist China.

Diplomatic sphere: In the hands of those who are appointed or elected to handle the dealings between nations.

*Apart from the military need, as I saw it, to neutralize **sanctuary protection** given the enemy north of the Yalu, I felt that military necessity in the conduct of the war made necessary (1) the intensification of our economic blockade against China, (2) the imposition of a naval blockade against the China coast, (3) removal of restrictions on air **reconnaissance** of China's coastal area and of Manchuria, (4) removal of restrictions on the forces of the Republic of China on Formosa [Taiwan], with **logistical support** to contribute to their effective operations against the Chinese mainland.*

*For entertaining these views, all professionally designed to support our forces in Korea and to bring hostilities to an end with the least possible delay and at a saving of countless American and allied lives, I have been severely criticized in **lay circles**, principally abroad, despite my understanding that from a military standpoint the above views have been fully shared in the past by practically every military leader concerned with the Korean campaign, including our own **Joint Chiefs of Staff**.*

*I called for reinforcements, but was informed that reinforcements were not available. I made clear that if not permitted to destroy the enemy built-up bases north of the Yalu, if not permitted to utilize the friendly Chinese force of some 600,000 men in Formosa, if not permitted to blockade the China coast to prevent the Chinese Reds from getting **succor** from without, and if there was to be no hope of major reinforcements, the position of the command from the military standpoint forbade victory.*

*We could hold in Korea by constant maneuver and in an approximate area where our supply line advantages were in balance with the supply line disadvantages of the enemy, but we could hope at best for only an indecisive campaign with its terrible and constant **attrition** upon our forces if the enemy utilized its full military potential.*

I have constantly called for the new political decisions essential to a solution.

*Efforts have been made to distort my position. It has been said in effect that I was a **war-monger**. Nothing could be further from the truth. I know war as few other men now living know it, and nothing to me—and nothing to me is more revolting. I have long advocated its complete abolition, as its very destructiveness on both friend and foe has rendered it useless as a means of settling international disputes. . . .*

But once war is forced upon us, there is no other alternative than to apply every available means to bring it to a swift end. War's very object is victory, not prolonged indecision.

In war there can be no substitute for victory.

There are some who for varying reasons would **appease** *Red China. They are blind to history's clear lesson, for history teaches with unmistakable emphasis that appeasement but* **begets** *new and bloodier wars. It points to no single instance where this end has justified that means, where appeasement has led to more than a* **sham** *peace. Like* **blackmail,** *it lays the basis for new and successively greater demands until, as in blackmail, violence becomes the only other alternative. Why, my soldiers asked me, surrender military advantages to an enemy in the field? I could not answer.*

Some may say to avoid spread of the conflict into an all-out war with China. Others, to avoid Soviet intervention. Neither explanation seems valid, for China is already engaging with the maximum power it can commit, and the Soviet will not necessarily mesh its actions with our moves. . . .

The tragedy of Korea is further heightened by the fact that its military action was confined to its territorial limits. It condemns that nation, which it is our purpose to save, to suffer the devastating impact of full naval and air bombardment while the enemy's sanctuaries are fully protected from such attack and devastation.

Of the nations of the world, Korea alone, up to now, is the sole one which has risked its all against **communism** *The magnificence of the courage and* **fortitude** *of the Korean people defies description. They have chosen to risk death rather than slavery. Their last words to me were "Don't scuttle the Pacific." I have just left your fighting sons in Korea. They have done their best there, and I can report to you without reservation that they are splendid in every way.*

It was my constant effort to preserve them and end this savage conflict honorably and with the least loss of time and a minimum sacrifice of life. Its growing bloodshed has caused me the deepest anguish and anxiety. Those gallant men will remain often in my thoughts and in my prayers always.

I am closing my 52 years of military service. When I joined the Army, even before the turn of the century, it was the fulfillment of all my boyish hopes and dreams. The world has turned over many times since I took the oath at **West Point,** *and the hopes and dreams have*

Appease: Conciliate; to make agreeable.

Begets: Bears; brings about.

Sham: False; fake.

Blackmail: Forcing a person to do something (pay money, change a position) under the threat of exposing a wrongdoing committed by that person.

Communism: An economic system that does not include the concept of private property. Instead, the public (usually represented by the government) owns the goods and the means to produce them in common.

Fortitude: Determination.

West Point: A U.S. military academy.

Douglas MacArthur was well loved in Japan. Here, a painter puts the finishing touches on a sign in front of a Tokyo business wishing MacArthur good luck in the upcoming U.S. presidential election, March 1948.
Reproduced by permission of the Corbis Corporation.

all since vanished, but I still remember the refrain of one of the most popular barracks ballads of that day which proclaimed most proudly that old soldiers never die; they just fade away. And like the old soldier of that ballad, I now close my military career and just fade away, an old soldier who tried to do his duty as God gave him the light to see that duty. Good bye.

What happened next . . .

Joseph C. Goulden, in *Korea: The Untold Story of the War*, sums up the impact of MacArthur's speech, noting that it is full of "factual and logical holes" but that "his performance ranked as one of the more powerful political experiences of the mid-twentieth century. Many congressmen wept openly as he finished; so, too, did men and women around the country who heard and saw the speech on radio and television."

MacArthur left Washington, D.C., for New York, where he was greeted by a jubilant nineteen-mile parade through Manhattan attended by an estimated 7.5 million people.

General Matthew B. Ridgway (1895–1993) took over MacArthur's Far East Command and held a defensive line near the 38th parallel, the dividing line between North and South Korea. Truce negotiations with the communist forces began in July 1951.

Did you know . . .

- According to author James Michener, who was a war correspondent in Korea, the press played a big part in stirring up the public in favor of MacArthur and against Truman: "One radio man had to interview seventeen soldiers before he got one who would allow his voice to break and ask pathetically why they were doing this to his general. What the other sixteen said would have made better—but unwanted—stories."

Where to Learn More

Goulden, Joseph C. *Korea: The Untold Story of the War.* New York: Times Books, 1982.

Michener, James A. "Introduction," to *Tokyo and Points East,* by Keyes Beech. Garden City, NY: Doubleday, 1954.

Web sites

"AP Stenographic Transcript of General MacArthur's Address to Congress, April 19, 1951, as Checked Against Official Record." Harry S. Truman Library, Student Research File, B File, Korean War Dismissal of General Douglas MacArthur, President's Secretary's Files. [Online] http://www.theforgottenvictory.org/macarthur.htm (accessed on August 14, 2001).

Mao Zedong

"Nuclear Weapons Are Paper Tigers" from "Talk with the American Correspondent Anna Louise Strong"

Interview held in August 1946; text published in Beijing in 1961 and in the United States in 1969

In 1927, Chinese leader Chiang Kai-shek (1887–1975) started a military offensive in an attempt to reunite the country under his rule. At that time, China was fragmented and in the hands of hundreds of warlords, local military governors who wrested control of parts of the country since no central government was in power. In Chiang's offensive to take control, he allied with the communists, a rapidly growing movement in China at the time. (Communists believe that private property should be eliminated, that goods and the means of their production should be owned by the community as a whole rather than by specific individuals and should be available to all as needed.) After the communists helped Chiang's troops to capture Shanghai, the troops turned around and massacred the communists, killing as many as three quarters of the group. After that, Chiang Kai-shek and his Nationalist forces worked for decades to eliminate communists in China.

Mao Zedong (Mao Tse-tung; 1893–1976), one of the survivors, helped to assemble a small group of communists in central China that rapidly grew into a formidable force. Also in the Red Army, as the communist forces were called, from these

Mao Zedong (center) greets a group of his army officers in Beijing, the capital of the newly founded People's Republic of China, September 1949.

Reproduced by permission of AP/Wide World Photos.

early days were Peng Dehuai (P'eng Teh-huai; 1898–1974), the future leader of Communist Chinese forces in the Korean War (1950–53), and Zhou Enlai (Chou En-lai; 1898–1976), the future premier and foreign minister of Communist China. In 1934, a successful offensive by Chiang's army forced the communists to flee, resulting in the one-year, eight-thousand-mile, combat-ridden Long March. At the end of it, a communist force of about ten thousand men settled in a new base. Mao Zedong was the clear leader. Chiang continued to make unsuccessful efforts to eliminate the communists, but in the 1930s Japan began to occupy more and more of China, and for a time the communists actually allied with Chiang's Nationalist army to fight the mutual enemy.

When World War II drew to a close in 1945, the Chinese Communists and the Chinese Nationalists resumed the conflict for rule. The United States backed Chiang Kai-shek. When he made his "paper tiger" statement in 1946, Mao Zedong was facing an opponent (the United States) that had recently dropped atomic bombs on two Japanese cities, killing hundreds of thousands of civilians.

After decades of occupation and civil war, China did not have the technology or resources that other large nations had. Instead, Mao is saying in the paper tiger statement that a Communist China would have the true source of power: the will of the people. Another more grisly aspect of Mao's tough stance toward the possible atomic bombing of China is his attitude that the huge death toll would not hurt China. China, with its great population, could endure.

Things to remember while reading this excerpt from "Nuclear Weapons Are Paper Tigers":

- Mao Zedong wrote many books about politics and on warfare. In *On Protracted War* he theorized that a weak army could conquer a strong one if the people who were fighting believed in their cause.

Excerpt from "Nuclear Weapons Are Paper Tigers," in "Talk with the American Correspondent Anna Louise Strong"

*The atom bomb is a **paper tiger** which the U.S. **reactionaries** use to scare people. It looks terrible, but in fact it isn't. Of course, the **atom bomb** is a weapon of mass slaughter, but the outcome of a war is decided by the people, not by one or two new types of weapon.*

*All reactionaries are paper tigers. In appearance, the reactionaries are terrifying, but in reality they are not so powerful. From a long-term point of view, it is not the reactionaries but the people who are really powerful. In Russia, before the **February Revolution** in 1917, which side was really strong? On the surface the **tsar** was strong but he was swept away by a single gust of wind in the February Revolution. In the final analysis, the strength in Russia was on the side of the **Soviets** of Workers, Peasants and Soldiers. The tsar was just a paper*

Paper tiger: Something that appears to be dangerous or threatening but upon close examination is not.

Reactionaries: People who distrust any kind of social or political change; here, meaning people who do not believe in the communist revolution.

Atom bomb: A powerful bomb created by splitting the nuclei of a heavy chemical that results in a violent and destructive shock wave as well as radiation.

February Revolution: The first of the Russian revolutions of 1917, in which people rebelled because of food shortages and other miseries, leading to the abdication (stepping down) of the tsar.

Tsar: The Russian emperor or ruler.

Soviets: Councils.

Hitler: Adolf Hitler (1889–1945), leader of Germany from 1933 to 1945.

Mussolini: Benito Mussolini (1883–1945), dictator of Italy from 1922 to 1945.

Imperialism: Governing by forcibly imposing one country's rule over another country or territory.

Chiang Kai-shek: (1887–1975) leader of the anticommunist Nationalist Chinese.

millet: Grain.

Reaction: Resistance to progress.

tiger. Wasn't **Hitler** once considered very strong? But history proved that he was a paper tiger. So was **Mussolini,** so was Japanese **imperialism.** On the contrary, the strength of the Soviet Union and of the people in all countries who loved democracy and freedom proved much greater than had been foreseen.

Chiang Kai-shek and his supporters, the U.S. reactionaries, are all paper tigers too. Speaking of the U.S. imperialism, people seem to feel that it is terrifically strong. Chinese reactionaries are using the "strength" of the United States to frighten the Chinese people. But it will be proved that the U.S. reactionaries, like all the reactionaries in history, do not have much strength. In the United States there are others who are really strong—the American people.

Take the case of China. We have only **millet** plus rifles to rely on, but history will finally prove that our millet plus rifles is more powerful than Chiang Kai-shek's aeroplanes plus tanks. Although the Chinese people still face many difficulties and will long suffer hardships from the joint attacks of U.S. imperialism and the Chinese reactionaries, the day will come when these reactionaries are defeated and we are victorious. The reason is simply this: the reactionaries represent **reaction,** we represent progress. (Mao, pp. 100–01)

What happened next . . .

Mao Zedong and the Communists drove the Nationalists to the island of Taiwan (formerly Formosa) off of mainland China in 1949 and proclaimed the People's Republic of China. When the war broke out in Korea less than a year later, Mao watched with concern. Although China was terribly depleted from years of war, he believed that the North Koreans should be supported in their efforts. As the United Nations forces, supporting South Korea, raced north after the successful Inchon landing in September 1950, Communist China gave repeated warnings to the Western powers that they would not sit by while American troops approached their border with North Korea. Along with trying to negotiate through the United

Nations, which did not recognize Communist China as a nation (they still recognized Chiang's Nationalists, though defeated in the Chinese Civil War), Mao was preparing his troops to enter the Korean War. In October 1950, the Chinese launched their first offensive.

The devastation wrought by the dropping of the atomic bomb on Nagasaki, Japan, August 1945. *Reproduced by permission of Archive Photos, Inc.*

Did you know . . .

- Many of the top generals of the Chinese army did not wish to enter the Korean War, fearing that U.S. technology and the atomic bomb would overpower their already weakened forces.

- The casualties for the Chinese army in the Korean War were estimated by the Joint Chiefs of Staff (the president's and the secretary of defense's war advisors) in 1953 to be 909,607: 401,401 killed, 486,995 wounded, and 21,211 missing. Some modern historians believe these figures are too high.

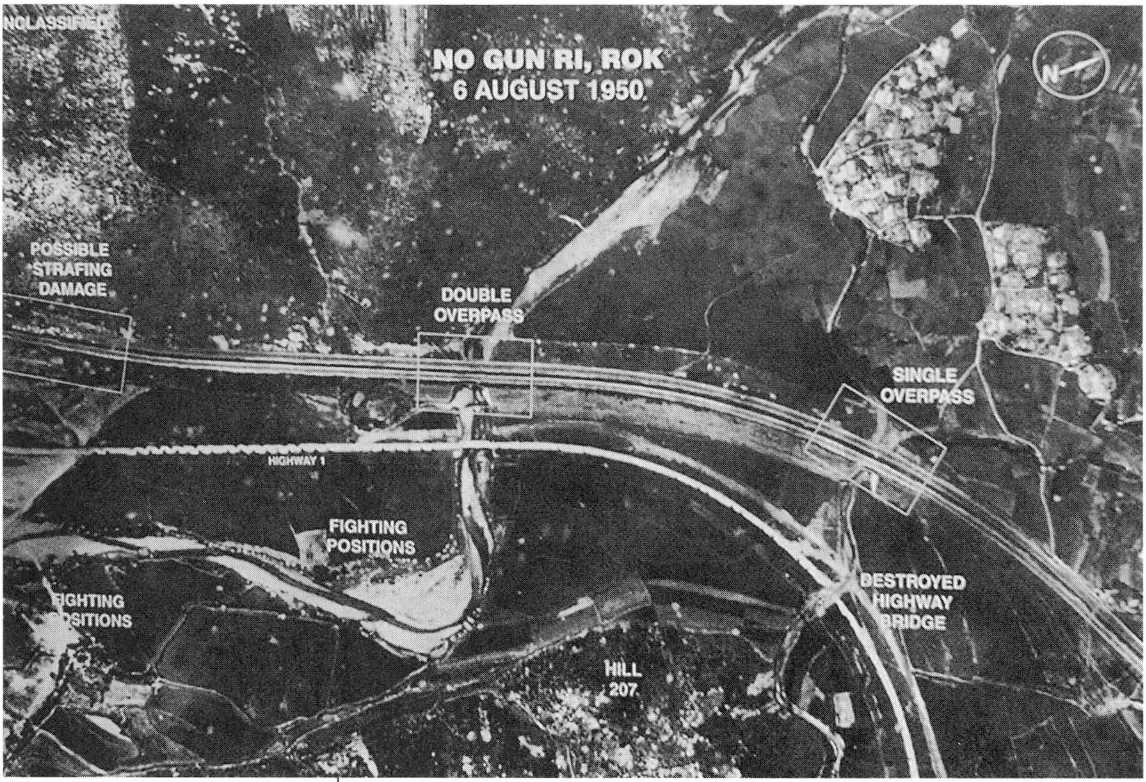

NO GUN RI, ROK
6 AUGUST 1950
POSSIBLE
STRAFING
DAMAGE
DOUBLE
OVERPASS
SINGLE
OVERPASS
HIGHWAY 1
FIGHTING
POSITIONS
DESTROYED
HIGHWAY
BRIDGE
HILL
207

This reconnaissance photo taken on August 6, 1950, shows the area of No Gun Ri, indicated by Korean witnesses as the site where U.S. forces killed South Korean civilians in July 1950. *Reproduced by permission of AP/Wide World Photos.*

National Archives, tracking down and then interviewing more than one hundred Korean War veterans, and reconstructing the unit movements of a First Cavalry battalion to prove that it was in fact at No Gun Ri at the time in question (which the U.S. Army had denied). The investigation provided substantial documentation supporting the survivors' accounts. For its report on No Gun Ri, the Associated Press won a Pulitzer Prize.

Things to remember while reading this excerpt of "Bridge at No Gun Ri: Survivors' Petition":

- Murder of civilians is against the laws and customs of war as expressed in the Articles of War, the military laws ruling the armed forces during the Korean War. Anyone who intentionally murders or rapes civilians during wartime is subject to the death penalty or life in prison.
- The Associated Press's search for eyewitnesses on the U.S. side was successful: "Six veterans of the 1st Cavalry Divi-

sion said they fired on the refugee throng at the South Korean hamlet of No Gun Ri, and six others said they witnessed the mass killing. More said they knew or heard about it. . . . Ex-GIs agreed on such elements as time and place, and on the preponderance of women, children and old men among the victims."

- The U.S. Army had noted at least one incident in which North Korean soldiers infiltrated into American lines of defense by posing as refugees, according to the Associated Press report. At the time of the No Gun Ri incident, the First Cavalry Division had issued the order: "No refugees to cross the front line. Fire everyone trying to cross lines. Use discretion in case of women and children."

Excerpt from "Bridge at No Gun Ri: Survivors' Petition"

Eun-yong Chung, Representative of Petitioners of No Gun Ri Incident

His Excellency Bill Clinton

President, The United States of America

September 10th, 1997

Dear Mr. President:

We, the remaining families of the Korean War victims who were killed or wounded by U.S. soldiers from July 26th to 29th, 1950, are petitioning for your recognition of the incident, a formal apology and ***compensation****. . . .*

Even though it has been 47 years since the slaughter of July 26th through July 29th, 1950, the incident still lives in our hearts and our minds daily. We are still suffering from the vivid memory of this unforgettable day.

Some survivors live with permanently disfigured bodies (without one eye or nose and so on). Others are in sorrow because they live without their families. About 400 souls roam around high above the killing field. . . .

Compensation: Money to repay the loss.

The atrocious act was not committed during warfare. We request that you review the following references sincerely and take proper measures to allow us our basic human rights.

Summary of the Incident

The following is an account and testimony of those who survived the incident:

At the beginning of the Korean War, around noon of July 23, 1950, two American soldiers and one Korean policeman arrived at Chu Gok Ri, Yongdong Eup, Yongdong Gun, North Chungchong Province. They ordered the villagers to **evacuate** *the village at once, because that area would become a dangerous battle field.*

Most of the villagers who heard that command took refuge in Im Ke Ri (a mountain village), which was located about 2 **kilometers** *away from their hometown.*

On the evening of July 25th, 1950, a group of American soldiers rushed into Im Ke Ri and ordered the villagers to gather together. They promised to take the villagers to a safe place, towards Pusan (City).

About 500 to 600 **refugees**, *led by the American soldiers, walked through Chu Gok Ri, towards the south. When the group of refugees arrived at Ha Ga Ri, Yongdong Eup, which is about 1.5 kilometers away from Chu Gok Ri, it was late in the evening.*

The American soldiers then led all of the refugees into a nearby stream, and ordered them to stay there that night. Overnight, many refugees witnessed a long parade of U.S. troops and vehicles towards Pusan.

At dawn, July 26th, the refugees had found that the U.S. soldiers had disappeared. Therefore, the refugees marched south on their own, following the Seoul-Pusan freeway where no one else was there except the refugees.

Around noon of July 26th, 1950, when the refugees group arrived at No Gun Ri, Hwanggan Myon, Yongdong Gun, suddenly four or five American soldiers appeared and stopped them from moving ahead. These soldiers commanded the refugees to stand on the railroad tracks and inspected the personal belongings of the refugees. Of course the American soldiers could not find any weapon.

However they sent a radio message for a machine gun and bomb raid towards the refugees. Then the soldiers fled. Shortly afterwards, planes flew over and dropped bombs on the refugees, and fired machine guns at the refugees.

Evacuate: To remove people from a dangerous area or a military zone.

Kilometer: A metric measure equivalent to 0.62 mile.

Refugees: People who are forced to flee their homes to escape danger.

From this unlawful and brutal attack many refugees were killed. Those who survived escaped into a water tunnel just below the railroad. After a while, U.S. soldiers forced the survivors out of the small water tunnel and pushed them all into larger tunnels nearby.

Then from July 26th to July 29th, 1950, U.S. soldiers constantly fired bullets at both openings of the tunnels, killing lots of people each time. The refugees had to make **barricades** with the dead bodies, and hid under blankets hoping that bullets wouldn't reach the inside. From the 26th to the 29th, the villagers had nothing to eat nor to drink.

Whoever stepped out from the tunnels was immediately shot. Only a few men managed to escape during the nights.

U.S. medics visited the tunnels a couple of times during the period. U.S. soldiers were supposed to treat the wounded. However they were just observing the situation of the refugees.

The U.S. soldiers disappeared on the 29th.

We can never imagine why U.S. soldiers had to kill these innocent refugees over the four-day period. However, one thing we are sure of is that it was not an accident. Also it didn't happen during a combat with the North Korean Army. The U.S. soldiers deliberately killed the innocent villagers of Im Ke Ri, Chu Gok Ri, etc.

We are testifying that U.S. soldiers assaulted Korean civilians before North Koreans occupied the areas of the massacre. At this time 118 people have been identified as victims, 100 people were murdered, and 18 people were left with severe injuries. There is an estimated 400 people who were killed. . . .

Please conduct a thorough investigation on the survivors and the actual site, and find out which of the 1st Cavalry Division committed such a grave mistake. We want the truth, justice and due respect for our basic human rights.

We thank you for your kind attention again. May God bless you and your country.

Respectfully yours,

(SIGNATURE) Eun-yong Chung, Representative of Petitioners of No Gun Ri Incident

Barricades: A barrier or an obstacle.

William B. Kean (center, no helmet), who told his troops that all civilians in the No Gun Ri battle zone should be treated as the enemy, confers with his subordinates near the front line in South Korea, August 1950. *Reproduced by permission of AP/Wide World Photos.*

What happened next . . .

Three-and-a-half years after the petition was filed, on January 11, 2001, President Bill Clinton, in cooperation with the South Korean government, finally replied to the petitioners, acknowledging (but not apologizing for) the loss of lives at No Gun Ri.

Eun-yong Chung, the representative of the survivors who signed the petition, lost his five-year-old son and three-year-old daughter at No Gun Ri; both were killed in the massacre. Chung was in his seventies at the 1997 signing of the survivors' petition.

The United States proposed building a memorial near No Gun Ri dedicated to Korean civilians who lost their lives in the war. It also planned to establish a scholarship fund for Korean students in memory of the dead.

Did you know . . .

- A one-year U.S. Army study in 2000 concluded that U.S. soldiers killed unarmed Korean civilians, but that they had acted without intention, due to the confusion of the surroundings. The study denied the accusations that the soldiers were acting on orders from their commanders.

- Major General William Kean, commander of the Twenty-fifth Infantry Division, which was stationed near the First Cavalry at the time of the No Gun Ri killings, issued a memo to all commanding officers in his division, saying, as reported by the Associated Press: "All civilians seen in this area are to be considered as enemy and action taken accordingly." Kean's order is a violation of the rules of war, according to most historians.

Where to Learn More

Becker, Elizabeth. "Army Admits G.I.'s in Korea Killed Civilians at No Gun Ri." *New York Times,* January 12, 2001, pp. A1 and A8.

Web sites

"Bridge at No Gun Ri: Survivors' Petition." Associated Press (AP). [Online] http://wire.ap.org/APpackages/nogunri/petition.html (accessed on August 14, 2001).

McIntyre, Jamie. "All-encompassing Probe Ordered into Alleged Korean War Massacre." CNN.com. [Online] http://www.cnn.com/US/9909/30/korea.pentagon.02 (accessed on August 14, 2001).

"President Clinton Statement on No Gun Ri, January 11, 2001." The United States Embassy, Seoul, Republic of Korea. [Online] http://www.usembassy.state.gov/seoul/wwwh42zv.html (accessed on August 14, 2001).

Sang-Hun Choe, Charles J. Hanley, and Martha Mendoza. "Bridge at No Gun Ri." Associated Press (AP). [Online]http://wire.ap.org/APpackages/nogunri/story.html (accessed on August 14, 2001).

Paik Sun Yup

From Pusan to Panmunjom: Wartime Memoirs of the Republic of Korea's First Four-Star General
Published in 1992

Paik Sun Yup (1920–) was only twenty-nine years old when the war broke out in Korea in 1950, but he was already a colonel and the commander of the First Division of the army of the Republic of Korea (ROK; South Korea). On the scene from the first day of conflict, Paik would be one of the principal players in the war until its end three years later. A highly talented military leader, he had been trained as a soldier in Manchuria, a large territory in northern China, and had served in the Manchurian army in World War II (1939–45). During the Korean War, Paik became Korea's first four-star general.

Toward the end of the war, South Korean President Syngman Rhee (1875–1965) strongly opposed truce talks between North and South Korea, but he requested that Paik represent South Korea at Panmunjom, where the negotiations were being held. This was difficult for Paik, for he, too, opposed ending the war before Korea could be once again unified. He had been born and raised in Pyongyang, now the capital of North Korea, and his home was barred to him by the demilitarized zone (DMZ), the line of division between North and South Korea. The excerpt of his memoirs below describes some of his thoughts when the war ended.

Things to remember while reading this excerpt from *From Pusan to Panmunjom:*

- The North Koreans so strongly outmatched the South Koreans when they invaded on June 25, 1950, that on July 1, one week later, the South Korean (ROK) army could account for only about 40,000 of its 98,000 men. Some American estimates put this figure even lower. More than one-half of the ROK Army was disabled or killed in that first week.

- The ROK army lacked training and experienced leadership and they were terribly short of weapons and ammunition. Knowing this, the Chinese, who were allied with the North Koreans against the ROK, would often find the spots where the ROK was defending a position and infiltrate (penetrate into the unit) there.

Excerpt from From Pusan to Panmunjom

*At 10:00 A.M. on July 27, 1953, the **Armistice** Agreement documents were signed and exchanged, and the cease-fire became effective twelve hours later, at 10:00 P.M. The fighting was over at last.*

*An urgent call had woken me at home on the morning of June 25, 1950. I really didn't have the heart for what followed. I dashed from my home to the 1st Division, then south to the Naktong River, then north to the Chongchon River, then back and forth in between—fighting bloodily all the time. The war managed to exchange the "**38th parallel**" for the "**DMZ**" and drench mountains of Korean soil with oceans of blood; it had not done a hell of a lot more.*

*Once the armistice was a **fait accompli**, President **Rhee** accepted it almost casually.*

*The cease-fire caused a measure of anguish in the officers and men of the Korean army, because it **perpetuated** the division of our*

Armistice: An agreement to temporarily stop fighting.

38th parallel: The 38th degree of north latitude as it bisects the Korean Peninsula, chosen by Americans as the dividing line between what was to be Soviet-occupied North Korea and U.S.-occupied South Korea in 1945.

DMZ: Demilitarized zone; an area in which military presence and activity are forbidden.

Fait accompli: French term, meaning an accomplished deed.

Rhee: Syngman Rhee (1875–1965), president of the Republic of Korea (ROK) from 1948 to 1960.

Perpetuate: To make continue.

nation. *The lengthy armistice negotiations had given us enough time, however, to accept the reality that we could do nothing at all about it. Indeed, I saw General [Mark W.] Clark in Seoul right after the armistice was signed and he seemed more distressed over the cease-fire than I did. I couldn't understand it at the time; after all, Clark had helped his nation achieve a major national goal, ending the war in Korea. I learned the reason for his distress much later from his book,* From the Danube to the Yalu. *He had become, he said, the first American commander not to accept surrender from the enemy.*

I had faced the bitterness of leaving my home behind and moving into South Korea, only to face the horror of another split in the nation. I felt like unification was more remote now than ever before. The return of peace to Korea, even the impermanent peace of an armistice, was most **providential** *in one way, however. The killing stopped at last. So many of my* **subordinates** *had been killed that I literally could not count them. Nor could any mind hope to grasp the immensity of the suffering these deaths brought to so many fathers, mothers, brothers, sisters, and wives. The bombing and the* **barrages**

Republic of Korea troops move out single file towards Korea's east-central front near Lookout Mountain, July 1953. *Reproduced by permission of AP/Wide World Photos.*

Providential: Happening as if by the intervention of God.

Subordinates: People under his command.

Barrages: Constant artillery fire.

Communists: People who adhere to a system of government in which one party (usually the Communist Party) controls all property and goods and the means to produce and distribute them; in this case, the North Koreans and Chinese.

Interminable: Long, never-ending.

Staved off: Fended off; prevented.

Infamy: Disgrace.

Cold war policy of containment: The general policy of Western (anticommunist) nations during the cold war (1945–91) of keeping communist nations within their current borders.

Expunge: Erase.

Grenade: A small explosive weapon that can be thrown.

Bayonet: A knife that is attached to the end of a rifle so that it can be used as a spear.

Pusan Perimeter: A 100-mile long, 50-mile wide area in southern Korea in which the U.S. and ROK armies mounted a defense.

were still. Our people would die in the terrible explosions no more.

I had no regrets about our soldiers. They put their lives on the line with no hope of reward, and they fought the **communists** to the death. But I had a few regrets as a commander. I was on the battle-field virtually the entire war, first as a commander of a division, then a corps, and finally as chief of staff. And I believe we could have fought a little better.

We faced enormous deficiencies, to be sure. We were a fledgling force, dreadfully inferior in training. We lacked the equipment of a modern army, and our commanders were often incompetent. These inadequacies made it all but impossible for Korean units to be tough enough to maintain our defensive positions. But this situation had nothing to do with the quality of our soldiers. If there was a lack of will, then we must turn to our commanders to find it. . . .

During the war, I thought we would be able to unify Korea by force of arms. That ardent desire, shared by sixty million Koreans to this day, was not to be, evaporating beneath the **interminable** talks at Panmunjom. We gained no victory, true enough, but we **staved off** a defeat that the **infamy** of surprise attack had nearly made a sure thing, and we established the **cold war policy of containment** by bringing the enemy's predatory aggression up short.

My memory shall never **expunge** the scenes of Korean soldiers, soldiers sacrificing their lives to place explosives on enemy tanks in the first days of the war, soldiers who fought with **grenade** and **bayonet** and died in the rugged mountains within the **Pusan Perimeter**, soldiers who fought desperately to gain every possible inch of ground before the armistice brought the curtain down. These heroes will live always in my heart. (Paik, pp. 244–45, 253–54)

What happened next . . .

After the Korean War, with help from the United States, the Republic of Korea Army built a seven hundred thousand-man force and greatly modernized its equipment, training, and logistics system. General Paik Sun Yup served two tours of duty as chief of staff of the army, through the year

1959, when he became chairman of the Joint Chiefs of Staff, serving as a war advisor to South Korea's leader. He retired from that position just as the political climate in South Korea forced Syngman Rhee to resign and flee to Hawaii. Paik went on to successful careers in diplomacy, government, and business.

In the year 2001, the DMZ in Korea stood as it did in 1953.

Did you know . . .

- In July 1951, Eighth Army commander General James A. Van Fleet (1892–1992) established the Field Training Command to retrain the ROK soldiers. "A training center was hastily constructed south of Sokcho," Paik recalled in his memoirs. "Training lasted nine weeks and consisted of basic individual, squad, platoon, and company training. The center started from scratch, assuming nobody knew anything. Every man in a division, with the exception of its commander, was required to undergo the training, and when the training was over, a unit had to pass a test before being assigned to the front." Paik continued: "By the end of 1952, all ten ROK Army divisions had completed the training. Units that completed the course lost 50 percent fewer men and equipment in combat than did units that had not had the training. Furthermore, divisions that completed the course and returned to the front revealed an élan [spirit] and confidence quite superior to what they had shown before going through the training."

Where to Learn More

Alexander, Bevin. *Korea: The First War We Lost*. New York: Hippocrene Books, 1986, revised edition, 2000.

Paik Sun Yup. *From Pusan to Panmunjom: Wartime Memoirs of the Republic of Korea's First Four-Star General*. Dulles, VA: Brassey's, 1999.

Toland, John. *In Mortal Combat: Korea, 1950–1953*. New York: William Morrow, 1991.

Bill Shinn

**The Forgotten War Remembered:
Korea, 1950–1953; A War Correspondent's
Notebook and Today's Danger in Korea**

Published in 1996

When the North Korean army invaded the Republic of Korea (ROK) on June 25, 1950 to start the Korean War, it took them four days to reach the South Korean capital city of Seoul. While the ROK troops fought a losing and bloody battle to hold them off, the families of Americans were evacuated, and then the South Korean government and American embassy personnel fled the city. Knowing the communist troops were coming in, thousands of Seoul's citizens gathered what belongings they could and joined the throngs of fleeing civilians on the roads heading south.

Bill Shinn was born in what is now North Korea in 1918. In August 1945, when the Soviet army came into his homeland to accept the Japanese surrender after World War II, he was overjoyed by the liberation of his people. His joy was brief, as he witnessed many atrocities at the hands of the Soviet soldiers, who were cruel and violent in their dealings with the Japanese and with wealthy or educated Korean people. Shinn left his home within two weeks of the Russian occupation, leaving behind his parents and three sisters; he was never to see or even hear from them again.

In 1945, Shinn found his way to the United States, where he finished a bachelor's degree and went on to get a degree in international law. In 1950, he took a job with the Associated Press (AP) as a reporter and went on to become a correspondent covering Korea. At the start of the war he and his wife, Sally, were living in Seoul. They had a young son, Johnny, and Sally was pregnant.

Things to remember while reading this excerpt from *The Forgotten War Remembered:*

- More than one million civilians who lived in North Korea at the time of Soviet occupation in 1945 became refugees in the south within one year.

- When the North Koreans entered Seoul, they arrested anyone who was in any way involved in Syngman Rhee's (1875–1965) South Korean government, most foreigners, Christian missionaries, educators, and a lot of other innocent people. Any journalist for the South Korean or American newspapers would have been certain to be arrested.

Excerpt from The Forgotten War Remembered

[On June 27, 1950, it was clear that the North Koreans would soon enter Seoul, South Korea. Shinn had been witness to the flight of the ROK government and many other officials and their families from Seoul.]

As the sounds of guns could be heard closer and closer, rows of **refugees** and wounded South Korean soldiers were streaming into Seoul . . . Amidst this panicky situation, many Koreans—young and old, men and women—began fleeing southward carrying their meager belongings on their heads or backs.

Toward dusk, I, too, decided to flee. I went to the AP [Associated Press] office from the Chosun Hotel, where I was covering the war news, to collect important papers, and rushed home.

My wife, who had been anxiously waiting for my return, reported that two men calling themselves "members of a security unit" had come about an hour earlier and searched for my Ford car. "They shouted at me, 'Where is the dark-blue old car?' They left because I declared that we don't have any car at all," she said.

If I had been at home at that time, I would have been taken away by them. The so-called "members of a security unit" must have been either North Korean agents or members of the South Korean Workers (Communist) Party who became active in preparation for the entry of the North Korean army into Seoul. What they were looking for was not the Ford car; it was me working as a correspondent for AP, an "American imperialist news agency," as the **Communists** would call it. I was saved thanks to the fact that the Ford car was then at the parking lot of the Chosun Hotel where I was gathering information.

At about 8:00 P.M., when I had finished my first meal at home in three days, I heard a big explosion outside. A bomb had been dropped. . . .

We had to flee at once. We hastily packed our essential belongings and fled in the old Ford. Amidst **sporadic** whines of small

Refugees: People who are forced to flee their homes to escape danger.

Communists: People who adhere to a system of government in which one party (usually the Communist Party) controls all property and goods and the means to produce and distribute them; in this case, the North Koreans.

Sporadic: Occasional.

Bill Shinn with his Ford, October 1950. *Reproduced by permission of AP/Wide World Photos.*

firearms, I drove desperately, without headlights on, toward the Han River bridge, the only exit from Seoul to the south. We felt relieved when we reached the bridge shortly after 10 P.M., believing that we would be able to save our lives once we safely crossed the bridge. But to our **consternation**, *we were stopped at gunpoint by South Korean military police at the entrance and ordered not to cross the bridge. "No one is allowed to cross!" the* **MP** *shouted. . . .*

[*The Shinn family crossed the bridge at 11:45 P.M. Two-and-a-half hours later, the South Koreans blew up the Han River Bridge, which was packed with soldiers and fleeing civilians at the time. Hundreds were killed and the escape route for thousands more was gone.*

[*Shinn took his family to Shinwon-ri, a small farming village where his younger brother was staying with a friend named Kim Jong-wook. Leaving his wife and child behind, on June 28, Shinn traveled on foot fifteen miles south to Suwon, where the ROK government was temporarily residing. After witnessing the communist aircraft fire on the city, Shinn decided he had better get back to his family immediately to evacuate them from the area entirely. Setting off in the evening, he walked through the night.*]

Consternation: Dismay; sense of dread.

MP: Military police.

Walking wearily at dawn, I could see South Korean soldiers limping along with their rifles upside down. As I moved further north, gruesome dead bodies lying in the roadside ditches greeted my eyes.

When I got to Shiwon-ri at last, not a soul could be seen in the village. Kim Jong-wook's house, where my family had taken refuge, was vacant and as silent as a grave. Realizing that all villagers had fled, I stood aghast, almost fainting. I looked around in a daze. Three men, who appeared to be North Korean soldiers, were standing guard on a small hill at the back of the village, and many others were moving southward along the Seoul-Suwon route across the rice field. I had entered an enemy-occupied zone!

Trembling with fear, I tried to escape. My old Ford had been left at Kim's house, but I could not find the key. . . . I broke open the dashboard, connected wires to start the motor, and frantically drove the car along a narrow lane. At a point about 300 yards from Kim's house, three North Korean soldiers suddenly emerged and ordered me to halt, blocking my way.

*Apparently assured that I was like a rat in a trap, they took their eyes off me for a moment to look around the neighborhood. Since any South Korean working for an American organization was to be shot to death, I immediately decided to throw away my wallet which contained my AP reporter's ID card, American **greenbacks**, U. S. postage stamps. . . .*

[The North Koreans finally accepted the gift of Shinn's car and allowed him to proceed on foot. During the next two days on the run, Shinn had many close brushes with the enemy. As he was driven back to Suwon by ROK soldiers, he saw the village of Shiwon-ri, where he had last seen his family, engulfed in flames. Shinn then headed for Taejon, where the South Korean government had relocated.

[In September 1950, the United Nations forces, supporting the South Koreans, began their first real victories with the landing at Inchon. Seoul was recaptured at the end of that month, after heavy fighting and the near-destruction of the ancient city and its treasures. Shinn had never heard from his family, but when he arrived in Seoul on September 30, he was immediately informed of their whereabouts. His wife had kept a diary throughout the ordeal.]

Sally Shinn's Diary

[Written in the form of a letter to her husband]

*On the night of June 29, fierce fighting continued near Shinwon-ri and North Korean soldiers were approaching the village. We fled the village together with Kim Jong-wook's family to his brother's home deep in a steep mountain in Kwangju-kun (county). Farmers in the out-of-the-way hamlet were so poor that we barely **staved off** hunger*

Greenbacks: Paper money.

Staved off: Fended off; prevented.

Korean refugees fleeing the war, June 1951. *Reproduced by permission of Archive Photos, Inc.*

Barter: Trading.

Personal effects: Belongings.

Fugitive: Moving from place to place to escape someone (usually the law).

Eluding: Quietly avoiding.

by **barter** of **personal effects** for food. Because it was too much of a burden on the part of the poor family of Mr. Kim's brother, I decided to go to my parents' home in Seoul.

Your younger brother, Wha-kyoon, who had been living a **fugitive** life in Seoul, **eluding** Communist search for young South Koreans to induct into the North Korean Army, was informed of my whereabouts by Mr. Kim's relatives. He kindly came to the remote village to take me to Seoul. I was about to collapse many times while trudging along the rugged mountain trails with Johnny. As a pregnant woman, I barely held out from hunger and fatigue thanks to the few vitamin pills on hand.

On our way, we came across Communist soldiers. They ordered Wha-kyoon to show them his hands. I trembled with fear when they yelled at him, "Your hands are clean enough. You are not a laborer," and threatened to take him away. With bare life, we managed to arrive in Seoul in three days. . . .

I and Johnny went to my parents' home at Yongchon in the western district of Seoul. . . .

Tribulation persisted even after I moved to Yongchon-dong. Unable to buy food, we sustained life by eating dumplings in soy soup each day. While furious battles continued, we lived in an air-raid shelter built by the Japanese on the hillside of a rocky mountain during World War II. More than 20 persons used the shelter, about the size of 20 square feet with a small public toilet outside. I had to bring meals from my parents' home 100 yards down at the foot of the mountain. Being in the last month of pregnancy, I had to carry diapers and swaddling clothes for the baby.

The most terrifying was the United Nations air raids during the furious street fights for the recapture of Seoul. While bringing meals from my parents' home, I saw gruesome corpses scattered around, and many old women dying from bomb **shrapnel**. Although their targets were the Communist troops, I felt sorry that the bombs dropped by American Air Force planes hit many South Korean civilians.

Despite all the hardships I and little Johnny had, my waking and sleeping thoughts were about you because I had no way of knowing your whereabouts since you had gone to Suwon from Shinwon-ri on the early morning of June 29. (Shinn, pp. 66–67, 72, 132–33)

Tribulation: Adversity; calamity; terrible problems.

Shrapnel: Fragments of the exploded ammunition.

What happened next . . .

As soon as the United Nations forces recaptured Seoul, Bill Shinn found his wife and son on September 30, 1950. Sally Shinn gave birth to a second child on October 30. Shinn covered the entire Korean War (1950–53) for the Associated Press and later worked in top-level positions in other news agencies.

The city of Seoul changed hands four times during the Korean War. The ancient city was destroyed by bombing and firefights, its treasures looted or burned.

One of the results of the Korean War was the permanent separation of families and loved ones. Bill Shinn dedicated his book: "To my mother and father, left behind when I fled Soviet-occupied North Korea fifty years ago and whose fate remains unknown."

Did you know . . .

- According to Shinn, during their occupation, the North Koreans killed 165,000 civilians (nonmilitary people). In Seoul alone, 9,500 people were executed by the communists. The South Koreans, when they recaptured the city, were also very intent on rooting out any communists. In early November 1950, Shinn witnessed and reported on an ROK mass execution of civilians suspected of having helped the communists.

Where to Learn More

Alexander, Bevin. *Korea: The First War We Lost.* New York: Hippocrene Books, 1986, revised edition, 2000.

Shinn, Bill. *The Forgotten War Remembered: Korea, 1950–1953; A War Correspondent's Notebook and Today's Danger in Korea.* Elizabeth, NJ: Hollym International, 1996.

Web sites

"Bridge at No Gun Ri: Mass Executions." Associated Press (AP). [Online] http://wire.ap.org/APpackages/nogunri/executions_doc2.html (accessed on August 14, 2001).

Harry S. Truman

*"President's Address: Korean War Dismissal
of General Douglas MacArthur"*
Delivered on April 11, 1951

When it was decided that U.S. Army general Douglas MacArthur (1880–1964), commander of the United Nations forces in the Far East, must be relieved of command because of his insubordination, it was obvious that it must be handled very carefully. MacArthur was beloved by the press, the Republican Party, and a good portion of the American public. And President Harry S. Truman (1884–1973), a Democrat, was already in trouble at home over the Korean War (1950–53). Despite precautions, the firing of the revered seventy-one-year-old general did not go smoothly. According to the plan, Secretary of the Army Frank Pace (1912–88), who was in the Far East at the time, would bring MacArthur the notice of his dismissal at 10 A.M. on April 12, 1951. But the communications system failed; Pace did not receive the notice. Before anything else could be done, the newspapers got the scoop about MacArthur's firing. Truman had no choice then but to send the orders to MacArthur directly and to order a press conference. He delivered the address excerpted below that night.

Harry S. Truman greets
Douglas MacArthur upon
his arrival at Wake Island on
October 14, 1950.
*Reproduced by permission of
AP/Wide World Photos.*

Things to remember while reading this excerpt from the "President's Address":

- The difference between limited versus unlimited war had become the biggest bone of contention between President Truman and General MacArthur. Truman and his staff, by the spring of 1951, believed that the costs of an all-out war with the Chinese, who were fighting on the side of the North Koreans, were too extreme and dangerous. They decided to use their military strength to hold a defensive line, keeping South Korea free of invasion from the north, and tried to use negotiation to end the war. MacArthur, on the other hand, believed that "there is no substitute for victory," and was willing to risk a larger war in order to destroy the enemy.

- As a military commander, MacArthur's duty was to carry out the orders of the president and the Joint Chiefs of Staff regardless of his personal opinions. The Joint Chiefs is an agency within the Department of Defense serving to advise the president and the secretary of defense on matters of war and to coordinate battle plans among the branches of the U.S. military.

- The Soviet Union, which was established in 1922, was comprised of fifteen republics. During the cold war, a period of heightened political tension between the United States and the Soviet Union that lasted from the end of World War II in 1945 to the dissolution of the Soviet Union in 1991, the U.S. and other Western (noncommunist) governments were fearful that the Soviets were trying to create a communistic bloc of nations opposed to the Western powers.

- The Soviet Union was not in favor of a war in Korea, and initially its premier, Joseph Stalin (1879–1953), did not give North Korean premier Kim Il Sung (1912–1994), a fellow communist, permission to invade the south. Even when Stalin gave his approval to Kim, he did so reluctantly and never sent any troops. Though Mao Zedong (Mao Tsetung; 1893–1976), the leader of the newly formed People's Republic of China, likewise was reluctant to engage in the war, Communist China did come to the aid of the North Koreans.

Excerpt from "President's Address: Korean War Dismissal of General Douglas MacArthur"

I want to talk plainly to you tonight about what we are doing in Korea and about our policy in the Far East.

In the simplest terms, what we are doing in Korea is this: We are trying to prevent a Third World War.

*I think most people in this country recognized that fact last June. And they warmly supported the decision of the Government to help the **Republic of Korea** against the **communist** aggressors. Now, many persons, even some who applauded our decision to defend Korea, have forgotten the basic reason for our action.*

Republic of Korea: South Korea.

Communist: Governments in which one party (usually the Communist Party) controls all property and goods and the means to produce and distribute them; in this case, the North Koreans and Chinese.

It is right for us to be in Korea. It was right last June. It is right today.

I want to remind you why this is true.

The communists in the **Kremlin** *are engaged in a monstrous conspiracy to stamp out freedom all over the world. If they were to succeed, the United States would be numbered among their principal victims. It must be clear to everyone that the United States cannot—and will not—sit idly by and await foreign conquest. The only question is: When is the best time to meet the threat and how?*

The best time to meet the threat is in the beginning. It is easier to put out a fire in the beginning when it is small than after it has become a roaring blaze.

And the best way to meet the threat of aggression is for the peace-loving nations to act together. If they don't act together, they are likely to be picked off, one by one. . . .

[The communists] want to control all Asia from the Kremlin. This plan of conquest is in flat contradiction to what we believe. We believe that Korea belongs to the Koreans, that India belongs to the Indians—that all the nations of Asia should be free to work out their affairs in their own way. This is the basis of peace in the Far East and everywhere else.

The whole communist **imperialism** *is back of the attack on peace in the Far East. It was the Soviet Union that trained and equipped the North Koreans for aggression. The Chinese communists massed 44 well-trained and well-equipped divisions on the Korean frontier. These were the troops they threw into battle when the North Korean communists were beaten.*

The question we have had to face is whether the communist plan can be stopped without general war. Our Government and other countries associated with us in the **United Nations** *believe that the best chance of stopping it without general war is to meet the attack in Korea and defeat it there.*

That is what we have been doing. It is a difficult and bitter task.

But so far it has been successful.

So far, we have prevented World War III.

So far, by fighting a **limited war** *in Korea, we have prevented aggression from succeeding, and bringing on a general war. And the ability of the whole free world to resist communist aggression has*

Kremlin: The seat of the Soviet government

Imperialism: Governing by forcibly imposing one country's rule over another country or territory.

United Nations: An international organization founded in 1945 comprised of member nations whose goal is to promote international peace and good relations among nations; their forces were defending the South Koreans.

Limited war: A war with an objective other than the enemy's complete destruction, as in holding a defensive line during negotiations, as opposed to an unlimited war, in which the combatant nations use every means within their power to pursue the goal of completely defeating the enemy.

been greatly improved. We have taught the enemy a lesson. He has found out that aggression is not cheap or easy. Moreover, men all over the world who want to remain free have been given new courage and new hope. They know now that the champions of freedom can stand up and fight and that they will stand up and fight. . . .

We do not want to see the conflict in Korea extended. We are trying to prevent a world war—not to start one. The best way to do that is to make it plain that we and the other free countries will continue to resist the attack.

*But you may ask why can't we take other steps to punish the aggressor. Why don't we bomb Manchuria and China itself? Why don't we assist **Chinese Nationalist** troops to land on the mainland of China? If we were to do these things, we would become entangled in a vast conflict on the continent of Asia and our task would become immeasurably more difficult all over the world.*

*What would suit the ambitions of the Kremlin better than for our military forces to be committed to a full scale war with **Red China?***

It may well be that, in spite of our best efforts, the communists may spread the war. But it would be wrong—tragically wrong—for us to take the initiative in extending the war. The dangers are great. Make no mistake about it. Behind the North Koreans and Chinese communists in the front lines stand additional millions of Chinese soldiers. And behind the Chinese stand the tanks, the planes, the submarines, the soldiers, and the scheming rulers of the Soviet Union.

Our aim is to avoid the spread of the conflict. . . .

I have thought long and hard about this question of extending the war in Asia. I have discussed it many times with the ablest military advisers in the country. I believe with all my heart that the course we are following is the best course.

I believe that we must try to limit the war to Korea for these vital reasons to make sure that the precious lives of our fighting men are not wasted; to see that the security of our country and the free world is not needlessly jeopardized; and to prevent a third world war.

*A number of events have made it evident that General **MacArthur** did not agree with that policy. I have therefore considered it essential to relieve General MacArthur so that there would be no doubt or confusion as to the real purpose and aim of our policy.*

It was with the deepest personal regret that I found myself compelled to take this action. General MacArthur is one of our greatest

Chinese Nationalist: The ruling party led by Chiang Kai-shek in China from the 1920s until 1949, when the Nationalists were defeated by the Communists in the Chinese Civil War and forced to withdraw to the island of Taiwan (formerly Formosa).

Red China: Communist China; the People's Republic of China.

MacArthur: Douglas MacArthur (1880–1964), U.S. Army general and commander of the United Nations forces in the Far East during the Korean War.

military commanders. But the cause of world peace is more important than any individual.

The change in commands in the Far East means no change whatever in the policy of the United States. We will carry on the fight in Korea with vigor and determination in an effort to bring the war to a speedy and successful conclusion.

We are ready, at any time, to negotiate for a restoration of peace in the area. But we will not engage in **appeasement***. We are only interested in real peace. . . .*

This is our military objective—to repel attack and to restore peace.

In the hard fighting in Korea, we are proving that collective action among nations is not only a high principle but a workable means of resisting aggression. Defeat of aggression in Korea may be the turning point in the world's search for a practical way of achieving peace and security.

The struggle of the United Nations in Korea is a struggle for peace.

The free nations have united their strength in an effort to prevent a third world war. That war can come if the communist rulers want it to come. But this Nation and its allies will not be responsible for its coming.

We do not want to widen the conflict. We will use every effort to prevent that disaster. And in so doing, we know that we are following the great principles of peace, freedom, and justice.

Appeasement: Making something agreeable at the sacrifice of one's principles.

What happened next . . .

Lieutenant General Matthew B. Ridgway (1895–1993) succeeded MacArthur as the commander of the United Nations forces in the Far East. Lieutenant General James A. Van Fleet (1892–1992) took over Ridgway's command of the Eighth Army in Korea.

In July 1951, truce talks with the Chinese and North Koreans began. At the request of Ridgway, who didn't trust the enemy, combat continued throughout the two years of negotiations, at the cost of thousands of lives.

Truman decided not to run for another term as president in 1952. MacArthur tried to win a Republican nomination, but failed. Dwight D. Eisenhower (1890–1969), the moderate Republican who took office, followed in Truman's footsteps with a limited war policy accompanied by peace negotiations.

Did you know . . .

- Although Truman dismissed MacArthur for his inflammatory public statements that threatened an all-out war with China, Truman, too, considered defeating the Chinese through all means available. On November 30, 1950, at a press conference, Truman stated that the use of the atomic bomb (two of which the United States had dropped on Japan with devastating effect to bring World War II to a close) was always under consideration in the Korean War. His statement, like some of MacArthur's, spread panic throughout the world.

Where to Learn More

Alexander, Bevin. *Korea: The First War We Lost*. New York: Hippocrene Books, 1986, revised edition, 2000.

Varhola, Michael. *Fire and Ice: The Korean War, 1950–1953*. Mason City, IA: Savas Publishing, 2000.

Web sites

"President's Address, 11 April 1951." Harry S. Truman Library. [Online] http://www.theforgottenvictory.org/macarthur.htm (accessed on August 14, 2001).

Ted White

"The Killing Ground"

Collected in *No Bugles, No Drums: An Oral History of the Korean War*, published in 1993

Fighting in Korea had taken a new shape by the spring of 1951. U.S. Army general Matthew B. Ridgway (1895–1993), commander of the United Nations forces in Korea, had successfully put an end to the panicked retreats that characterized the early fighting, and the Chinese had put a stop to the UN forces' rapid advance to the northern borders of Korea. The UN forces, nonetheless, held their own against the Chinese in their huge spring offensive in April 1951, which was ongoing when infantryman Ted White arrived. A pattern had emerged. The Chinese attacked, then disappeared for a period to recuperate. The Eighth Army forces then advanced northward in Ridgway's famous counteroffensives: operations with names like Ripper, Killer, and Rugged. Then, the recovered Chinese would attack again. This became known as "accordion" or "yo-yo" warfare.

Many eyewitness accounts by Korean War soldiers of this period express serious doubt about the purpose of the fighting, and Ted White's is no exception. Many lives were lost on both sides in order to gain a hill, which might easily be lost again the next day. The fighting was brutal and had no apparent end in sight.

African American troops of the Twenty-fifth Infantry Division advance in the rugged terrain of Korea, so close to the enemy they can reach them with grenades, September 1951. *Reproduced by permission of the Corbis Corporation.*

Ted White was an infantryman in the Twenty-fourth Regiment of the Twenty-fifth Infantry Division, the last all-African American unit in the U.S. Army.

Things to remember while reading this excerpt from "The Killing Ground":

- At about the time that Ted White first found himself in Korea, U.S. Army general Douglas MacArthur (1880–1964) was relieved of command. Ridgway took his place as commander of the United Nations forces in Far East. General James A. Van Fleet (1892–1992) took over Ridgway's position as commander of the Eighth Army.

- The Eighth Army had been moving its defensive line up the peninsula since January 1951. In April it was north of the 38th parallel (which officially divided North and South Korea before the war) at the lines Ridgway had named Utah and Wyoming. Then the Chinese spring offensive

After we dug our foxholes we left the hill. That's what usually happened. We'd move out and attack a ridge or a hill, dig foxholes to spend the night in, then move out again in the morning, or sometimes even before we got all the way dug in.

Once we attacked four ridges in one day, one after another. Rumors had started that the Chinese [who were allied with the North Koreans, against the Americans] were going to hit us with one of their

was launched, and by May 19
back south of the 38th parallel
"No Name" line, extending a
Seoul to Yangyang on the east co
the Kansas line, which was just n
With minor changes, that is whei
for the next two years.

Excerpt from "The Killing G.

What happened was, me and a bunch of fe.
down to the recruiting office and enlist. This was Sep.
just turned nineteen. The war was a couple months
we decided we'd do something for our country, becu
was doing much of anything else.

I had no idea what the **38th parallel** was. I didn
what was happening in Korea. I wasn't even sure I knew
was. All I knew was, there was a war on.

I went to Fort Jackson, South Carolina, for basic train
there for **infantry** training. Then I got sent to Korea. It wa.
here, and then I was gone.

The 24th **Regiment** was just north of the Han River, an
day I joined the unit we were **strafed** and **napalmed** by c
planes. I came in with some other replacements, and the co
we were assigned to (E Company) sent somebody down this
pick us up, and when we got to the top of the hill they told us
off to dig **foxholes.** As soon as we got ready to dig in about six
planes came over and strafed us and dropped napalm. I didn't h
a hole dug yet, so I hid behind a rock. There was a big boulder n
where I'd started to dig, and I got behind it, and as this business we
on, I probably tried to crawl under it. I didn't know what was hap
pening, because it was the first time I'd ever been under fire. The
napalm burned some guys real bad. One was killed. He was lying
there on the ground like a charred piece of wood. An officer finally got
on the radio and told them to call it off.

Ted White: The Killing Ground

big offensives, so after that we moved a little more careful. We still advanced every day, but we did it slow, and that gave us a little more time to eat and sleep.

We ate C **rations**. I don't remember any hot meals. We ate everything cold, out of cans. There was stuff like franks and beans, corned beef hash, spaghetti, ham and lima beans. There was always a lot of trading. Ham and lima beans I don't think nobody wanted. We gave a can to a Chinese prisoner once, and even he wouldn't eat it. On the other hand, everybody wanted the cans of fruit. Can of peaches, or fruit cocktail, it made your day. . . .

I didn't know too much about the Chinese being in the war. I got there in April of 1951, and the big Chinese attacks had come in November and December and January. A lot of the other fellas were new, too, so I didn't have people telling me what to expect.

When we got hit it was the start of the biggest battle of the Korean War. As I understand it, something like three hundred thousand Chinese attacked all across the front. Of course, at the time I wasn't thinking about no front except my own front. We could hear them coming, because they'd blow bugles and horns and whistles, trying to work on your mind. Then an **artillery** flare went up, a real bright light, and there they were. Thousands of them, kind of jogging across the rice paddies below us and up the sides of the hill. I remember telling myself, "Just survive, Theodore. Just survive. You gotta survive this somehow."

We stayed up on that hill for two nights. The Chinese wouldn't attack in the daytime because they were afraid of our planes. But at night we got them with artillery. That's what stopped them. I was just a rifleman, firing an **M-1**, trying to save my butt. What killed them Chinese was the artillery. It was a terrible thing to see. Bodies flying into the air, and pieces of bodies. When they charged they'd be so close together you couldn't miss.

But they had so many men. During the daytime you could see hundreds of bodies lying out there on the hillside, and you'd think, How could they take any more of that? But the next night they'd do it again.

Finally they just overpowered us, there was so many of them. We started to retreat. One company would be the rear guard while the rest of the regiment moved back to another position. Then a different company would hold that position while the rest of the regiment moved again.

Rations: Food provision.

Artillery: Large, mounted firearms, such as rockets, guns, and howitzers.

M-1: An M-1 "Garand" .30 caliber rifle, the primary rifle used by UN forces.

Sometimes we'd take up a position and hold it for a while, until it seemed like we'd be overrun. But at the last minute we'd always get the word to pull back. Now what I understand is, that business was General **Ridgway**'s idea. He was still out to kill as many Chinese as possible, and the longer a unit held on to a position, the longer the artillery could stay forward and blow the hell out of the Chinese. . . .

[*After the May conflicts, the Twenty-fourth Regiment retreated back to a line north of Seoul and then held. The Chinese eventually vanished. Patrols were sent out to find them, and then the Twenty-fourth went on the offensive again.*]

In June we were advancing again, taking hills, and one of the worst fights I was in took place about that time.

They put a **squad** of us out on a hill two hundred yards in front of the main lines. About twenty guys. We went out there and dug our foxholes, two guys to a hole, and then for every hole they gave us a machine gun.

Only twenty guys, and we get ten machine guns.

I'm thinking, Lord, what are they gonna do to us out here?

We had a machine gun in each hole, we had rifles, we had .45 pistols, and we had **grenades**. Plus, they zeroed us in with artillery. They told us, "You stay out here, and if you see Chinese you open fire. And you hold this hill."

Well, it dawned on us then. Somebody was planning to kill themselves some Chinese, and we were the bait. I learned later that another company had been ordered out to that hill, and they refused to go. They disobeyed the order, and they were charged with **mutiny**.

But we went. And not too long after it got dark—I don't recall the exact time—I saw the Chinese coming. I could see them against the skyline. The way they came strutting by, I could tell they didn't know we were there. They were looking up at the ridge two hundred yards away, where our main line was. They paid us no attention at all.

I woke the guy who was in the hole with me, and when the first Chinese got within about fifty yards of us I opened up with the machine gun.

That started it. We fought all night long. We didn't dare move out of our holes, because they kept sending artillery down on us. And even if we left our holes and somehow made it back to our own lines, we'd be shot by our own guys.

Ridgway: Matthew B. Ridgway (1895–1993), U.S. Army general and commander of the United Nations forces in Korea during the Korean War.

Squad: A unit consisting of riflemen.

Grenades: Small explosive weapons that can be thrown, usually with a pin that was pulled to activate them and a spring-loaded safety lever that was held down until the user wanted to throw the grenade; once the safety lever was released, the grenade would explode in seconds.

Mutiny: Rebellion against the forces of authority.

So we were there to stay. I had no confidence we could hold, but we had to hold. There was no place for us to go.

Actually I was too scared to think about being overrun. They kept coming in waves, and I kept firing. I fired my machine gun all night long. Everybody else was firing. And the artillery was dropping all around us. The artillery did a good job keeping them off us.

And all night long I'm thinking, These people are crazy. They're dying in droves, and they just keep coming on.

But all that night we didn't lose a man, and when they broke off the attack at daylight we could see what we'd done to them. There were dead Chinese all over the ground. Hundreds and hundreds of them. And they were only the ones their people couldn't drag away in the dark.

*Everybody on that hill was recommended for a **Bronze Star**. I never got one, but I understand the recommendation went in. (White, pp. 125–29)*

Bronze Star: A military decoration awarded for bravery.

What happened next . . .

By mid-June 1951, the UN forces had established a defensive line at the 38th parallel. The Chinese and North Koreans had built a strongly entrenched defensive line of their own on the north side, with reinforced bunkers, underground chambers that were almost impossible to penetrate with air fire. The war became stationary (or unmoving), but remained vicious, as the enemies fought for the same hills over and over. In July, the United Nations and the Chinese and North Koreans began to negotiate a truce that would take two years to complete. In the meantime, the killing continued.

Did you know . . .

- The Twenty-fourth Regiment of the Twenty-fifth Infantry Division was disbanded by the army on October 1, 1951. The men of this all-black unit were absorbed into other units—a move that began the racial integration of the Eighth Army in Korea. Army history held that the Twenty-fourth had disgraced itself by repeatedly "breaking and running" from combat. Recent historians and veterans have questioned the old perspectives on the Twenty-fourth's actions. Racism within the army meant that the unit did not receive proper leadership and the soldiers were poorly trained. But there is also evidence that the Twenty-fourth Regiment performed just as well in combat as other troops, and that in many cases it distinguished itself.

Where to Learn More

Blair, Clay. *The Forgotten War: America in Korea, 1950–1953.* New York: Times Books, 1987.

Tomedi, Rudy. *No Bugles, No Drums: An Oral History of the Korean War.* New York: John Wiley and Sons, 1993.

Web sites

United States Army. "African Americans in the Korean War." Fiftieth Anniversary of the Korean War Commemoration Site. [Online] http://korea50.army.mil/history/factsheets/afroamer.html (accessed on August 14, 2001).

Larry Zellers

In Enemy Hands: A Prisoner in North Korea
Published in 1991

When the North Koreans captured cities and villages in South Korea in the first months of the Korean War (1950–53), they arrested people they thought were anticommunist. Among those arrested was Larry Zellers, a Methodist missionary and schoolteacher in the town of Kaesong near the 38th parallel, the dividing line between North and South Korea. In a prison in the North Korean capital of Pyongyang, Zellers joined a group of eighty-seven civilians from many countries, the United States, France, Britain, Russia, Australia, Belgium, and others. Many had been in Korea as Christian missionaries; others were diplomats and businessmen and their families. The ages of this group of internees ranged from six months old to eighty-two years old. In October 1950, with United Nations forces (allied with the South Koreans) rapidly advancing up toward Pyongyang, the North Koreans decided to move these civilian internees.

When the first marches took place, the internees created systems to help the old and sick. They managed the first part of the trip, the twelve miles from Manpo to a mining town, with great difficulty. There they learned that they were to be placed in the hands of the North Korean army to join with captured American troops in a 120-mile march to the city of Chunggang-jin in the far north. The march, later known as the Death March, was led by a brutal North Korean major called "The Tiger."

Things to remember while reading this excerpt from *In Enemy Hands:*

- The North Koreans, like the communist nations of the Soviet Union and China, did not accept organized religion within their society.

- After the fall of Seoul, the capital of South Korea, many missionaries were arrested by the North Koreans, among them Bishop Patrick Byrne, the Apostolic Delegate to South Korea, several elderly priests and nuns, and the Australian priest Philip Crosbie, who would later write a book about the experience. They were brought before a People's Court and interrogated in front of five hundred South Koreans who sided with the communists. The missionaries were told to renounce their country and their church. None did. The crowd was hostile to the missionaries and foreigners in general, at times screaming for their deaths.

Excerpt from In Enemy Hands: A Prisoner in North Korea

[On October 31, 1950, Zellers and the rest of the group of eighty-seven civilian internees were being turned over to the North Korean prison system. As they waited in uncertainty, a North Korean major strode up to their area of the prison camp. The major spoke to the group, using British internee Herbert A. Lord , director of the Salvation Army in Korea, as a translator.]

"We are going on a long march. I am in command, and I have the authority to make you obey. From now on, you will be under military orders." There was a pause. *"You see,"* he said, pointing to his military **epaulette**, *"I have the authority. Everyone must march. No one must be left behind. You must discard at once anything that can*

Epaulette: An ornamental fringed shoulder pad denoting high military rank.

be used as a weapon. After all, you are my enemy, and I must consider that you might try to do me harm." Having said this in a strong, clear voice, he proceeded down the line of assembled prisoners, pausing to inspect each one. Father Paul Villemot, an eighty-two-year-old French priest, stood at the very head of the line, leaning heavily on a wooden cane. The major marched up to him and tapped the cane with his **swagger stick.** "Throw that away. That is a weapon."

The major moved swiftly on down the line of prisoners, looking at what each one was carrying. When he came to me, he tapped the rolled-up straw sleeping mat slung across my shoulder. "That can be used as a weapon. Throw it away."

With one task out of the way, the major returned to the front of the group and once more addressed us. Apparently trying to justify what he had just said and done, he continued as before. "You are my enemy, and I must protect myself from you." By this time, several members of the group were trying either directly or through Commissioner Lord to reason with the major. The **consensus** was that many of the prisoners would not be able to make a long march. I remember Father Villemot speaking up in French with Monsignor Quinlan [an Irish Catholic missionary] translating: "If I have to march, I will die." Similar sentiments were voiced by others.

"Then let them march till they die. That is a military order," the major concluded. So saying, he gave the order to move out.

By this point the major had earned his new name: by common consent, he was referred to as the The Tiger. Soon the long march ahead of us would also have a name—the Death March. The man to lead it was in a hurry, and we could never move fast enough to satisfy him.

To the east, we could see the American **POWs** also lining up and preparing to march. . . .

[The first night of the Death March the internees were marched until midnight in sleet and snow. Many had inadequate footwear and wore the clothes they had been wearing at the time of their capture, in the warm days of June or July. The next day several weak and ill POWs fell behind in the march. The Tiger held their group leader responsible and, as punishment, bound his hands and shot him in the back of the head, in front of the all the internees, young and old. The next night it was bitterly cold and most of the men and the POWs slept outside again. During the night ten POWs froze to death, and another eight were too weak to go on. The Tiger gave orders to bury all eighteen—the dead and the eight that could not march—and ordered the guards not to leave mounds where they buried them. Many of the older nuns and priests were having such a difficult time walking that

Swagger stick: A stick carried by hand by military officers, usually covered in leather and tipped in metal.

Consensus: General agreement.

POWs: Prisoners of war.

the others set up a system of helping them. But they all were starving and weak and it was becoming more and more clear that they weren't all going to make it.]

[On the fourth day of the march,] when the order was given to begin the march on this November 3, the women were told to wait for transportation. Some of the weaker ones had had great difficulty the day before, even with the help of the entire group. Nevertheless, I remember that we had some **misgivings** as we marched away, leaving only Commissioner Lord to look after the women's group. At noon we were ordered to move into a field to wait for the women to catch up. . . .

[When the women had caught up,] two French nuns plus Madame Funderat and Commissioner Lord were still missing. Soon Mother Eugénie appeared on the road all alone except for a guard. She was extremely distraught at having had to leave Mother Béatrix behind, but the guard had ordered her to do so when Mother Béatrix fell far behind the group. Arriving in Korea in 1906, Mother Béatrix had devoted her whole life to working with the poor and the aged. She was seventy-five years old.

Not long after that, we were greeted by the strange sight of Commissioner Lord assisting Madame Funderat by means of a rope tied to each. Lord was exhausted, and I wondered how he could go on, considering his heart problem. . . .

When we resumed march after the noon meal, we were forced to leave Madame Funderat behind with the promise that she would be looked after. Neither she nor Mother Béatrix was ever seen again.

Normally, two people would have had no difficulty assisting a third, but all of us had been on a starvation diet for about a month. Although our bodies had not yet wasted away as much as they would later on, we were little more than living skeletons. Our bones were covered with cracked, dirty skin; we had scruffy beards and long, dirty, matted hair. Our ragged summer clothes and hollow eyes completed the testimony to our depleted condition.

Little clusters of people from our various groups were scattered up and down the road for miles that afternoon. Monsignor Quinlan and Father Crosbie were trying to assist the oldest member of our group. Father Villemot, who had come to Korea in 1892, was eighty-two years of age on the Death March. Not having teeth, he could not eat the half-cooked corn that the local villagers prepared for us. As the old man's strength failed, Bishop Quinlan and Father Crosbie were

Misgivings: Nagging doubts.

required to carry more and more of the burden. Slowly, these three men dropped behind and were soon out of sight. At one time Father Villemot begged to be left to die in a farmyard. Finally, he was permitted to ride in an oxcart. . . .

Toward evening, more POWs fell out of line, unable to keep up. As we walked past them, we tried to encourage them to keep walking as long as possible. Some did make a new effort, but others remained by the side of the road. Later, we heard many gunshots behind us; we knew what was happening.

*On this particular afternoon, I noticed something different. The guard who marched by my side was not like most of the others. My burden became greater near nightfall, and I was **obliged** to fall behind rather than abandon the malnourished, weak, and frail Anglican nun by the side of the road to die alone. The main body of marching prisoners was miles ahead. Darkness was fast approaching, but this guard stayed by my side, offering encouragement. As other groups of two fell behind—one stronger, one weaker, but together trying to trade a little time in exchange for a life—each couple was assigned a guard, and the decision was his whether to tolerate the delay. Many did not. The sound of the gun was heard in the gathering darkness. (Zellers, pp. 84–85, 106–08)*

Obliged: Compelled; duty bound.

What happened next . . .

The Death March lasted nine days and was completed on November 8, 1950. Out of eighty-seven civilians and about seven hundred soldiers, about one hundred people died during the march. Many who survived the march would soon die in the North Korean prison from the extreme deprivation—lack of food, heat, sleep, and medical attention—and unsanitary conditions experienced during and after the march.

The survivors endured very bad conditions in North Korean prisons for the next two and a half years. By April 1953, when the peace talks began to progress, those who had survived prison were emaciated (dangerously thin), sick, dirty, and frail. At that time, they were taken to the North Korean capital of Pyongyang, where for some time they were well fed, provided with new clothing, and allowed daily baths. The

North Koreans wanted publicity about the humaneness with which they treated the prisoners, but none in the group was willing to go along with them.

Did you know . . .

- According to Larry Zellers, as many as twenty people a day died in the prison camp where he was interned.

- When the United Nations and the communist forces (North Korean and Chinese) exchanged prisoner lists, the United Nations expected the communists to be holding a good portion of the missing: 11,500 Americans and 88,000 South Koreans. The communist list, however, showed only 3,198 Americans, 7,142 South Koreans, and 1,200 other UN prisoners of war. The communists claimed that many soldiers had died of disease while in prison and others had been killed when UN air attacks had struck prisoner of war camps.

Where to Learn More

Crosbie, Philip. *March Till They Die*. Dublin: Browne & Nolan, c. 1955.

Toland, John, *In Mortal Combat: Korea, 1950–1953*. New York: William Morrow, 1991.

Zellers, Larry. *In Enemy Hands: A Prisoner in North Korea*. Lexington: University Press of Kentucky, 1991.

Web sites

"Tiger Survivors: Civilian Internee Prisoners." [Online] http://www.tigersurvivors.org/civbios.html (accessed on August 14, 2001).

Where to Learn More

Books

Acheson, Dean. *Present at the Creation: My Years in the State Department.* New York: W. W. Norton, 1969.

Alexander, Bevin. *Korea: The First War We Lost.* New York: Hippocrene Books, 1986, revised edition, 2000.

Allen, Richard C. *Korea's Syngman Rhee: An Unauthorized Portrait.* New York: Charles E. Tuttle, 1960.

Ambrose, Stephen E. *Eisenhower, Soldier and President.* New York: Touchstone Books, 1991.

Apel, Otto F., Jr., M.D., and Pat Apel. *MASH: An Army Surgeon in Korea.* Lexington: University Press of Kentucky, 1998.

Baik Bong. *Kim Il Sung: Biography.* 3 vols. Tokyo: Miraisha, 1969–70.

Beech, Keyes. *Tokyo and Points East.* Garden City, NY: Doubleday, 1954.

Blair, Clay. *The Forgotten War: America in Korea, 1950–1953.* New York: Times Books, 1987.

Blair, Clay. *Ridgway's Paratroopers.* New York: Dial Press, 1985.

Bradley, Omar N. *A Soldier's Story.* New York: Henry Holt, 1951.

Bradley, Omar N., and Clay Blair. *A General's Life.* New York: Simon & Schuster, 1983.

Breen, Michael. *The Koreans: Who They Are, What They Want, Where Their Future Lies.* New York: St. Martin's Press, 1999.

Chace, James. *Acheson: The Secretary of State Who Created the American World.* Cambridge, MA: Harvard University Press, 1999.

Ch'en Jerome, ed. *Mao.* Englewood Cliffs, NJ: Prentice-Hall, 1969.

Conquest, Robert. *Stalin: Breaker of Nations.* New York: Viking Penguin, 1991.

Crozier, Brian. *The Man Who Lost China: The First Full Biography of Chiang Kai-shek.* New York: Scribner, 1976.

Clark, Mark W. *From the Danube to the Yalu.* New York: Harper Brothers, 1954.

Cowdrey, Albert E. *United States Army in the Korean War: Medic's War.* Washington, DC: United States Government Printing Office, September 1987.

Crosbie, Philip. *March Till They Die.* Dublin: Browne & Nolan, c. 1955.

Cumings, Bruce. *Korea's Place in the Sun: A Modern History.* New York: W. W. Norton, 1997.

Cumings, Bruce. *The Origins of the Korean War,* Volume 1: *Liberation and the Emergence of Separate Regimes,* and Volume 2: *The Roaring of the Cataract: 1947–1950.* Princeton, NJ: Princeton University Press, 1981.

Darby, Jean. *Douglas MacArthur.* Minneapolis, MN: Lerner, 1989.

Dean, William F., Major General, as told to William L. Worden. *General Dean's Story.* New York: Viking Press, 1954.

Deane, Hugh. *The Korean War: 1945–1953.* San Francisco: China Books, 1999.

Dolan, Sean. *Chiang Kai-shek.* New York: Chelsea House, 1988.

Domes, Jurgen. *Peng Te-huai: The Man and the Image.* Stanford, CA: Stanford University Press, 1987.

Edwards, Richard. *The Korean War.* Vero Beach, FL: Rourke Enterprises, 1988.

Eisenhower, Dwight D. *The Eisenhower Diaries.* Edited by Robert H. Ferrell. New York: W. W. Norton, 1981.

Ferrell, Robert H. *Harry S Truman and the Modern American Presidency.* Boston: Little, Brown, 1983.

Goulden, Joseph C. *Korea: The Untold Story of the War.* New York: Times Books, 1982.

Griffith, Robert. *The Politics of Fear: Joseph R. McCarthy and the Senate.* Lexington: University of Kentucky Press, 1970.

Hart-Landsberg, Martin. *Korea: Division, Reunification, and U.S. Foreign Policy.* New York: Monthly Review Press, 1998.

Hastings, Max. *The Korean War.* New York: Simon & Schuster, 1987.

Higgins, Marguerite. *War in Korea: The Report of a Woman Combat Correspondent.* Garden City, NY: Doubleday, 1951.

Hooker, Richard. *MASH: A Novel about Three Army Doctors.* New York: William Morrow, 1968.

Hoyt, Edwin P. *The Day the Chinese Attacked Korea, 1950: The Story of the Failure of America's China Policy.* New York: McGraw-Hill, 1990.

James, D. Clayton. *The Years of MacArthur,* Vol. 3. Boston: Houghton Mifflin, 1985.

Khrushchev, Nikita. *The Crimes of the Stalin Era.* New York: The New Leader, 1962.

Kim Il Sung. *On Juche in Our Revolution.* Pyongyang, North Korea: Foreign Languages Publishing House, 1980.

Kim, Joungwon Alexander. *Divided Korea: The Politics of Development, 1945–1972.* Cambridge, MA: East Asian Research Center, Harvard University, 1975.

Knox, Donald. *The Korean War: Pusan to Chosin, An Oral History.* New York: Harcourt Brace, 1987.

Liem, Channing. *The Korean War: An Unanswered Question.* Albany, NY: The Committee for a New Korea Policy, 1992.

MacArthur, Douglas. *A Soldier Speaks.* Westport, CT: Praeger, 1965.

Manchester, William. *American Caesar: Douglas MacArthur, 1880–1964.* Boston: Little, Brown, 1978.

May, Antoinette. *Witness to War: A Biography of Marguerite Higgins.* New York: Beaufort Books, 1954.

Marrin, Albert. *Mao Tse-Tung and His China.* New York: Puffin, 1993.

Marrin, Albert. *Stalin.* New York: Viking Kestrel, 1988.

Matray, James I. *Historical Dictionary of the Korean War.* New York: Greenwood Press, 1995.

McCullough, David. *Truman.* New York: Simon & Schuster, 1992.

McLellan, David S. *Dean Acheson: The State Department Years.* New York: Dodd, Mead, 1976.

McLellan, David S., and David C. Acheson, eds. *Among Friends: Personal Letters of Dean Acheson.* New York: Dodd, Mead, 1976.

McNair, Sylvia. *Enchantment of the World: Korea.* Chicago: Children's Press, 1986.

Miller, Merle. *Plain Speaking: An Oral Biography of Harry S Truman.* New York: G. P. Putnam, 1950.

Nahm, Andrew C. *Historical Dictionary of the Republic of Korea.* Metuchen, NJ: Scarecrow Press, 1993.

Noble, H. J. *Embassy at War.* Seattle: University of Washington Press, 1975.

Oliver, Robert T. *Syngman Rhee: The Man Behind the Myth.* New York: Dodd, Mead, 1960.

Paik Sun Yup. *From Pusan to Panmunjom: Wartime Memoirs of the Republic of Korea's First Four-Star General.* Dulles, VA: Brassey's, 1992.

Paschall, Rod. *Witness to War: Korea.* New York: Perigree Books, 1995.

Peng Dehuai. *Memoirs of a Chinese Marshal: The Autobiographical Notes of Peng Dehuai (1898–1924).* Translated by Zheng Longpu and edited by Sara Grimes. Beijing: Foreign Languages Press, 1984.

Perret, Geoffrey. *Old Soldiers Never Die: The Life of Douglas MacArthur.* New York: Random House, 1996.

Poats, Rutherford M. *Decision in Korea.* New York: McBride, 1954.

Ridgway, Matthew B. *The Korean War: How We Met the Challenge, How All-Out Asian War Was Averted, Why MacArthur Was Dismissed, Why Today's War Objectives Must Be Limited.* Garden City, NY: Doubleday, 1967.

Ridgway, Matthew B. *Soldier: The Memoirs of Matthew B. Ridgway.* New York: Harper, 1956.

Roe, Patrick C. *The Dragon Strikes, China and the Korean War: June-December 1950.* Novato, CA: Presidio, 2000.

Sandberg, Peter Lars. *Dwight D. Eisenhower.* New York: Chelsea House, 1986.

Sandler, Stanley, ed. *The Korean War: An Encyclopedia.* New York: Garland Publishing, 1995.

Shinn, Bill. *The Forgotten War Remembered: Korea, 1950–1953; A War Correspondent's Notebook and Today's Danger in Korea.* Elizabeth, NJ: Hollym International, 1996.

Simmons, Robert R. "The Korean Civil War." In *Without Parallel: The American-Korean Relationship since 1945,* edited by Frank Baldwin. New York: Pantheon Books, 1973.

Solberg, S. E. *The Land and People of Korea.* New York: HarperCollins, 1991.

Spurr, Russell. *Enter the Dragon.* New York: Newmarket, 1988.

Suh Dae-sook. *Kim Il Sung: The North Korean Leader.* New York: Columbia University Press, 1995.

Summers, Harry G., Jr. *Korean War Almanac.* New York: Facts on File, 1990.

Terrill, Ross. *Mao: A Biography.* New York: Simon & Schuster, 1993.

Toland, John. *In Mortal Combat: Korea, 1950–1953.* New York: William Morrow, 1991.

Tomedi, Rudy. *No Bugles, No Drums: An Oral History of the Korean War.* New York: Wiley, 1993.

Truman, Margaret. *Harry S Truman.* New York: William Morrow, 1973.

Varhola, Michael J. *Fire and Ice: The Korean War, 1950–1953.* Mason City, IA: Savas Publishing, 2000.

Webster's American Military Biographies. Springfield, MA: G. & C. Merriam Company, 1978.

Whelan, Richard. *Drawing the Line: The Korean War, 1950–1953.* Boston: Little, Brown, 1990.

Whiting, Allen S. *China Crosses the Yalu: The Decision to Enter the Korean War.* Stanford, CA: Stanford University Press, 1960.

Zellers, Larry. *In Enemy Hands: A Prisoner in North Korea.* Lexington: University of Kentucky Press, 1991.

Web sites

"Cold War: Episode 5: Korea: 1949–1953." CNN Interactive. [Online] http://www.cnn.com/SPECIALS/cold.war/episodes/05/ (accessed on August 14, 2001).

Cold War International History Project, Woodrow Wilson International Center for Scholars. [Online] http://cwihp.si.cdu (accessed on August 14, 2001).

Feldman, Ruth Tenzer. "Women in the War." Cobblestone: Korean War Fiftieth Anniversary Issue. [Online] http://korea50.army.mil/cobblestone/29.html (accessed on August 14, 2001).

"The Forgotten Victory." Korean War Veterans National Museum and Library. [Online] http://www.theforgottenvictory.org/ (accessed on August 14, 2001).

Matray, James I. "Korea's Partition: Soviet-American Pursuit of Reunification, 1945–1948." [Online] http://www.mtholyoke.edu/acad/intrel/korpart.htm (accessed on August 14, 2001).

"President Clinton Statement on No Gun Ri, January 11, 2001." The United States Embassy, Seoul, Republic of Korea. [Online] http://www.usembassy.state.gov/seoul/wwwh42zv.html (accessed on August 14, 2001).

"President's Address, 11 April 1951." Harry S. Truman Library. [Online] http://www.theforgottenvictory.org/macarthur.htm (accessed on August 14, 2001).

Project Whistlestop: The Truman Digital Archive Project. [Online] http://www.whistlestop.org (accessed on August 14, 2001).

Sang-hun Choe, Charles J. Hanley, and Martha Mendoza. "Bridge at No Gun Ri." Associated Press (AP). [Online] http://wire.ap.org/APpackages/nogunri/story.html (accessed on August 14, 2001).

Savada, Andrea Matles, ed. "North Korea: A Country Study." The Federal Research Division, Library of Congress. [Online] http://lcweb2.loc.gov/frd/cs/kptoc.html (accessed on August 14, 2001).

Savada, Andrea Matles, and William Shaw, eds. "South Korea: A Country Study." The Federal Research Division, Library of Congress. [Online] http://lcweb2.loc.gov/frd/cs/krtoc.html (accessed on August 14, 2001).

State of New Jersey. "U.S. Military Biographies: Korea." [Online] http://www.state.nj.us/military/korea/biographies/yup.html (accessed on August 14, 2001).

"Tiger Survivors: Civilian Internee Prisoners." [Online] http://www.tiger-survivors.org/civbios.html (accessed on August 14, 2001).

Truman Presidential Museum and Library. [Online] http://www.trumanlibrary.org/ (accessed on August 14, 2001).

United States Army. Fiftieth Anniversary of the Korean War Commemoration Site. [Online] http://korea50.army.mil/index.html (accessed on August 14, 2001).

United States Army. "African Americans in the Korean War." Fiftieth Anniversary of the Korean War Commemoration Site. [Online] http://korea50.army.mil/history/factsheets/afroamer.html (accessed on August 14, 2001).

United States Army. "Korean War Medal of Honor Recipients." United States Army. [Online] http://www.army.mil/cmh-pg/mohkor2.htm (accessed on August 14, 2001).

United States Army. "Prisoners of War in the Korean War." Fiftieth Anniversary of the Korean War Commemoration Site. [Online] http://korea50.army.mil/history/factsheets/pow.html (accessed on August 14, 2001).

United States Army. "Women in the Korean War." Fiftieth Anniversary of the Korean War Commemoration Site. [Online] http://korea50.army.mil/history/factsheets/women.html (accessed on August 14, 2001).

Weathersby, Kathryn. "Soviet Aims in Korea and the Origins of the Korean War, 1945–50: New Evidence from Russian Archives." Cold War International History Project, Woodrow Wilson International Center for Scholars. [Online] http://cwihp.si.edu (accessed on August 14, 2001).

Webb, William J. "The Korean War: The Outbreak" (army brochure). [Online] http://www.army.mil/cmh-pg/brochures/KW-Outbreak/outbreak.htm (accessed on August 14, 2001).

Index

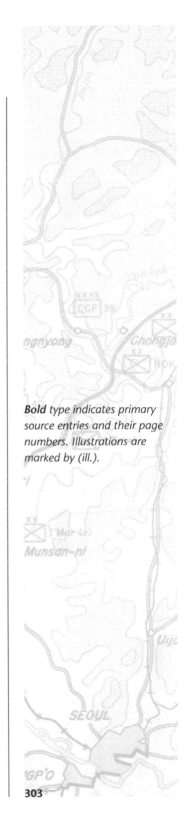

Bold type indicates primary source entries and their page numbers. Illustrations are marked by (ill.).

Atomic bombs, 191, 192–193,
    193 (ill.), 249, 281
Austin, Warren, 102

B

B-29A Superfortress, 64
Bailey, Sydney, 196
Bayonets, 84
Beech, Keyes, 215–222, 224, 229
Bicycle Corps (National Police),
    29 (ill.)
Biological warfare, 182–183
Blair, Clay, 52
Blair House meetings, 49–51
Bloody Gulch, 77
Bloody Ridge, 166–168, 167 (ill.)
Bombing campaigns, 195
    Kaesong, 165
    MacArthur, Douglas, 81–82,
        147–148
    UN Forces bombing, 273
    Yalu River, 124–125
Bowling Alley, 83, 86
Bradley, Omar N., 49
**"Bridge at No Gun Ri:
    Survivors' Petition,"
    253–259**
Browning automatic rifle (M-
    1918A2), 84
Byrne, Patrick, 292

C

C rations, 287
Cafferata, Hector A., 139
Caldwell, William, 68
Calvert, Philip A., 219
Canney, John J., 218
Capitalism, 17
Casualties, 72, 169, 198–199, 251
CCF. *See* Chinese
    Communist Forces
Cease-fire. *See* Armistice
Chaffee tanks (M-24), 85
Changjin Reservoir. *See* Chosin
    Reservoir
Cheju-do, South Korea, 33–36
Chiang Kai-shek, 12–13, 13 (ill)
    Chinese Nationalists, 191,
        247–248
    MacArthur, Douglas, 148

Mao Zedong, 33, 91, 250
    United States support, 110–111,
        118, 248
Chieh Fang, 163
*China Crosses the Yalu: The
    Decision to Enter the Korean
    War* (Whiting), 102
China Lobby, 110–112
China (Mainland), 113 (ill.). *See
    also* Chinese Nationalists;
    Communist Chinese Forces
    armistice, 197
    Chipyong-ni, 152
    demarcation line, 164
    entry into Korean War, 102,
        109–126
    government of, 12–13
    Iron Triangle, 155–157
    MacArthur, Douglas, 153
    Mao Zedong, 33
    relations with Japan, 11–13
    relations with Soviet Union,
        12–13
    relations with U.S., 33,
        109–112, 161, 248–251
    vs. Taiwan, 91–92, 250
    United Nations and, 49–50,
        102, 117–118
    White, Ted, 283–289
    Yalu River, 195
    Yudam, 218–221
Chinese Civil War, 12–13
Chinese Nationalists, 12–13, 118,
    191, 247–248
Chinese People's Volunteers
    (CPV), 118–126, 132,
    150–151
Chipyong-ni, South Korea, 152
Chosin Reservoir, 131 (ill.),
    135 (ill.)
    Communist Chinese Forces,
        135–137, 141
    Fox Company, 139–141
    MacArthur, Douglas, 134
    memoirs, 217–221
    Task Force Drysdale, 135–136
    Tootsie Rolls, 136
    U.S. Marines, 131–143, 178
    Yudam, South Korea, 137–141
Chou En-lai. *See* Zhou Enlai
Chun Doo Hwan, 200–201
Chunchon, South Korea, 41–42
Church, John H., 69

Clark, Mark W.
  armistice, 263
  bombing campaigns, 195
  Eisenhower, Dwight D.,
    189–191
  Koje-do, 186
  Rhee, Syngman, 196
  unlimited warfare, 192
Clinton, William J., 70, 255, 258
Cold War, 15–26, 18 (ill.), 19 (ill.),
  32–33, 277. *See also*
  Communism
Coleman, John, 209–210, 212
Colson, Charles, 184–186
Committee for the Preparation of
  Korean Independence
  (CPKI). *See* People's
  Committees
Communism. *See also* Cold War
  in China, 111–113, 116–118,
    247–249
  juche, 232
  Kim Il Sung, 232
  in North Korea, 201–202, 243
  POW camps, 177, 178
  in South Korea, 269
  in Soviet Union, 3, 15–16,
    161–162
  Truman, Harry S., 278–279
Communist Chinese Forces (CCF)
  Chosin Reservoir, 135–137, 141
  military organization, 112–113
  military strategy, 115, 130–131,
    150–151
  military training, 114
  in Seoul, 147
  trench warfare, 159
Communist Party (China),
  12–13, 112
Communist Party (Korea), 9–10
Communist Youth League, 10
Containment, 50
Corsairs (F-4UID), 64–65, 116 (ill.)
CPKI (Committee for the
  Preparation of Korean
  Independence). *See* People's
  Committees
CPV. *See* Chinese People's
  Volunteers
Crane, Lionel, 225, 229
Crosbie, Philip, 292, 294
Cult of personality, 202, 233
Cumings, Bruce, 21

D

Davies, John, 225, 229
*The Day the Chinese Attacked
  Korea, 1950* (Hoyt), 115, 123
Dean, William F., 56, 66–67
Deane, Hugh, 193
Death March, 292–295
Decision in Korea (Poats), 96
Demarcation line, 164, 172
Demilitarized zone (DMZ), 172,
  203, 203 (ill.), 261
Democratic People's Republic of
  Korea (DPRK). *See*
  North Korea
Desegregation, military, 150,
  289–290
DMZ. *See* Demilitarized zone
Doctor's Draft Act, 207
Dodd, Francis T., 184–186
Doyle, James H., 229
*The Dragon Strikes, China and the
  Korean War: June-December
  1950* (Roe), 123, 138

E

Eisenhower, Dwight D.
  atomic bombs, 191
  Chance for Peace speech, 193
  Clark, Mark W., 190–191
  election, 189–190
  foreign policy, 191
  Korean War, 190–191
  limited warfare, 191, 281
  Malenkov, Gerogy M., 191
  Rhee, Syngman, 196
  Truman, Harry S., 191
  unlimited warfare, 197
  Van Fleet, James A., 190–191
Elections, Korean, 28, 29 (ill.),
  30, 236
Eun-yong Chung, 255, 258
Evacuations, helicopter, 213
Executions, mass, 45–48, 48 (ill.)
Executive Order 9981, 150

F

F-86A Sabre, 65 (ill.)
F-4UID Corsairs, 64–65, 116 (ill.)
Far East Policy. *See* Foreign policy

FEAF, 64–65

"Fire and Ice" (Beech), 215–222

Fire and Ice: The Korean War, 1950–1953 (Varhola), 65

Foreign policy
  Eisenhower, Dwight D., 191
  MacArthur, Douglas, 91–92, 101, 239–244
  Truman, Harry S., 91–92, 101, 153, 279–280
  United States Joint Chiefs of Staff, 49

The Forgotten War: America in Korea (Blair), 52

The Forgotten War Remembered: Korea, 1950–1953; A War Correspondent's Notebook and Today's Danger in Korea (Shinn), 267–274

Forward surgical teams. *See* MASH units

Fox Company, 139–141

Fox Hill. *See* Toktong Pass

From Pusan to Panmunjom: Wartime Memoirs of the Republic of Korea's First Four-Star General (Paik), 43–44, 52, 83, 115–116, 122, 133, 200, 261–265

From the Danube to the Yalu (Clark), 36, 263

G

Garand .30 caliber rifle (M-1), 84

Gonzalez, Ernest, 178

Goulden, Joseph C., 47, 97, 100–101, 143, 169, 244

"The Great Gamble at Inchon" (Higgins), 223–230

Grenades, 84

Gromyko, Andrei A., 161

Guerrilla warfare, 33–36, 147

H

Hagaru, South Korea, 138, 141–143, 221

Haichi Shiki, 119

Han River Bridge, 44–45, 270

Harriman, Averell, 92

Heartbreak Ridge, 148 (ill.), 168 (ill.), 169

Heavy weapons, 84

Hickey, Doyle, 154 (ill.)

Higgins, Marguerite, 52, 61, **223–230**, 224 (ill.)

Hitler, Adolph, 250

Hodge, John Reed, 20–21, 23

Home by Christmas offensive, 129–133, 217

Hoover, Herbert, 234

Howitzer (M1), 85

Howitzer (M-114), 85

Howitzer (M-101A1), 85

Hoyt, Edwin, 115, 123

Hua, Teng, 116

I

In Enemy Hands: A Prisoner in North Korea (Zellers), 291–296

In Mortal Combat: Korea, 1950–1953 (Toland), 157, 164–165

Inchon, South Korea, 89–108, 93 (ill.), 100 (ill.), 228 (ill.)
  Higgins, Marguerite, 223–230
  MacArthur, Douglas, 86, 224

Independence, Korean, 8–9, 13–14, 20–22, 36, 234–235

India, 196, 198

International trusteeship, 20–21, 27, 234

Iron Triangle, 155–157, 166

Isolationism, Korean, 6

J

Japan. *See also* Japanese occupation; Pacific Campaign
  cultural assimilation, 12
  relations with China, 11–13
  in South Korea, 21–22
  surrender of, 17, 19–20
  treatment of women, 11 (ill.), 13

Japanese occupation, 3–14, 6 (ill.), 20, 231–233, 232 (ill.)

Jaskilka, Sam, 219

Joint Task Force 7, 93–94

Journalism, war. *See* War correspondents

Ridgway, Matthew B., 159–160
Truman, Harry S., 276, 279
vs. unlimited, 192–193
Litzenberg, Homer L., 217–218
Lord, Herbert A., 292–294
Luce, Henry, 110

M

M-24 Chaffee tanks, 85
M-1 Garand .30 caliber rifle, 84
M-114 Howitzer, 85
M-26 Pershing tanks, 85
M-4 Sherman tanks, 85
M-1911A1 .45 caliber rifle, 84
M-1918A2 Browning automatic
    rifle, 84
M-101A1 Howitzer, 85
M1 Howitzer, 85
MacArthur, Douglas, 154 (ill.),
    224 (ill.), 240 (ill.), 276 (ill.)
    "Address to Congress,"
    239–245
    attack on North Korea, 103–107
    bombing campaigns, 81–82,
        147–148
    Chiang Kai-shek, 148
    Congressional address, 239–245
    dismissal of, 154–155, 239–240,
        275–281
    foreign policy, 91–92, 101,
        240–244
    Higgins, Marguerite, 52, 223
    Hodge, John Reed, 21
    Home by Christmas offensive,
        129–133, 217
    Inchon, South Korea, 86,
        89–90, 93, 224
    invasion of South Korea, 50–52
    Japanese surrender, 19–20
    limited warfare, 148
    Paik Sun Yup, 52
    politics, 244 (ill.), 281
    the press and, 245
    Rhee, Syngman, 51–52, 65, 97
    Ridgway, Matthew B., 101, 149
    Seoul, South Korea, 95–97
    Taiwan, 91–92
    Truman, Harry S., 52–53, 103,
        154–155, 240
    United States Joint Chiefs

of Staff, 90–93, 101, 124,
    148, 153
unlimited warfare, 192, 242
Walker, Walton H., 71, 145
warmongering, 147–149
Yalu River bombings, 124–125
Machine guns, 84
Malenkov, Georgy M., 191
Malik, Jacob A., 117, 161
Manchukuo, 11, 13
Manchuria, China, 7–11, 13, 17
Mao Tse-tung. *See* Mao Zedong
Mao Zedong, 13, 248 (ill.)
    Chiang Kai-shek, 33,
        90–91, 250
    interview with, 247–252
    Kim Il Sung, 37, 277
    Korean War, 118
    military tactics, 115, 124
    **"Nuclear Weapons Are Paper
        Tigers," 247–252**
    Peng Dehaui, 118, 120
    People's Republic of China,
        33, 49
    U.S. Marines, 137
March First Movement, 8–9,
    8 (ill.)
Marshall, George C., 125
Marx, Karl, 232
MASH: An Army Surgeon in Korea
    (Apel), 207–213
MASH units, 60 (ill.), 207–213,
    208 (ill.), 211 (ill.)
Mass executions, 45–48, 48 (ill.)
McCarthy, Joseph, 114–115,
    115 (ill.)
McCarthyism. *See*
    Anticommunism
Michaelis, John, 83, 83 (ill.)
Michener, James, 245
MiG-15s, 64
Military government, 20–23, 200
Military spending, 55
Military strategy
    Chinese People's Volunteers,
        119, 123–124, 150–151
    Communist Chinese Forces,
        115, 130–131
    Mao Zedong, 115, 124
    U.S. Army, 116
Military training, 23 (ill.)
    Communist Chinese
        Forces, 114